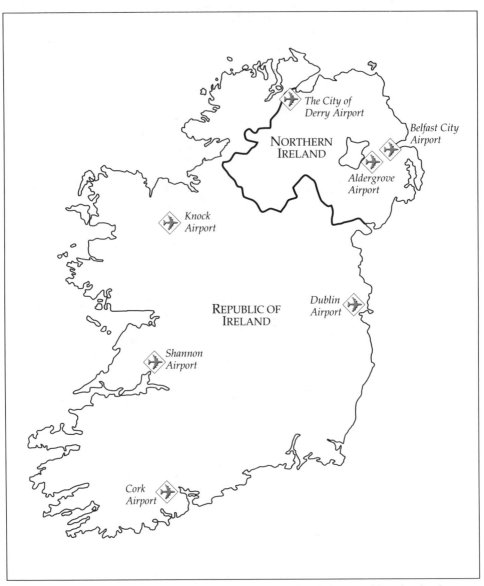

Map showing international airports in Northern Ireland and the Republic of Ireland.

BORDER CROSSINGS

DEVELOPING IRELAND'S ISLAND ECONOMY

Edited by

MICHAEL D'ARCY AND TIM DICKSON

Gill & Macmillan

Published in Ireland by
Gill & Macmillan Ltd
Goldenbridge
Dublin 8

with associated companies throughout the world

0 7171 2383 9

Print origination by Typeform Repro
Printed in Ireland by ColourBooks Ltd, Dublin

1 3 5 4 2

Contents

Preface

Nobody made a greater mistake than he who did nothing because he could do only a little.

—Edmund Burke

> Two roads diverged in a yellow wood
> And sorry I could not travel both
> And be one traveller, long I stood
> And looked down one as far as I could
> To where it bent in the undergrowth . . .
> —Robert Frost, *The Road Not Taken*

The idea for this book came to us during a telephone call between Dublin and London on the day of the IRA ceasefire in August 1994. The real inspiration, however, was a series of conversations we had in the late 1980s when overlapping professional interests—and the bond that joins Irishmen of all persuasions when they find themselves away from home—periodically brought us together in Brussels.

It seemed to us then—as indeed it does now—that the best hope for a permanent end to the dreadful suffering of Northern Ireland over the last quarter century lay in a wider European context. If economic and political barriers were tumbling everywhere else, perhaps the Irish border and the associated myths on both sides of it could be viewed in a different light. If the centre of European economic and political power was moving eastwards—to the Belgian capital and possibly one day beyond—perhaps those on the periphery of the single market had a compelling new incentive to make common cause. If federalism and (especially) regionalism were on the march in Europe, perhaps divisions driven by separate national identities were finally in retreat.

These are big political issues, however, and to the extent that it is possible when writing about Ireland, North and South, this is avowedly not a political book. Its subject matter in this new era of peace is the *economic* rationale for increased cross-border trade and for greater economic co-operation between Belfast, Dublin, London, and Europe.

We firmly believe that trade is a healthy means of improving understanding of other people's cultural differences, and therefore a not insignificant influence in an Irish dimension. But that is not the justification for this book. The only case for developing an island economy, we would maintain, is that it brings new opportunities for higher living standards for both parts of Ireland in a rapidly changing international market, and hence helps consolidate the peace.

The indispensable role of the European Union and the United States in accelerating that process has been highlighted during the preparation of this book. The EU's ECU300 million special initiative to support peace and reconciliation, for example, was formally launched in Belfast in April 1995 by Jacques Santer, President of the European Commission. Over four hundred representatives of every shade of political opinion, and of every variety of economic activity, attended.

The White House Conference in Washington DC followed in May 1995, bringing together political and business leaders from both parts of the island for a highly successful three days of discussion. Shoulder to shoulder they told potential American investors and joint-venture partners that the island of Ireland—notably Northern Ireland and the border counties—is a good location for business.

Instinctively we feel that the case for working side by side *in Ireland* rather than back to back is a strong one. The best way to prove it, we calculated, was to examine the issues from a variety of angles with the help of expert witnesses. Hence our delight at being able to line up, in remarkably quick time, the distinguished business people, academics, policy-makers and other commentators who have generously contributed essays to this book. We are deeply indebted to them.

We also want to thank Gill & Macmillan, especially our guide and fellow 'team' member Finola O'Sullivan. From first sight of the concept to the day of publication Finola has been behind this book. Our wives, Kay and Sally, and children, Michelle, Cathal, Matthew, Emily, Annabelle, and Alice, have all been a tower of strength. We also want to acknowledge the help and support of Tim's brother-in-law and sister Kerry and Libby O'Halloran, who put us in touch with the publisher, Sir George Quigley, the *Financial Times,* Séamus Boyle of the Northern Ireland Partnership, Alan Gillespie of Goldman Sachs, John Dowdall, Ted Smyth, Julie O'Neill, Alan Matthews, David Begg, Helen Gallivan, Kingsley Aikens, Seán Ó hÉigeartaigh, John Malone, Michael McGrath, Karen Molloy, the ESRI researchers Nuala O'Donnell and Niamh Sheridan, Tom Walsh and all the company executives who responded to our questionnaire.

Michael D'Arcy	Tim Dickson
Dublin	London
Spring 1995	Spring 1995

Biographical Notes

Editors

Tim Dickson was born in Dungannon, Northern Ireland in 1954, and read history at Cambridge University. He joined the *Evening Chronicle* newspaper in Newcastle upon Tyne as a graduate trainee. He has been a journalist with the London *Financial Times* for seventeen years—including spells in the paper's Brussels bureau and on its Lex column—and currently edits the daily Management Page.

Michael D'Arcy was born in Dublin in 1956 and read history and politics at University College Dublin. He is principal of the Dublin based independent public policy advisors, D'Arcy Smyth & Associates, which he founded in 1981. He advises public and private sector clients operating in the domestic and international arenas and has served on a variety of official sectoral working groups and task forces in both Dublin and Brussels.

Contributors

Tony O'Reilly is chairman, president and chief executive officer of the H. J. Heinz Company, which has annual sales of $8 billion in food products around the world. Through his controlling investment in Fitzwilton plc he has invested in Northern Ireland through the acquisition of the Wellworths retail chain, one of the two largest employers in Northern Ireland. He is chairman of Waterford Wedgwood and of Independent Newspapers and a major investor in Arcon International Resources, which is building the largest lead-zinc mine in Europe. He is founding chairman of the Ireland Funds, the largest philanthropic organisation for Ireland overseas.

Peter Sutherland SC is deputy chairman of the British Petroleum Company plc and a director of other companies. He is also chairman of the European

Institute of Public Administration in Maastrict. He is a Senior Counsel of the Irish Bar and is a member of the English and New York Bars. Having served as Attorney General of Ireland between 1981 and 1985 he was appointed Commissioner of the European Communities. From 1989 to 1993 he was chairman of Allied Irish Banks. He was Director-General of GATT and later the World Trade Organisation until he relinquished his position in May of 1995.

Jonathan Bardon is a Faculty Advisor at the Belfast Institute of Further and Higher Education. Born and raised in Dublin, he came to Belfast after graduating in 1963 and has been teaching there ever since. He is the author of books on the history of Ulster, Belfast and Wood Quay, and he was scriptwriter for the UTV/Channel 4 series *Understanding Northern Ireland* and for numerous BBC schools history programmes. He is chairman of the Cultural Traditions Group and he chaired the DENI Education for Mutual Understanding and Cultural Heritage working groups in 1989 which helped to shape the Northern Ireland Curriculum for schools.

John Bradley is a research professor at the Economic and Social Research Institute, Dublin, and formerly worked at the Central Bank of Ireland. His research and publications cover a wide area of applied economic policy and are at present focused on the periphery of the European Union, on which he directs teams from Greece, Ireland, Portugal and Spain in a research programme on the implications of EU regional policy. Since 1993 he has co-directed a programme of North-South research on the two economies of Ireland, financially assisted by the International Fund for Ireland and carried out in collaboration with the Northern Ireland Economic Research Centre.

Jim Walsh is a senior lecturer in the Department of Geography in Maynooth College and chairman of the Regional Studies Association in the Republic of Ireland. He has written extensively on the geography of economic development in Ireland; his most recent research has been on strategic planning for local and regional development.

Peter Brennan is a graduate of the University of Dublin (Trinity College) and since 1986 has been director of the Irish Business Bureau, Brussels, which represents the EU interests of the Irish Business and Employers' Confederation and the Chambers of Commerce of Ireland. He is also a director of IBEC, with responsibility for European and international affairs. Until 1986 he worked in the Irish civil service; this included two tours of duty at the Irish Permanent Representation to the EU.

Gerry McAlinden is chief executive of the Northern Ireland Centre in Europe, an independent organisation representing the interests of a range of sectors in the region among the institutions of the European Union and other European regions. He worked in the public service in Northern Ireland with the Department of Economic Development before spending several years with the European Commission, where he dealt with rural development issues. He has a BA and an MBA from the Open University, and in his earlier career he taught in a rural college in western France for four years.

John Simpson was for many years a senior lecturer in economics at Queen's University, Belfast. He has been involved in various capacities in economic development agencies, north and south, and has served as a member of the National Economic and Social Council, Dublin, and as an economic adviser in government departments in Northern Ireland. At present he is a member of the Economic and Social Committee of the European Communities and is serving as a specialist adviser to the Northern Ireland Committee of the House of Commons during its inquiry on job creation in Northern Ireland. He has also served as chairman of various non-departmental public bodies, including the Eastern Health and Social Services Board, the Probation Board for Northern Ireland, and the former Youth Employment Service Board.

Bill Hodges was permanent secretary of the Department of Agriculture, Northern Ireland, from 1989 until his early retirement in 1994. At present he is chairman of Industrial and Trade Exhibitions Ltd, which organises Ireland's top food exhibitions in Dublin and Belfast. He is also a director of An Bord Bia, the Irish Food Board.

Eugene Regan has a master's degree in economics from University College, Dublin, and a master's degree in international law from the Vrije Universiteit of Brussels, and was called to the Irish Bar in 1985. He has been an economist with the Irish Farmers' Association, director of the Brussels office of the IFA, chief executive of the Irish Exporters' Association, and a member of Peter Sutherland's cabinet at the European Commission. At present he is a director and general manager of Agra Trading Ltd.

William Poole is director of the IBEC-CBI North-South Business Development Programme (a joint initiative of the Irish Business and Employers' Confederation and the Confederation of British Industry in Northern Ireland), based in the offices of the CBI in Belfast. At present he chairs a Northern Ireland Government Committee on Energy Efficiency in Transport. He holds primary degrees in agriculture and science from Queen's

University, Belfast, and postgraduate degrees in business administration from the University of Ulster. He previously worked as manager for Imperial Chemical Industries in Northern Ireland.

Geoff MacEnroe is director of the IBEC-CBI North-South Business Development Programme, based in the offices of the Irish Business and Employers' Confederation in Dublin. He previously worked in the construction industry and with the Irish Trade Board, where he held positions in Dublin, Brussels, and Tokyo. He holds primary degrees in engineering and in economics and politics from University College, Dublin, and studied production engineering at the University of Aston in Birmingham.

Joyce Irwin, a native of Belfast, joined the International Division of the Ulster Bank in 1979 and became manager of trade finance in 1985. Since 1994 she has been on secondment to the Department of Trade and Industry under the auspices of the United Kingdom government's Export Promotion Initiative.

Colum MacDonnell is chief executive of the Irish Exporters' Association and chairman of the Service Industries Research Centre at University College, Dublin. He was responsible in the mid-1980s for developing the Irish Trade Board's policies for promoting Ireland's international services earnings.

Harford Robb left his native Belfast in 1956 after attending Queen's University and qualifying as a chartered accountant. He has worked in Australia, India, the United States, and several European countries. In 1968–80 he established the all-Ireland consulting practice of Arthur Andersen, and was an early member of Co-operation North. Based outside London since 1980, he has worked with many smaller companies as an investor and board member. In 1993 he accepted a short-term appointment as joint chair in cross-border business enterprise at University College, Dublin, and the University of Ulster, which was funded through the Irish and British governments by Interreg.

Inez McCormack is Northern Ireland Regional Organiser of Unison, whose members, largely low-paid women, work in the health and public services. She is a member of the Executive Committee and the Northern Ireland Committee of the Irish Congress of Trade Unions. She was a founder-member of the North's Fair Employment Agency and also of the Equal Opportunities Commission, of which she was legal vice-chairwoman. She is a signatory of the Seán MacBride Principles of Fair Employment and has written and broadcast extensively on social and economic matters in Northern Ireland.

Maureen Gaffney is chairwoman of the National Economic and Social Forum. She was educated at University College, Cork, and the University of Chicago. A psychologist by profession, she is a senior lecturer in psychology in Trinity College, Dublin, and also a member of the Law Reform Commission. She writes a column for *The Irish Times* and is a well-known broadcaster on radio and television.

Austin Smyth holds the chair of transport within the Department of Civil Engineering and Transport at the University of Ulster, Jordanstown, with particular responsibility for the development and maintenance of its research capability and consultancy. He was awarded a PhD for postgraduate research into urban modal choice and transport policy, and has worked in transport consultancy in the United States, Russia, the Middle East, the Netherlands, the United Kingdom, and Ireland.

Gerry McAleavy is senior lecturer in the School of Education of the Faculty of Social and Health Sciences and Education, University of Ulster, Newtownabbey.

Gerard Parr is lecturer in the School of Information and Software Engineering of the Faculty of Informatics, University of Ulster, Derry. The authors would be particularly interested in giving further information on the ACTOR project.

Paul Tansey MA MBA is a journalist and columnist. A former assistant editor of *The Irish Times*, he now writes a weekly economics column for the *Sunday Tribune*. He is a partner in Tansey, Webster and Associates, economic consultants, authors of *The Economic Effects of Tourism in Ireland* (1995).

Douglas Hamilton is a senior economist with the Northern Ireland Economic Council, an independent advisory body to the government, specialising in regional and industrial development and policy issues, with a specific interest in indigenous industry, inward investment, and the role of development agencies such as the IDB. In addition to writing a number of reports for the Economic Council on the Northern Ireland economy he has published on economic and industrial development and policy matters in the Republic of Ireland.

Shane Molloy joined Lever Brothers Ireland, part of Unilever, in 1973 on completing a MBA at the Cranfield School of Management. Having held a series of marketing and sales posts, mainly in Ireland, but also in the UK, he became Managing Director in 1988. He was appointed to the Board of Lever Europe in March 1995 as General Manager, Operations with responsibility for ten countries. He has primary degrees from the College of Commerce and UCD and after University worked in the marketing research and dairy industries.

Editors' Introduction

The contributors to this book all write from different perspectives, but a number of common themes have emerged. One of the most basic, yet easiest to overlook, is that the island economy at the centre of our thinking is neither a theoretical construction nor a romantic fiction. It already exists, and in certain respects it is vibrant and multidimensional.

The volume of cross-border trade may be small in absolute terms—2.8 and 3.6 per cent of the Republic's imports and exports, respectively—but recent evidence suggests that cross-border economic activity is fast picking up. A powerful case for expanding it—notably the opportunity for companies on both sides to extend their home markets before turning to more difficult markets overseas—is spelt out in the chapter by Bill Poole and Geoff MacEnroe. They point out that proportionately more of the new business opportunities arising from growing cross-border trade may be available for those selling into the Republic from the North, rather than vice versa. On the basis of relative GDP and population figures the North-South trade balance—currently £350 million in the South's favour—ought to be in the other direction.

A much more subtle picture of co-operation and integration, however, emerges from a reading of the whole. North-South differences are not to be denied, but the chapter by Shane Molloy, managing director of Lever Brothers Ireland, offers a fascinating insight into future possibilities. Creating a single island structure for inward distribution, he explains, made economic sense for his company' and has had a positive effect on the bottom line. Those who responded to our questionnaire (see appendix 1) highlight other and varied benefits to individual businesses of adopting a single island structure.

The adverse trade balance referred to above, incidentally, does not mean that the Northern establishment or the people in the North—too easily characterised as defensive and isolationist—are hostile to economic interaction with their island neighbours. Tourism flows in recent years show that the number of visitors to the Republic from Northern Ireland has been significantly greater than in the other direction. In the transport sector, funding for the Belfast–Dublin cross-border rail project was approved earlier and more enthusiastically by the Department of the Environment in Belfast than it was by the relevant authorities in Dublin. And as Peter Sutherland writes in his chapter on trade, 'the staggering communication deficit between Belfast and Dublin, whether by air or road, speaks volumes for the indifference of successive administrations, particularly on the southern side of the border.'

Sutherland's contribution is an eloquent reminder of the global economic realities facing both parts of Ireland as the next millennium approaches. Integrating technologies, sharply divergent demographic trends in developed and developing countries and the embracing of market-oriented reforms by formerly communist states are among the pressures intensifying the competition for mobile capital and labour-intensive industries.

Between now and 2015 the number of new jobs required to keep unemployment rates unchanged in the developing world will exceed the current populations of Europe and North America combined.

Sutherland touches briefly on the development of integrated regional economic areas that extend beyond the nation-state, a global geopolitical phenomenon that we consider highly relevant to the future prosperity of Ireland, North and South. The European Community and the North American Free Trade Agreement are, of course, the most visible manifestations of this; but the argument goes further.

The chairman of the Ulster Bank, Sir George Quigley, not a contributor to this book but someone who is rightly cited in a number of places for his role in promoting North-South economic dialogue, outlined (in a speech to an ESRI conference in March 1995) his concept of the island as a 'natural economic zone.' Citing Japan's most famous management guru, Kenichi Ohmae, former head of the Tokyo office of the management consultancy firm McKinsey, he argued that the lines on the global economic map that really matter are not imposed by political fiat. Sometimes they are parts of states, sometimes they overlap existing national boundaries (e.g. San Diego and Tijuana, Hong Kong and southern China, the growth triangle of Singapore and its neighbouring Indonesian islands, and the triangle across the Strait of Malacca that links Medan, Penang, and Phuket). Complex and sensitive political challenges result, but, as Quigley points out, 'the political scientists are coming up with increasingly innovative ideas for what are elegantly described as soft functional areas: overlays added for limited purposes over existing boundary lines and neither prejudicing nor modifying those boundaries.'

The crucial point, we believe, is that sovereign political structures can co-exist with the notion of regional frameworks, less precise configurations which nevertheless often make more sense to business people than the traditional nation-state.

The thesis of this book is that both parts of the island of Ireland will benefit if more business people, politicians and policy-makers start thinking in such terms, and do so now.

We are confident that they will gain new understandings and insights from the short history of Ireland's partition by Jonathan Bardon and the economic background so ably sketched in by John Bradley and Jim Walsh. Bardon undertook with sensitivity and style the unenviable task of condensing five hundred years into five thousand words, including his own memorable image of the Belfast buzzard. Bradley astutely analyses the economic consequences of violence and evaluates the impact of three possible economic scenarios for a permanent peace. Walsh vividly reminds us how and why prosperity has spread unevenly across both parts of the island and the need for 'a perspective on the spatial organisation of the economy.'

Such disparities—regional, social, and economic—highlight the need for substantial inward investment, a subject dealt with by Douglas Hamilton. He carefully maps out the extent of foreign ownership North and South, the respective records of the IDB and IDA, and the potential of the peace, including increased policy co-ordination between Belfast and Dublin.

The attraction to American companies of the Republic's 10 per cent manufacturing tax—a key weapon in the IDA's armoury—is underlined by Dr Tony O'Reilly in an upbeat personal perspective. 'The island as a whole can now be marketed as a gateway to Europe,' he writes, drawing attention to the seventy million people of Irish descent throughout the world, into which his American Ireland Fund has so successfully tapped. 'American investment in Ireland is a win-win for both countries. The United States gains new markets in Europe; Ireland avails itself of new technology and capital to create jobs and economic growth.'

The importance of the European Union, however, can hardly be overstated as a facilitator for increased economic integration. The benefits that have already been gained from encouraging co-operation in the border regions— areas that are remote from the centre of economic and political power on both sides—are highlighted from different perspectives by Gerry McAlinden and Harford Robb, yet with strikingly similar conclusions. The EU has also brought about a degree of harmonisation in cross-border transport policy— though, as Austin Smyth explains, serious questions need to be addressed concerning the allocation of resources, the cost-effectiveness of current plans, and the adequacy of key cross-border road and rail links in the medium and long term. Bill Hodges and Eugene Regan—one of three North-South writing 'teams' we put together for this project—vividly demonstrate the overlapping interests of Northern Ireland and the Republic in that most European of all sectors, food and agriculture.

Brussels also has a role to play in telecommunications and information technology, which, as Gerry McAleavy and Gerard Parr demonstrate, represents a formidable resource for assisting in the regeneration of rural areas, expanding training and education, and opening up new possibilities for public debate and communication across communities.

Services, being the 'art of the possible', as Joyce Irwin and Colum MacDonnell crisply observe, also offer great opportunities, especially when effectively allied to new technology. While there is similarity on both sides of the border, they suggest, there are differences of market focus that would justify joint ventures in third markets.

The single currency debate, meanwhile, looms large in several contributions, and though many other factors will doubtless influence the final outcome of the Maastricht Treaty negotiations, policy-makers in London and Dublin should appreciate its impact on the island economy. There is no great evidence at the moment that an unstable exchange rate is a major hindrance to cross-border trade: perceived payment difficulties and a lack of market information are probably the biggest impediments. But if peace comes dropping fast, the continued presence of two separate currencies—and divergent macro-economic policies—could be a deterrent to further economic integration.

As Peter Brennan puts it in arguing for a common London-Dublin approach to priority European issues, 'the competitive equilibrium of the island could be adversely affected if one of our economies operated outside the monetary and economic disciplines that will be required of full EMU members and one operated inside it.'

The single currency debate is not the only economic difficulty, as John Simpson's essay underlines. Comparing the dependence of the two parts of the island on external financial support—in Northern Ireland's case the financial transfers from the British Treasury, in the Republic's case the transfers from Brussels—he brings clarity and objectivity to an often misunderstood issue. High public expenditure in both parts of the island, but particularly in the North, should be a source of long-term concern for both governments, and a sharing of provision in some areas is surely worth considering.

At the heart of the book is the island's most pressing problem: unemployment. The contributions from Maureen Gaffney and Inez McCormack make clear that radical solutions will be necessary if a dangerously large minority is not to be excluded from the island's future prosperity. As Gaffney says, 'We know that the rising tide does not lift all boats.'

The main message, however, is that the opportunities are there today for business people, politicians and policy-makers with the will and imagination to grab them. Partition and twenty-five years of violence have certainly exacerbated the different structures of the two economies; but many similarities remain, and the common external challenge has seldom been greater. These are the cross-border stepping-stones for those who wish to use them.

The scale of the opportunity must be accompanied by an appreciation of the limits to cross-border integration, and a hard headed realism about the future. Misunderstanding, suspicion and bitterness are never quickly overcome.

Other relationships, notably the North's potential to develop fuller trade, business and economic contacts with the British mainland, must be accommodated. The impact of a different exchange rate policy on the South's trading links with the UK should be acknowledged.

Perhaps Paul Tansey's warning, in a paper highlighting the immediate prospects for tourism growth, is apposite. Peace, he says, should not be jeopardised by 'the imposition of grandiose structures.' Much better, he adds, 'that border crossings be built on the firm foundations of mutual economic benefits.'

Part 1

Outside Perspectives: The Case for an Island Economy

1 Letter from America

A. J. F. O'Reilly

It was my friend Sir George Quigley, chairman of the Ulster Bank and the Northern Ireland Economic Council, who popularised the term all-island economy. By this he means the island functioning as a natural economic zone, with both parts working together pragmatically, at all levels and in all sectors (public and private), in whatever way and to whatever extent is to their mutual benefit, to add value to what they are doing.

In a business sense, an all-island economy entails not only actively developing existing trade links but also promoting all kinds of co-operative relationships between companies to exploit their growth potential and attack new markets. It will be important to seize strategic opportunities, like the creation of an economic corridor between Belfast and Dublin, to produce the synergy, for the benefit of east, west, north, and south, that one would expect to see between cities of this size only a hundred miles apart.

This is not a parochial agenda. Whatever its political configuration, the island can position itself better than either part can do separately to respond to the opportunities and demands of the global economy.

An economic zone of this kind is essentially market-driven, but there are obstacles to its vigorous development (for example a poor transport infrastructure, which reduces accessibility) that it falls largely to governments to address. For example, only 15 per cent of the Belfast–Dublin route is motorway.

In Sir George's view, the optimum condition for progress towards the island economy is that both parts of the island should be growing strongly. With peace this should happen, and the opportunity to accelerate the pace should not be lost.

During the past twenty-five years the entire island has suffered from the cancer of violence, which ate away at our prosperity and self-esteem. In addition to the terrible human tragedy, vast resources of money and energy have been diverted from productive enterprise. The peace process has now lifted a cloud from the island and opened up a host of possibilities and opportunities. For the people on the island, it is akin to the sense of relief that accompanied the end of the Cold War. Nothing could be more important to us than sustaining this peace process.

The key to lasting peace in Ireland is in economic development and prosperity. Because we have a small home market of five million people, outside investment is essential to sustain economic growth. For some investors the island suffers from low population density and peripheral location, an island behind an island. As I will discuss below, these factors become advantages when attracting tourists and selling an image of environmental purity in a post-Chernobyl Europe. But when it comes to encouraging business leaders to invest in Ireland as distinct from anywhere else in Europe, we must minimise the political and bureaucratic barriers that divide the already small domestic markets. For example, it is extraordinary to think that some 5 per cent of the South's total exports go to the North, while the North supplies only 4 per cent of the South's imports. The good news is that in the first eight months of 1994, North–South trade has increased by 22 per cent, and South–North trade has increased by 11 per cent.

However, contrast this minimal trading with Canada and the United States, which share a 3,000-mile border. Following the NAFTA agreement, businesses on both sides of that border are rationalising their manufacturing and distribution facilities. For instance, the Heinz factory in Leamington, Ontario, packs vegetarian beans, junior baby foods and bulk tomato paste for sale throughout North America. Likewise, Heinz USA in Pittsburgh makes private-label soup, pickles and single-serve ketchup, among other things, for continent-wide distribution.

As this century comes to a close, global competition for investment capital has become more intense. New and emerging economies are entering the market economy and offering incentives for inward capital and growth. Billions of dollars are switched from country to country at the touch of a keyboard. Capital is ruthlessly seeking the best rate of return, without regard to ideology, race, or religion. Power centres have moved from traditional elites to high-technology industries and to the Asia-Pacific region. The information revolution is challenging conventional wisdom everywhere.

In these circumstances the island of Ireland cannot afford to stand on ceremony or be less aggressive in its business orientation than competing emerging economies. We must not lose the unique opportunity provided by the peace dividend to industrialise and provide jobs for all our people. There is now a danger that over-regulation from Brussels will act as an impediment to business development in Europe, particularly in the peripheral regions. Ireland must muster all its resources to play in the 'World Cup'. We are competing not with each other, North and South, not even with Britain, but with the other continents of the world. We have to benchmark our productivity and standards against the best work practices in Europe, Asia-Pacific, or North America.

The Industrial Development Authority was one of the first agencies in the world to recognise that we have to play in the world league. It has showcased Ireland's many advantages to attract a thousand overseas companies to Ireland. Four hundred of these are American, which earned an average annual rate of return on their investment of 25 per cent since the 1970s—four times the world average. This investment has transformed our economy: between them the companies employ four out of ten of all Irish workers employed in manufacturing; they represent 70 per cent of the country's exports and 55 per cent of its industrial output. All this from a standing start no more than thirty-five years ago.

The Industrial Development Board in Northern Ireland has obviously been hampered by twenty-six years of violence. Against this background it has had its successes. Last year it attracted thirteen overseas investments, totalling £216 million sterling and creating a potential 2,300 jobs. Now in co-operation with the IDA in a new environment of peace it should become very successful. President Clinton's White House conference was particularly welcome because it highlighted the investment attractions on both sides of the border. American investment in Ireland is a win-win for both countries: the United States gains new markets in Europe, and Ireland avails itself of American technology and capital to create jobs and economic growth.

The island as a whole can now be marketed as a gateway to Europe. The best talents of the public and private sectors should examine how we can do things better collectively. Economies of scale must be pursued ruthlessly in the face of special interests and 'turf wars'. The attractions that the IDA has successfully projected can be promoted by both North and South. There is an educated work force, the language of global business, important tax incentives, capital grants, excellent raw materials, and pro-business political systems.

A word about tax incentives. Corporations do not talk publicly about this very much, but financial analysts will quickly judge the quality of a company's management by how efficiently it manages its tax rate. The US corporate tax rate, including federal and state tax, is approximately 39 per cent, but there are American companies that have a tax rate in the twenties. That is why the 10 per cent manufacturing tax is so important in the South. I would respectfully suggest that the North be granted a similar tax regime by the British government. In private conversation with American business leaders and bankers, the 10 per cent tax is constantly highlighted as a very important incentive. The North already has a special political status, and according it a special tax status should not be a major challenge if the result is more jobs and a self-sustaining economy that enhances the peace process.

Clearly, North and South must work together to make the island package even more attractive. As I said earlier, there are very few developed countries whose main cities are not connected by motorways. Belfast and Dublin should be connected by a motorway-based economic corridor. Two years ago Heinz located a frozen food factory in Dundalk, half way between these two cities, so that we could benefit from a choice of ferries and airports to Britain and the Continent. We now employ over three hundred people at this factory and are planning to expand its operations to include Weight Watchers products. Our managers are very happy with the quality of our work force and the supply of high-quality food materials, and we intend to grow this facility. Our products are produced in the South near Dundalk and are exported through the North via the port of Larne.

There are also major opportunities for co-operation in tourism, agriculture, health, and fisheries. Back in 1988 I said to an Irish Management Conference in Killarney that Ireland enjoys a unique image of purity, greenness, and tranquillity. Our peripheral location, which proved a barrier to the Romans, can now be marketed as a true advantage in an overpopulated and polluted world. We must try to bring together the dairy, beef and seafood interests in a renewed and high-quality campaign for a 'Garden of Ireland'. We could look to New Zealand, which has successfully pursued a low-cost private enterprise policy as the garden of the South Pacific. An increase in foreign investment in the Irish food sector will increase the capacity for branded exports and help develop consistent standards of high quality. In addition, both parts of Ireland have tremendous attractions for tourism, with golf and fishing as well as with their cultural and heritage diversity. For example, the North has only begun to tap into its rich 'Scotch-Irish' tradition in the United States and Canada.

Finally, a word of caution. If the island of Ireland is to prosper in the twenty-first century it must focus on the global consumer. Price and value and service with a smile are the elements gaining universal appeal. A culture of begrudgery does not have universal appeal, especially where envy and prejudice disguise themselves as public policy to the detriment of community development. The global competition of the twentieth century was ideological—a struggle to convert people from one political belief to another. The global competition of the twenty-first century will hopefully be more commercial—a struggle to understand and to satisfy the consumers of the world. Business and financial leaders must co-operate with politicians and officials to succeed in this new world. The leadership shown by the respective employer organisations in Ireland, North and South, is exemplary. The mission of the CBI and IBEC is simple: to increase trade between both parts of Ireland, creating more attractive markets for international investment. The engine of growth is private enterprise, and it must be fuelled by infrastructural development and a pro-business environment. The tax systems must encourage investors and savers rather than punish them. At the same time, more people must be trained and motivated to have the freedom to join the productive wealth-producing culture of a new, peaceful island. In Ireland and around the world, men and women, when given the opportunity, will choose economic independence.

This fact has been confirmed to me when working for the American Ireland Fund which for twenty years has provided new opportunities to thousands of Irish people. Once a single chapter in New York, the Ireland Funds have grown to become the largest Irish charitable organisation raising funds internationally. Over $60 million has been raised for projects, many of which have difficulty in receiving alternative funding when they are at the start-up stage. These have ranged from integrated religious schools in Belfast to the WIN business park in Newry. The Funds are active in America, Australia, Canada, France, Germany, Great Britain, Japan, New Zealand and South Africa and this year will hold fifty-one events in thirty-two cities. The Funds recognise the best hopes of a vast Irish diaspora, enabling Ireland's extended family and friends overseas to make a positive and peaceful contribution to Ireland's future.

The island of Ireland has over the past two thousand years endured many hardships; but its people have demonstrated an extraordinary capacity for leadership, creativity and hard work around the world. Now the five million people on the island have a unique opportunity to drive for the economic benefits of peace within the framework of the European Union and the wider framework of free-market globalism. With a network of seventy million people of Irish descent in the world and with the good will that the Irish universally enjoy there will be no shortage of allies. But to prosper, the five million people on the island must be prepared to abandon the patterns of the past that have set them at odds with each other economically as well as politically. Now, at last, with the bonds of enmity broken, they can join forces in a wider European framework to be creative and imaginative in developing one community of interest for the whole island.

2   *Letter from Geneva*

Peter Sutherland

For the rest of the world, and for the great majority of Irish people, North and South, the appalling and tragic violence of the last twenty-five years has been not merely inexplicable but riddled with cruel ironies. Here we have a small island populated by people who pray to the same God and generally call themselves Irish (at least when abroad) who have not so ordered their affairs as to be able to live harmoniously together. And yet both parts have decided to be part of a European Union that requires them to cede sovereignty to an entity that supersedes the nation-state to which they give allegiance. Furthermore, both parts are living in a world of five-and-a-half billion people, who increasingly recognise the concept of global interdependence. It seems like a throwback to an earlier age to have witnessed in Ireland the inability to understand and build upon shared interests in facing the challenges of this globalisation. The evidence of this failure is dramatically illustrated by the failure to even create a single effectively functioning market for goods and services in Ireland, or to develop structures and bodies to advance common economic interests internationally. Hopefully this situation may now be changing.

The transformation of the world in the last fifty years has made little apparent impression on the Irish situation. During that period we have become aware of the enormous potential for rapid progress in burying historic enmities elsewhere. Much of that progress has been driven by economic co-operation. Trade has transformed the world from separate markets into a global market. Lurking within that global market are more profoundly integrated regional economic areas extending beyond the nation-state. This advance in international trade has been much faster than the extraordinary growth that has taken place in global industrial and agricultural production. Concurrently we have witnessed the startling impact of technological change in making the world smaller. Information technology and the effects of automation have brought about a greater revolution in societies everywhere than political events have achieved in history. With up to $1,000 billion dollars moved around global exchanges daily, having the potential to destabilise economies in minutes, the issue of national economic governance, for good or ill, has to be viewed as being significantly limited by external factors that cannot be controlled domestically. Even where decisions are taken domestically, such as in budget policy, global financial markets effectively place limits within which governments must seek to manoeuvre. In addition, of course, the age-old conflicts for political power in small geographical areas are increasingly absurd in a world threatened by a capacity for self-destruction through environmental disaster or nuclear war—both of which can be confronted only through international structures for global governance.

The purpose of this contribution is to set out some of the parameters of the challenges that face us in the area of trade. Trade remains the only viable means of creating a more prosperous and self-confident Ireland, and it will be advances in our economy based on trade that will most effectively transform our societies in a positive way through the creation of employment both in the North and in the Republic.

I

Following the last war, the visible evidence of material and spiritual collapse was so obvious, particularly in Europe, that the absolute need for new structures for multilateral co-operation was understood at least by Western leadership. In addition there was a fleeting recognition that originality, courage and sacrifice were needed if a new and better world was to be built from the ruins that were the legacy of the past. The lessons of the failure of the policies and structures adopted following the First World War were apparent and were so historically proximate as to defy being ignored. A lack of generosity in victory then had contributed towards the re-emergence of the old vices in international affairs. These were essentially related to a willingness to place self-interest above any sense of the rights of others. The economic factors that contributed to the rise of totalitarian rule were also increasingly understood. The extent of unemployment, the development of protectionism and the effects of the depression of the thirties generally acted as a catalyst for a small but highly influential group to become the founding fathers of a new order. One of them, Dean Acheson, subsequently wrote of 'being present at the creation.' He was referring to the creation of the Bretton Woods organisations and the new trading system, the GATT. It was no accident that the conference that produced the Havana Charter was called 'the United Nations Conference on Trade and Employment'.

At a regional level also, and particularly in Europe, which had been the cockpit of so much suffering through the preceding century, new ideas were stirring. Again they represented both a rejection of established verities regarding national sovereignty and a determination to create new structures. They recognised that interdependence was an inevitable reality in a new world that maintained a capacity to destroy itself virtually by the pressing of a button, but that interdependence, to develop in an ordered way, needed an institutional base. Monnet, Schuman, de Gasperi, Adenauer and those others who launched the process of European integration recognised that economic factors influence peace just as they clearly had in the past precipitated war. The Coal and Steel Community and the European Economic Community represent the most far-reaching attempt to harness economic self-interest to the process of fostering interdependence and, essentially, reducing extreme nationalism.

Today we also live in challenging times. The challenge for leaders now is perhaps even greater than ever before, because they head what Professor J. K. Galbraith has described as the 'Contented Society'. Relative affluence and the inexorable rise of consumerism have made politicians wary of being seen as even temporarily interfering with the comfort of the electorate. Sacrifice may be palatable in moments of crisis, but few believe that today we face a crisis at all.

While we have the benefit of the wisdom of the architects of the European Union and the Bretton Woods institutions (and we are not faced with the immense challenge of repairing war damage and massive conversion to peacetime activities), we live in a world where the undoubted victory of economic liberalism has fostered a belief that survival of the fittest is the only creed necessary for progress.

We also live in a world in which the institutions that have governed international affairs are generally under greater criticism than ever before. The United Nations, the IMF and World Bank and the European Union are increasingly the focus of virulent criticism.

II

Allowing for some inevitable oversimplification, the origins of the current challenge confronting international economic relations can be traced principally to four developments. They are largely independent, in the sense that any one of them could have occurred on its own, yet they interact in ways that multiply their separate impacts.

The first is the continuing integration of the world economy. Led by the liberalisation of exchange and capital restrictions, technological change, innovations in the organisation of international business operations, and the more open and secure trading environment made possible by GATT, the volume of world trade has expanded more rapidly than the volume of world output in nearly every year since the end of the Second World War.

As the world's trade-to-output ratio has steadily increased, national frontiers have become less and less relevant for private-sector decisions concerning investment, production, and consumption. The mirror image of more intense competition on world markets has been an increasingly defensive stance of import-competing industries, especially pronounced in the developed countries in periods when markets have grown slowly and even shrunk. Thus, even as the national economic interest becomes increasingly identified with an open international economic environment, the forces hostile to the openness clamour more loudly for assistance. Whether actually linked to trade or not, persistent social problems, including high rates of unemployment, are perceived by some analysts as the main 'costs' of liberal trade. From 1959 to 1973 the rate of unemployment in Europe was only about 2 per cent. In the United States it averaged about 5 per cent. Now the OECD has 36 million unemployed, and in the European Union it is about 12 per cent. In Ireland it is, of course, worse. In the United States, while unemployment has remained steady at between 5.5 and 7 per cent for nearly two decades, the real wages of workers have stagnated. This all provides fertile ground for those who argue for protectionism, even though their arguments have as much validity as that of the snake-oil salesman.

The second development is the sharply different demographic trends in the developed and developing countries. Very low or zero population growth rates in the OECD countries are aging the populations and bringing many attendant changes, not the least of which are the financial implications for national pension schemes. As for the developing countries, of the nearly two billion people who will be added to the world's population in the next twenty years, ninety-five out of each hundred will be born outside the current OECD area. One consequence is that between now and 2015 the number of new jobs required to keep unemployment rates unchanged in the developing world will exceed the current populations of Western Europe and North America combined. Again the economic implications are manifold, including competition for capital and a continuing shift in competitiveness in labour-intensive activities to high-population-growth countries. Nor is it a coincidence that migration, and the linkage between pressures for migration from low-income countries and trade barriers in the rich countries, are moving rapidly up the international agenda. World population was 1.5 billion in 1900; it has reached 5.5 billion today; it will be 10 billion in 2050. Consider furthermore some of the latest UN medium-term projections. Morocco will grow from 25 million to 46 million, Egypt from 52 to 90 million, Brazil from 150 to 246 million, Iran from 55 to 114, India from 853 to 1,512 million.

The third development is the spread of market-oriented reforms. In transition economies, reforms are liberating markets from government control and creating the basis for faster growth. Export-led growth strategies in developing countries have led to the rejection of import substitution. In both cases difficulties have arisen in this process, exacerbated by limits on export access to vital areas. But the trend remains clear. For much of the postwar period, more than three-quarters of the world's people lived in countries whose governments were sceptical of—and in some instances openly hostile to—the advantages of integration into world markets. India and Latin America provide obvious examples. That has changed, and the implications for international economic relations are enormous. Since 1982, for example, the developing countries have nearly doubled their share of world exports of manufactures, from 11 per cent to more than 20 per cent last year. One-third of the top twenty-five traders of goods and services are now developing countries.

The fourth development is the end of the Cold War. National economic 'competitiveness' has now become a rallying cry, and competition has increasingly been refocused from the political-military sphere to the economic sphere. While the notion of competition between countries and regions is rather simplistic in an era of greater global economic integration, where competition among enterprises is a much more relevant concept, it nonetheless seems to influence policy-making to a growing extent. And, as the interests that bound together traditional alliances have shifted, the cohesion that helped countries resolve economic problems can no longer be taken for granted, increasing uncertainty in the area of international economic relations. The European Union no longer survives in the uncomfortable stability of a divided world. Its membership is no longer defined by an Iron Curtain. Even its relationship with the United States has dramatically altered in the absence of the bipolar world that was there before.

Along with pressures for structural adjustment, issues of sovereignty can also generate frictions between countries. As advances in communications and transport shrink distances between people, and each country's activities become more intertwined with those of other countries, it is inevitable that countries will find that there are increased external influences on what used to be considered purely domestic policies. This is, of course, particularly true of the European Union. Indeed the range of policies considered as trade-related has steadily grown, from measures applied at the border on imported products to policies whose trade effects are incidental to their main purpose, such as production subsidies, taxation, investment, anti-trust and technical standards, and domestic regulations. New areas of attention include the protection of the environment, which has been accepted as being part of the future trade agenda. Other issues that have been raised include, for example, the relationship between the trading system and internationally recognised labour standards, the relationship between immigration policies and international trade, trade and competition policy, trade and investment, regionalism, and the interaction between trade policies and policies relating to financial and monetary matters.

The common element in these developments is continuous pressure for structural adjustments in patterns of production, investment, and world trade. From an economic efficiency perspective the challenge is to ensure that these adjustments take place in a timely and orderly fashion, while from a political perspective the challenge is to prevent adjustment pressures from generating trade tensions and an associated souring of political relations between countries that could lead in time to conflict.

III

How can we hope to cope with the immensity of these challenges? In the first instance we have to recognise that they can only be addressed in the context of some form of order. This order to the extent that it existed in the past was largely based on a concept of the balance of power (which some, such as Henry Kissinger, still see as an essential element in maintaining global stability). An aspect of the balance of power was a perception of the need for powerful players who would, when push came to shove, be willing to use their great power in order to maintain stability. In the past this imperialist role was more easily played than today. For example, the electorates of Europe, Russia and the United States have begun to clearly demonstrate that for whatever reasons, whether founded on morality or self-interest, they do not relish the prospect of foreign military adventures. Colonialism as historically understood is generally, and one hopes permanently, out of fashion. So if the balance-of-power logic is undermined by a more disengaged public base and a more disparate world, how are peace and progress to be maintained? How are the more powerful to be prevailed on to act in a manner consistent with the rights of others?

One element in a solution is related to the structures of trade. There is no more potent cause of international tension than trade. It was the recognition of this fact that promoted the most essential element, at least up to the present time, in the European integration process, namely its economic integration.

If there are no rules in trade then the resulting anarchy will inevitably lead to conflict. In *The Constitution of Liberty,* Friedrich von Hayek developed John Locke's very important idea of law as a guarantor of freedom: 'The end of the law is, not to abolish or restrain, but to preserve and enlarge freedom.

For in all the states of created beings capable of laws, where there is no law there is no freedom.' At the international level such norms not only ensure freedom for economic agents to operate in their commercial interest across national frontiers, they also enhance the freedom of governments in their trade policy interventions, by defining the scope of actions permissible within the confines of international law. The behaviour of all governments becomes more predictable when all accept the rules of the game.

In the spring of 1995 we witnessed the long-delayed birth of a new institution: the World Trade Organisation. Had the founding fathers of the Bretton Woods institutions had their way, this organisation would have been born as the International Trade Organisation in the late forties. It now stands as testimony to the willingness of the governments of well over 120 countries to accept disciplines in international trade. It further represents a recognition that multilateralism, rather than the power politics of bilateralism or unilateralism, is the best way to order our affairs in this difficult area. We should, however, recall that a rule-based system such as that now created in the largest treaty ever concluded is only as good as the credibility of its rules and procedures. It is a purely intergovernmental structure, largely relying on peer pressure for compliance with its rulings.

For several years before the successful conclusion of the Uruguay Round a number of developments had been contributing to a steady erosion of GATT's credibility. These included a failure to bring agriculture under GATT disciplines and the exclusion of textiles and clothing from the normal rules. I single both of these out for mention because they demonstrate some of the ambivalence that we in Europe can have at times towards a reasonable balance of rights and obligations in trade. The developed countries and, in particular, Europe and the United States ultimately had greater difficulty in concluding and ratifying the Uruguay Round than others. They were far more likely to cause the Round's collapse, and with it the whole multilateral system, than were the developing countries as a whole or in any one region. The greatest opposition came in areas where export opportunities for the developing world are not merely a counterpart to the access demanded by the developed world to their dynamic markets, but are an indispensable element in avoiding a world placed in turmoil by the maintenance of a divide between rich and poor. How can we in Western Europe look with confidence to the future if we deny the opportunity for growth to the vast population of the former communist bloc or if we exclude from our markets the products of the Maghreb? This is where leadership really counts. It is all very well to mouth the rhetoric of inclusion but if the deeds are a contradiction of the rhetoric then the future will bring its riposte. I am not one of those who believe, as Huntingdon suggests, that we are facing an imminent conflict between civilisations. I do, however, believe that division rather than reasonable harmony will be the result of policies in trade that seek to ignore the obligation to open one's own markets when at the same time one demands the opening of others. The political dilemma here is not an easy one but, as a recent report by the European Bank for Reconstruction and Development emphasises, the arguments for trade and not aid are overwhelming.

So in a time when some international institutions are criticised, a new one has been born. It provides a basis for some optimism in the area where the global economy will have its greatest impact on political developments: trade. It brings within an international discipline whole new areas, such as services and intellectual property. Perhaps most important of all, it creates a dispute settlement system that will have a decisive role in determining right and wrong in areas of trade conflict. Decisions will no longer be held hostage to a requirement that they be adopted by unanimity among the contracting parties. Unanimity will be required now to block decisions rather than to take them.

From the challenges facing international economic relations I draw the conclusion that there is a compelling need to enhance co-operative arrangements at the international level in order to promote coherence in economic policy-making. This need exists not only in the area of trade relations but also more generally in relation to other aspects of economic policy. Indeed, one decision taken in the Uruguay Round was that the World Trade Organisation should 'pursue and develop co-operation with international organisations responsible for monetary and financial matters,' and the director-general of the WTO was invited to pursue this question. Last year at the World Economic Forum in Davos, speaking personally, I argued that the existing high-level forums for the development of global economic policy initiatives were inadequate for the task that now faces them. Neither the G7 nor the G15 reflects a perspective that adequately represents the world economic community. Their authority to set political objectives in the economic area is thus not as effective as necessary. There is an urgent need to establish a structure for annual discussions of global economic policy that can provide, at the highest level, the necessary impetus for the implementation of specific commitments on new initiatives to address the challenges that I have enumerated earlier. Any co-operation between the WTO, the IMF and the World Bank must surely be premised upon a coherent policy that is broadly acceptable.

IV

Let me turn now to the European Union. In doing so I would underline that if Ireland is to play a real role in the development of global economic or indeed political strategies it can only realistically expect to do so in the context of our participation in the EU. There are those who have fostered the myth, for myth it is, that Ireland had decisive influence on world events in the past in, for example, the United Nations. The future of the European Union will determine the role—if any—that we as a people can play in addressing the challenges of a world that is changing more rapidly and less predictably than at any stage in its history. However, I would also like to emphasise a second and less insular point: in my opinion, the creation and maintenance of any world order requires the continuing integration of the European Union. More particularly, it requires the deepening of its institutional base.

The process of European integration may have been motivated originally by a desire to heal the division of a continent that had constantly re-enacted the worst moments of its own history. Now, however, the absolute need for its further development is both external and internal. The core principle of the EU is that it should develop through the sharing of sovereignty rather than by mere co-operation among nation-states. If that principle were to be weakened rather than strengthened then the prospects for the implementation of global strategies to influence change for the better would be significantly damaged. Let me give an example. If the European Union did not have the internal institutional framework that allowed for the articulation and implementation of a common external economic policy, then I believe we could never have concluded the Uruguay Round. If the members of the EU had spoken with individual voices they would no doubt have created a situation where consensus could not have been achieved globally. This in turn would have led inexorably to the collapse of a system, the GATT, that had served much of the world well since the last war.

One looks now with apprehension at the forthcoming debate on the next stage of the integration process, because should it fail, or even seriously falter, it is not merely the constituents of the EU that suffer. In this regard it is difficult to be optimistic. The recent experience of the Maastricht Treaty is a pointer to the risks we face. In addition, with the passing of those who learnt and remembered the lessons of history, we are now faced with a new generation, many of whom have yet to demonstrate that they appreciate what has been achieved—and what is at risk. More fundamentally, by reducing the debate on Europe to tabloid trivia, by failing to contest the xenophobic and racist trends now evident in parts of Europe (and the protectionist rhetoric that is extreme nationalism's economic concomitant), we have before us the imminent danger that we could not merely lose the momentum for integration but could reverse the process.

The European Union acting as an entity in international affairs either in the political or in the economic areas should be an instrument for moderation and tolerance. This should be the case precisely because the varied experience of its member-states develops shared principles pragmatically applied in a way that is less likely to be found in policies that are the result of purely national influences.

V

Before leaving the topic of European integration I would like to refer to Ireland.

In writing about a post-war Europe while in prison in 1942, Altiero Spinelli mentioned prophetically that Ireland and Yugoslavia were two places that needed a new overarching order to permit different communities to live and work together in harmony. It is a sad fact that when that new order was created for both parts of this island in 1973, by the time we both joined the EC, we abjectly failed to take advantage of it. The fact that the European experiment was primarily motivated by a desire for reconciliation in continental Europe was apparently not recognised as having any real relevance in Ireland, even though there were few communities in more need of reconciliation. Instead of using trade to create understanding, even the most elementary contact, we let the opportunity slip. Not merely did trade not grow between North and South, in some areas it significantly declined. As a result, we increasingly exacerbated myths about each other. We literally alienated ourselves. When John Taylor, the Ulster Unionist MP, expressed pleasant surprise about what he found in Kilkenny when he went there recently, he reflected, I am sure, an experience many might share.

Sir George Quigley, the prominent Northern Ireland businessman, has ploughed more or less a lone furrow in promoting cross-border trade, or at least he has had little official support until recently. The business communities, however, have now woken up to the possibilities. The staggering communication deficit between Belfast and Dublin, whether by air or road, speaks volumes for the indifference of successive administrations, particularly on the southern side of the border. Perhaps closed minds and fantasies could be removed if we developed better economic relations. Ireland could then be presented as a paradigm for others in demonstrating that economics and peace are inextricably bound together.

We all wish the end of violence to be crowned with political structures that will have the consent of all communities. We all clearly wish to see a lasting peace sustained by widespread agreement and mutual trust and confidence. As the political parties involve themselves in the search for agreement, it is important, I believe, not to lose sight of the economic and trade dimension so cruelly undermined by the years of violence. Ireland, North and South, shares the problem of high unemployment. If we are to tackle this scourge we can best do it together in co-operation, not only through trade with each other but also in co-operating to sell into the global market.

We have, it appears to me, identical economic interests and indeed claims on the policies of the European Union. Our economies have essentially shared characteristics. While our industrialisation histories are different, with the North having a much longer one, we share a similar agricultural base. We also share a need to develop an entrepreneurial culture. In the Republic our exports amount to 63 per cent of our GNP, and in recent years they have grown up to three times as fast as the economy as a whole, but many of our successes have been the result of the activities of non-indigenous firms. In the North the dependence is greater on the British market than is the case with the Republic, but overall we both need to develop markets in other places, such as Asia and Latin America. Surely there is much that can be done together in attracting inward investment and developing overseas markets?

Increasingly we will be compelled to raise our eyes from the microscopic issues of this small place to the vast challenges of the broader world that surrounds us. These challenges cannot be ignored and present far more of an opportunity than a threat. Perhaps if we talk more of them and seek to understand the dramatically changing times in which we live, our weary disputes may be placed in a perspective that will compel their resolution.

This chapter is adapted from a paper delivered to the inaugural conference of University College Cork, in January 1995.

Part 2

Economic and Historical Background

3 Ireland's Partition: A Brief History

Jonathan Bardon

It is worth being reminded that human beings had been living in Australia for some forty thousand years before the very first people set foot in Ireland. The oldest known habitation site, discovered in 1972, is Mount Sandel, near Coleraine, which suggests that the first intrepid Mesolithic arrivals came from Scotland over nine thousand years ago. Thereafter this aboriginal gene pool was steadily topped up by people moving westwards from the European continent. Ireland, however, was spared invasion by both the Romans and Germanic tribes; this enabled a Gaelic civilisation, Christianised in the fifth century, to come into full flowering in the early Middle Ages. It is misleading to regard the Gaels as a separate race, as so many Irish did until recently: their ties with the rest of western Europe were strong, and their culture was a compound of languages, beliefs and customs brought by successive incomers.

Until the early seventeenth century, Ulster was separated from the rest of Ireland to some degree by natural defences, in particular the largest drumlin belt in Europe, stretching from Donegal Bay across to Strangford Lough. Densely wooded and separated by treacherous wetlands, these low hills formed a frontier of some significance. This barrier, never completely impenetrable, should not be overemphasised, but it does explain in part why Ulster remained the most Gaelic province in Ireland until the reign of James I.

Ireland was thrown on the defensive by Viking raids from the end of the eighth century, but the north proved less attractive than the east and the south, where the Northmen made impressive settlements at Dublin, Waterford, Limerick, and elsewhere. In the eleventh century the Normans conquered England thoroughly and swiftly after the Battle of Hastings. By contrast, they overran only the fertile lowlands in Ireland a century later. Ulster was the least affected province: from 1177 John de Courcy, and those Anglo-Normans who came after him, took only the Down and Antrim coastlands. From 1300 onwards the English Crown's authority began to decline, eventually contracting to a few ports and an area around Dublin known as the Pale. By 1500 the Gaelic Irish had recovered all of Ulster save Carrickfergus, parts of

Lecale, and the tip of the Ards peninsula. Ulster, in short, was beyond the Pale.

Tudor Conquest and Stuart Plantation

In the sixteenth century, England became a great European power. During a period when international tensions were aggravated by religious bitterness, the Crown could not afford to let a hostile power unite with disaffected Irish and use the island as a base from which to threaten England from the west.

By the time Elizabeth came to the throne in 1588, much of Ireland had been recovered, but Ulster largely remained beyond the Crown's grasp. Heading a formidable coalition of all the Gaelic lords of the north, Hugh O'Neill of Tyrone for several years inflicted severe defeats on the English in the 1590s. Spanish help, however, caused Elizabeth to spare no expense, and eventually, a few days after the Queen's death in 1603, O'Neill capitulated. The final stages of this conquest were terrible: by burning corn and seizing cattle the English commanders caused mass starvation in Ulster and left bitter memories among the survivors.

James I's solution to the problem of Ulster was to settle Protestant English and 'Inland' Scots in the newly conquered territory. Piecemeal colonisation of the counties of Antrim and Down from 1603 onwards was strikingly successful. The 'Plantation of Ulster'—an ambitious scheme to colonise confiscated land in the rest of the province with the exception of County Monaghan—was launched in 1610.

For the future the tragedy was that Ulster was conquered and colonised at a time of intense religious division in Europe. In a sense, that conflict was frozen in time in the north, to survive to the present day. The plantation was neither a complete success nor a total failure. Not enough land was left for the native Irish, and yet the colonists did not come over in sufficient numbers to be able to manage their estates without Irish help. The incoming British felt deeply insecure, while the dispossessed Irish resented the intrusion of settlers with an alien language, alien customs, and alien religion.

Rebellion and International Conflict

Political instability across the Irish Sea on the eve of the English Civil War gave the Gaelic natives in Ulster the opportunity they sought. In 1641 they rose in furious rebellion and slaughtered great numbers of settlers. Soon after, the Scots and later Cromwell's forces exacted a fearful revenge in blood: the horrors of these times were etched into the folk memory of both sides.

After a period of peace and recovery under Charles II, Ireland was again dislocated by a bout of political turmoil. For a time the island became the cockpit of western Europe as England and the Netherlands attempted to halt Louis XIV's bid for domination. The forces of France and the Catholic King James II at first swept the country but then were routed at Derry and Enniskillen in 1689, at the Boyne in 1690, and most decisively at Aughrim on 12 July 1691, when seven thousand Irishmen were killed in an afternoon. These victories ensured the survival of the Plantation of Ulster, which began to attract a new influx of British settlers.

Oppression, Peace, and Prosperity

A typical tolerant Dutch Protestant, William III was overruled nevertheless by landlords in both the Dublin and Westminster parliaments. Further land confiscations were authorised, and a series of statutes enacted between the 1690s and 1720s, known as the Penal Laws, severely curbed Catholic rights. This code was designed to weaken the Catholic elite to prevent further rebellion; it was only partly effective, because (assuming that land was the sole source of wealth) it failed to prevent the rise of a new Catholic commercial middle class. In Ulster, however, Catholics were confined overwhelmingly to the lower rungs of society, with the exception of the town of Newry.

The Protestant victory was so decisive that the island was largely at peace for a century. Contrary to popular opinion, Ireland enjoyed increasing prosperity and was able to benefit from Britain's expanding colonial trade. In the seventeenth century Ulster's extensive sessile oak forests offered a quick cash return, but these were so ruthlessly plundered that in 1780 the bark from a single oak tree on the Conway estate was sold for £40. As the most northerly province, with much high ground and waterlogged soil, Ulster did not seem well placed for successful commercial agriculture. However, settlers from the north of England, Quakers in particular, established a flourishing domestic linen industry in south-central Ulster. Smallholders supplemented their income by spinning and weaving in their own homes and sold their webs in Lurgan, Armagh, Dungannon, and Lisburn. This area became a cradle of the first industrial revolution as drapers harnessed water to power wash-mills, rub-boards and beetling engines to finish the cloth for an expanding market. The Newry Canal (the first in Ireland or Britain) and the Lagan Navigation helped this trade and directed it away from Dublin to the flourishing ports of Newry and Belfast.

Sectarian Conflict, Rebellion, and the Union

It was among the farmer-weavers of the 'Linen Triangle' in mid-Ulster that sectarian conflict revived from the 1780s onwards. In fierce competition to gain access to scraps of land close to the markets, the weavers fought at fairs and in the countryside, Protestants calling themselves Peep o' Day Boys and Catholics naming themselves Defenders. The real border then was the Bann: east of the river, Protestants were numerous enough to feel secure. Influenced by the American and French Revolutions and determined to break the power of the ruling elite, the Protestant Ascendancy, the Presbyterian middle class of Belfast founded the Society of United Irishmen in 1791.

Meanwhile the sectarian warfare west of the Bann reached a crescendo, and in September 1795 the Peep o' Day Boys routed Defenders at the Battle of the Diamond and founded the Orange Order at Loughgall immediately afterwards. The United Irish were strongest in Belfast, Lisburn and Ballymena and won the support of Presbyterian farmers in Antrim and Down. These Protestants became revolutionaries in 1795 and sought the assistance of the French. After the Diamond, Defenders joined the United Irishmen wholesale and, being driven from County Armagh by the Orangemen, spread the revolutionary fire southwards.

When rebellion came in 1798 it was strongest in Leinster. The Orangemen kept mid-Ulster cowed while the Crown forces defeated the Protestant farmers easily enough at Antrim and Ballynahinch. The operation to crush the Leinster insurgents was on a much larger scale and may have left as many as forty thousand dead. Thoroughly frightened by belated French involvement, the Westminster government cajoled and bribed the thoroughly unrepresentative Irish Parliament into voting itself out of existence in 1800.

The Union: Poverty or Prosperity?

In the eighteenth century, Dublin was the second-largest city in the British Empire. After the Union the city's textile industry found it increasingly difficult to compete with the power-driven mills and factories of northern England. For the same reason the domestic linen industry in mid-Ulster and west Cork, and the domestic woollen industry throughout the rest of Ireland, suffered catastrophic decline. A rapidly rising population depended ever more heavily on what the overworked soil could produce. The potato, the staple food of about half the inhabitants, was destroyed by blight in the 1840s; about a million people died from hunger and famine fever, and about a million people emigrated.

There was a flight from the land, and those without the resources to go abroad often ended up in Belfast, which became the fastest-growing urban centre in the United Kingdom. At first growth depended on cotton produced by steam and water-powered machines. Finding it difficult to compete with Manchester, the mill owners transferred to the power production of linen yarn in the 1830s and 1840s and the power weaving of cloth in the 1850s and 1860s. During the American Civil War (when supplies of cotton wool were closed off) Belfast became the world centre of the linen industry.

The linen industry stimulated the growth of engineering firms (such as Mackie's, making textile machinery) and encouraged the Harbour Board to cut a deep channel at the mouth of the Lagan; the mud from this cut formed Queen's Island, and here Edward Harland began making vessels from riveted iron plates. The partnership of Harland and Wolff flourished in collaboration with the White Star Line, building ocean-going passenger liners. Wolff set up ropeworks nearby that soon became the largest in the world.

Belfast became a city in 1888 (it was then the largest in Ireland), and by 1900 it was one of the great cities of the Empire, with the biggest shipyard in the world launching the largest ships in the world, the biggest linen mill, the biggest tobacco factory, the biggest tea machinery works, the biggest ropeworks, the biggest aerated waters factory, and the biggest gasometer in the world ... but it was a city with severe problems.

Sectarian Conflict in the Nineteenth Century

In the eighteenth century the Protestants of Belfast were noted for their liberalism and tolerance (they paid for the first Catholic chapel in 1785 and attended the opening). In part this was because Catholics, few in number, posed no threat. In the nineteenth century an entirely new urban population emerged as Protestants and Catholics poured in from the surrounding Ulster countryside. These immigrants brought with them folk memories of past conflicts, massacres, and dispossession; they chose where they lived with care, clustering with their co-religionists in distinct districts. Protestant ones included Sandy Row, the Shankill, the Village, and most of east Belfast; Catholic ones included—in order of creation—the Markets, Short Strand, Hercules Lane (now Royal Avenue), the Pound Loney, the Falls, and the Bone; and these ghettos were separated by invisible frontiers.

The rapid growth of Belfast and the changing of frontiers between districts led to ferocious sectarian rioting. The worst were in 1857, 1864, 1872, and 1886. Much the same happened in Derry: the walled Protestant city expanded and Catholics settled in the suburbs, notably the Bogside. Riots ensued, though on a smaller scale than in Belfast.

The sectarian riots got worse, even though the proportion of Protestants in

Belfast rose to 75 per cent in the early twentieth century. This was due in part to the growing importance of the national question.

The Clashing of Aspirations, 1841–1941

Led by Daniel O'Connell, Irish Catholics campaigned peacefully for emancipation (achieved in 1829) and for repeal of the Act of Union, that is, the restoration of a parliament in Dublin subservient to Westminster (this failed in the 1840s, partly because of the Famine).

Parliamentary reforms in 1832, 1867 and 1872 made Westminster more representative of the people, now able to vote in secret. By 1886, 86 out of 100 Irish MPs were nationalists, seeking 'Home Rule', that is, devolution—a parliament in Dublin but with Ireland staying in the British Empire. In 1886 the Liberal government supported the nationalists and put forward the first Home Rule Bill. This failed to pass the Commons because of some desertions from the Liberal Party on the issue.

A second Home Rule Bill in 1893 passed the Commons but was defeated by the unrepresentative peers in the House of Lords. The return of Conservative governments put the question into cold storage.

In 1906 the Liberals returned to power and in 1911—in a constitutional crisis—virtually destroyed the power of the Lords (they could only delay the passing of a bill by two years).

The Road to Partition, 1912–21

As nationalist passion spread across Europe in the nineteenth century it became ever clearer that those who regarded themselves as distinct nationalities were not neatly divided from each other. The lands of the Crown of St Stephen, for example, claimed by Hungarians, included substantial Slovak, Romanian, Croat, Serb and Slovene minorities. In Ireland, particularly in Ulster, Protestants and Catholics increasingly believed that they formed two separate nations. Certainly they had profoundly divergent aspirations.

Nearly all Irish Catholics wanted national self-determination, either in the form of Home Rule or complete separation. Some Protestants, drawn largely from the intelligentsia, shared this aspiration, but the great majority were growing stronger in their determination to remain in the United Kingdom. Nationalists had the support of three-quarters of the Irish people and believed they had the right not only to decide their own destiny but also to rule the whole island. Unionists saw themselves as Britons (though perhaps with their own regional characteristics), and, in any case, the Gaelic Revival made them feel aliens in their own land. Northern unionists demonstrated that the prosperous industrial north-east was tied in with the British Empire, the source of raw materials and the market for ships, ropes, and other manufactured products: they feared that this prosperity would be threatened by a Dublin parliament determined to impose protective tariffs or to tax northern industry to subsidise impoverished farmers in the west and south. Unionists feared that their Protestant 'liberties' (the control of schools, for example) would be endangered by a Catholic-dominated parliament. In addition, unionists were convinced that Home Rule was only a staging post on the road to full Irish independence.

In gratitude for the support of Irish nationalists, the Liberal government put forward a third Home Rule Bill in 1912. The issues that emerged were very similar to those that crystallised in the 1840s and that remain central in Ireland today.

Unionists had the support of the Conservative opposition at Westminster, but the third Home Rule Bill could only be delayed, not stopped: it was certain to become law some time in 1914. Unionists decided to resist Home Rule by unconstitutional means if necessary. On 28 September 1912 unionists signed a Covenant pledging themselves to resist Home Rule for all of Ireland 'by all means which may be found necessary ...' In 1913 the Ulster Volunteer Force was formed, and in April 1914 a huge consignment of German arms was smuggled in.

Ireland was brought to the brink of civil war when nationalists formed the Irish Volunteers in November 1913.

'I have never heard that orange bitters will mix with Irish whiskey,' T. G. Agar Robartes, a Liberal backbencher, had observed at an early stage in the Home Rule debate. His amendment to exclude the four most Protestant counties of Ulster from the bill's operation was decisively rejected. By the autumn of 1913, however, the government reconsidered and proposed an amendment to allow Ulster counties to opt out for six years. 'Irish nationalists can never be assenting parties to the mutilation of the Irish nation,' the nationalist leader John Redmond declared. Fortunately for Redmond, the Unionists demanded the permanent exclusion of all nine counties, which the government refused to consider. The partition of Ireland, however, had become a real possibility by the time the Great War had broken out in 1914.

Most of both the unionist and nationalist paramilitaries in Ireland agreed to fight with Britain in its war with Germany. Protected by the Royal Navy and too far away for Zeppelin raids, Ireland was rarely so peaceful and never before so prosperous. Factories, mills, shipyards and farms worked flat out to meet the insatiable demands of the British war machine.

A minority of Irish nationalists believed that Britain's difficulty was

Ireland's opportunity. Organised by the secret Irish Republican Brotherhood, a rebellion broke out in Dublin on Easter Monday 1916. This was a conspiracy and not a popular insurrection (fewer than two thousand took part), and it was crushed in less than a week. But thereafter nationalist opinion began to shift because of the execution of republican leaders and because Home Rule had been put into cold storage. A new separatist party, Sinn Féin (meaning 'ourselves'), was launched in 1917 to obtain full independence. A blundering suppression and an attempt to impose conscription in 1918 increased support for Sinn Féin.

During this period northern unionists decided that partition was the only solution. In June 1916 the Ulster Unionist Council voted to seek the exclusion of the six north-eastern counties (to the dismay of unionists who had signed the Covenant in Donegal, Cavan, and Monaghan). The following year unionist delegates from the north pressed this demand at the Irish Convention, to the consternation of southern unionists. The general election of 1918—the first in which there was 'one man one vote' and some women voters— shattered the Irish Parliamentary Party: it was not only a triumph for Sinn Féin, now with 73 seats, but also for the Unionists, who increased their representation from 18 to 26. The balance of power had shifted significantly in favour of the Unionists, for not only did Sinn Féin abstain from Westminster but also Lloyd George's coalition was overwhelmingly Conservative: more than half the MPs were members of the Conservative Party.

While the Dáil voted for a republic and Volunteers of the Irish Republican Army waged their guerrilla war, the British government prepared what was in effect a fourth Home Rule Bill. The cabinet committee was chaired by Walter Long, a strong supporter of the Ulster Unionists. The bill, which became law as the Government of Ireland Act in December 1920, gave Home Rule to two parts of the island—the twenty-six southern counties and the six north-eastern counties—with devolution (a local parliament) in Dublin and Belfast; both parts were still to send some MPs to Westminster, and both parliaments were to send representatives to the Council of Ireland to discuss common concerns.

The Dáil and the IRA rejected this solution, and the fighting continued. The Ulster Unionists, in spite of some public grumping, found this arrangement suited them perfectly. Six counties, rather than the nine of historic Ulster, would give them a comfortable majority; and a Belfast parliament would, they believed, protect them from the day when a Liberal or Labour government (less friendly to Unionists) would take power at Westminster.

The IRA suffered some severe defeats in the spring of 1921, and Britain was tiring of the expense of the campaign. A truce was agreed in July 1921 and eventually negotiations between the British government and representatives of the Dáil began in the autumn. On 6 December 1921 the Anglo-Irish Treaty was signed: the twenty-six counties would become the Irish Free State, a dominion similar in status to Canada (virtual independence), Britain would retain naval bases, and the frontier would be revised by a Boundary Commission. Sir James Craig (later Lord Craigavon), the Prime Minister of Northern Ireland, was furious and declared that he would yield 'not an inch' of the region's territory.

It is worth observing that partition was a solution applied elsewhere by the peacemakers after the First World War, with boundary commissions in Silesia (to decide the frontier between Poland, Germany and Czechoslovakia in that province) and Schleswig-Holstein (to determine the border between Denmark and Germany).

The Creation of Northern Ireland and the Boundary Commission

The irony was that the only part of Ireland to resist Home Rule was the only part to get it: the Government of Ireland Act, 1920, gave Northern Ireland a local parliament subservient to Westminster. Elections for this parliament in Belfast (it generally met in the City Hall) took place in May 1921; Ulster Unionists won 40 seats, the Nationalists 6 seats, and Sinn Féin 6 seats.

On 22 June 1921 King George V came in person to Belfast to open the Northern Ireland Parliament, and there he made an appeal 'to all Irishmen to pause, to stretch out the hand of forbearance and conciliation ...' A truce between the IRA and the British government was made in July, and negotiations on the future of the island began in London.

Northern Ireland came to life during a period of violence far worse than any experienced in the nineteenth century. As the political future of the island hung in the balance, sectarian warfare began in Londonderry (from June 1920) and Belfast (from July 1920). Characterised by rioting, burning, shooting, and assassination, the violence got worse after the 1921 Truce and reached a peak of intensity during the first six months of 1922. Between July 1920 and July 1922 the death toll in the six counties was 557: 303 Catholics, 172 Protestants, and 82 members of the security forces.

The Northern Ireland government's response to the violence and to the IRA campaign in particular was to adopt a Special Powers Act to give the Minister for Home Affairs authority to detain suspects and set up courts with exceptional jurisdiction. An armed police force was created, and the Ulster Special Constabulary (formed by the British government in 1920) was greatly expanded.

The outbreak of the Irish Civil War in June 1922 (between those for and against the 1921 Treaty) gave the Northern Ireland government the breathing space to restore order on its own terms. The Civil War delayed the re-drawing of the border; fighting stopped in May 1923 (with defeat for the republicans), and it was the end of 1924 before the commission began work. Only minor adjustments to the frontier were recommended, and after details had been leaked to the press in November 1925, the Dublin and London governments agreed to suppress the commission's findings ... and so the border remained without alteration.

The Northern Ireland Problem

The British government by now assumed that the 'Irish question' had been solved and turned their attention elsewhere. Though Northern Ireland seemed remarkably peaceful (there was not one sectarian murder between 1923 and 1933), major problems remained—problems in part inherited from previous centuries. The Catholics, one-third of the population, felt they were worse off than when all of Ireland was in the UK. They were now ruled by their political opponents (with a permanent majority) and wanted to be in the Irish Free State. The Protestants, two-thirds of the population, had a comfortable majority but feared that the Catholics, with southern help and perhaps with British government approval, would one day get all of Ireland placed under a Dublin government. Catholics for a time refused to send MPs to Belfast or take part in local government. The Unionists used this opportunity to re-draw local government boundaries to their advantage, to make sure that most public appointments were in their own hands, and to use the special powers and police to stifle dissent. The situation has been described as one where the Unionists were 'governing without consensus'.

Economic Problems

The financial arrangements in the over-complex constitutional relationship between Belfast and Westminster had been worked out during the postwar boom. When that boom ended, the Northern Ireland government found it extremely difficult to make ends meet. Northern Ireland suffered an acute depression between the two world wars. Why? Political instability probably discouraged new light industries from being set up, but the real reasons had nothing to do with politics.

The economic climate had completely changed during the First World War. Other countries developed new export industries that competed with Ulster's staple industries. Northern Ireland was dangerously dependent on a limited range of export products: ships, textile engineering, linen, aerated waters, and tobacco. There was a world surplus of ships: Japan, Sweden, the United States and others now had their own shipbuilding firms; cotton (and later artificial fibres) competed effectively with linen; states imposed import duties on aerated waters; and the prices obtained by farmers for their food went down throughout the world. In addition, the colonies and dominions—formerly good customers—experienced severe economic difficulties in these years.

Unemployment, which became more acute in the early 1930s, averaged at least 25 per cent for men between the two world wars. In the 1920s Irish Free State governments did not attempt to create the siege economy advocated by Sinn Féin's founder, Arthur Griffith, mainly because they did not see how smuggling could be controlled. In the 1930s, however, de Valera introduced his own brand of 'autarky' during the 'Economic War' with Britain, and high protective tariffs were to remain until the Anglo-Irish Free Trade Area Agreement of 1965.

Partition Reinforced

Policies of protection pursued by Dublin, together with the partial abandonment of free trade by London, helped to make partition more deeply felt as a day-to-day reality. Grave economic difficulties in districts north and south of the Border were aggravated by the dislocation of trade, despite new opportunities for profitable smuggling. De Valera campaigned vigorously against partition, but his trade policies reinforced it.

De Valera's decision to keep the Republic neutral ensured that the Second World War was a starkly contrasted experience for people living on the same island but divided by a political frontier into citizens of two states. The Republic suffered no more than a few air raids and a fall in living standards. By contrast, Belfast lost more lives in one air raid by the Germans than any other city in the United Kingdom except London. Northern Ireland had a strategic role as a base against the U-boats and then as the first toe-hold for the Americans preparing for the Normandy landings. Living standards rose in the North as the region's industries and farms strove to feed the Allied war machine.

The Labour government elected in 1945 introduced an all-embracing welfare state, and the bill for additional expenditure was lifted by central government; this was the beginning of the 'annual subvention' that today plays such a big role in Northern Ireland's economy. The result was a vast improvement in educational opportunities, health care, and living standards. Though unemployment black spots reappeared in places like Derry, generally the prospects for the future looked bright.

Intercommunal divisions remained stubbornly alive and came to the surface in 1949 when the Republic left the Empire. The British government gave its famous promise—repeated in the 1985 Anglo-Irish Agreement and the 1993 Joint Declaration—that Northern Ireland would remain part of the United Kingdom as long as the majority there wished it to be.

Lord Brookeborough, Prime Minister of Northern Ireland for twenty years, faced an IRA campaign between 1954 and 1962. It had little support and mainly affected border areas. Internment in both the Republic and Northern Ireland reduced the IRA to a relatively powerless movement.

Brookeborough refused most demands for reform from constitutional nationalists. Terence O'Neill replaced him as Prime Minister in 1963 and immediately made improvement in community relations a central part of his programme. He sought to bring the benefits of modernisation to everyone in the region and not just to the Protestant majority. In the 1960s traditional industries declined rapidly, but, helped by a sustained boom in the western world, the Unionist government was very successful in attracting multinational companies—such as Goodyear, Grundig, and synthetic fibre firms—to set up in Northern Ireland. O'Neill went out of his way to visit Catholic schools and hospitals, and invited the Taoiseach, Seán Lemass, to Stormont in 1965.

Ian Paisley, founder and moderator of the Free Presbyterian Church, denounced O'Neill's conciliatory approach to the Catholic minority and gained growing support for his 'O'Neill must go' campaign. O'Neill raised Catholic expectations with his bridge-building gestures, but the small crop of practical reforms caused mounting frustration. There were ominous indications of future trouble: vicious riots in Divis Street, Belfast, in 1964, a petty dispute over the naming of a bridge across the Lagan and clashes with Paisley-led demonstrations in 1966, the revival of the UVF and the murder of Peter Ward, a Catholic, in Malvern Street, Belfast, in June 1966, and the formation of organisations seeking civil rights.

From Civil Rights to Civil Strife

The problems and divisions within the region had their origins long before the creation of Northern Ireland. The increase in living standards and in educational opportunities after the Second World War helped to create a new Catholic middle class (especially at student level at this stage), ready to lead a challenge to the status quo. The vast improvement in international communications brought pictures of events overseas into everyone's living-room. The Black civil rights campaign in the United States, the demonstrations against the Vietnam war, the student uprising in Paris in 1968 and the passive resistance to Soviet tanks in Prague in the spring of 1968 set powerful examples of action.

The main argument put by the civil rights movement was that full British standards were not being applied in Northern Ireland. The Cameron Report, commissioned by the Unionist government in 1969, was to substantiate this view. What had happened was that Westminster governments had failed to keep a close watch on political developments in Northern Ireland after 1922. Indeed London was grateful for the region's crucial support during the war, and Northern Ireland seemed to be a strategic asset at the height of the Cold War. Nationalists in the north had expended their energies futilely railing against partition. The Civil Rights movement was more challenging to the Unionist hegemony because it sought reform within Northern Ireland and attracted mass support.

In 1968–69 Northern Ireland moved rapidly from an apparent easing of tension to violence so intense that in news coverage throughout the world it vied with reports of the Vietnam war. In August 1969, British troops were put on active service in the streets of Derry and Belfast as people began to die, and Westminster desperately sought expedients and solutions while ancient hatreds welled to the surface and the issue of partition moved in from the wings towards centre stage. The Provisional IRA and other republican militants had as their primary aim the ending of British rule, while loyalist paramilitaries saw themselves as being front-line defenders of the Union. Partition remained, but the turmoil, killing and destruction of less than three years shattered the elaborate constitutional arrangement of 1920.

On 30 January 1972 paratroopers killed thirteen men in Derry during a demonstration against internment; this immediately became known as 'Bloody Sunday'. Some terrible IRA atrocities followed, while loyalist paramilitaries paraded openly in force. On 24 March 1972 Edward Heath, the British Prime Minister, told Faulkner that Westminster was taking over control of security. The Unionist government resigned. The Northern Ireland Parliament was suspended, and fifty years of devolved government came to an end.

Direct Rule: the Seventies

The British government sought to control the violence and—in co-operation with the Dublin government—to find a constitutional compromise, which included the sharing of power by Protestant and Catholic elected representatives.

At the end of 1973, following a conference at Sunningdale in Berkshire, Faulkner led a power-sharing government, including Gerry Fitt and members of the Social Democratic and Labour Party. A Westminster election soon after showed that most unionists opposed this arrangement, and in May 1974 a loyalist strike paralysed much of Northern Ireland and forced the break-up of the power-sharing administration.

Several other attempts by the British government to get local assemblies to work failed completely. Violence continued at a high level, the worst day being 'Bloody Friday', 21 July 1972, when in 65 minutes the IRA detonated twenty bombs in Belfast. The 'Peace People' in 1976 ran a well-publicised campaign to get the paramilitaries to stop the killing. But the killing went on: Earl Mountbatten and two boys were killed at Mullaghmore, County Sligo, and eighteen soldiers were killed at Warrenpoint, County Down, on one day, Monday 27 August 1979.

Towards the Anglo-Irish Agreement, 1979–85

In spite of appalling incidents, the level of violence was much reduced in the 1980s. Internment was phased out, and those imprisoned on terrorist charges were henceforth treated like other prisoners. IRA prisoners responded by refusing prison clothes and by smearing excrement in their cells; then in March 1981 Bobby Sands refused all food. He died, after being elected MP for Fermanagh-South Tyrone, on 5 May. The Conservative government still refused to grant the prisoners political status. By 20 August 1981 ten prisoners had starved themselves to death. There was a huge upsurge of feeling in the Catholic community.

Both the London and Dublin governments were alarmed by the increase in Sinn Féin's support: 13.4 per cent of the electorate by June 1983. Both governments were anxious to bolster the constitutional SDLP. A New Ireland Forum in the Republic (1983–84) recommended a choice of constitutional solutions. At first Margaret Thatcher, the Prime Minister, seemed to reject the choices offered her, but, in spite of the bombing of the Conservative Party conference in Brighton by the IRA on 12 October 1984, she was persuaded to make an agreement by the Taoiseach, Garret FitzGerald.

The Anglo-Irish Agreement was announced at Hillsborough on 15 November 1985. It included an intergovernmental conference to promote cross-border co-operation and created a secretariat of Northern Ireland and Republic civil servants at Maryfield just outside Holywood, County Down. The Republic was given a consultative role.

'Ulster Says No', 1985–90

Unionists of almost every persuasion were appalled by the agreement. They had not been consulted (the SDLP had); southern civil servants were in the North; the Republic could be consulted on Northern Ireland affairs; and it was seen as a first step towards the reunification of Ireland—though the agreement repeated the promise that Northern Ireland would remain in the United Kingdom as long as the majority there wanted it.

Years of non-co-operation and protest followed, but the British government stood firm; the agreement was designed to be immune to loyalist protest. However, there was closer co-operation between Dublin and London on security matters, and Sinn Féin's electoral support declined.

Towards the Joint Declaration, 1990–93

Violence increased again in the early 1990s; the Provisional IRA got large consignments of arms and explosives from Libya, and loyalist paramilitaries got weapons from South Africa. Members of the IRA were now the most experienced paramilitaries in Europe; their bombs were fewer but larger, doing severe damage in Belfast, provincial towns, and London. Loyalists stepped up their long-standing campaign of sectarian assassinations. Horrific incidents included eight men killed when their van was bombed by the IRA at Teebane, County Tyrone, and the shooting dead of five Catholics in a betting shop on the Ormeau Road, Belfast, in early 1992.

The London and Dublin governments strove to reach a new agreement while the SDLP leader, John Hume, had secret talks with Gerry Adams, president of Sinn Féin. Two horrific atrocities impelled the two governments towards a new accord: the killing of ten people on the Shankill Road, Belfast, by an IRA bomb on 23 October 1993 and the killing of seven people in Greysteel, County Londonderry, on 30 October 1993.

On 15 December 1993 John Major and Albert Reynolds launched the Joint Declaration at Downing Street, which reaffirmed the constitutional guarantee to Northern Ireland, stated that Britain no longer had any 'selfish strategic or economic interest' in Northern Ireland, acknowledged the right of self-determination but subject to the consent of a Northern majority, and held out the prospect of exploratory talks with Sinn Féin three months after an agreement to stop the IRA campaign of violence.

Appalling violence during the first half of 1994 seemed to indicate that the Downing Street Declaration had failed, but the whole situation was strikingly altered by the republican and loyalist ceasefires in the autumn.

Whatever the political commentators might say, the people themselves quickly decided that the Troubles were over. On a Saturday afternoon in early December 1994, the day the new Lagan bridge was opened for pedestrians, this writer waited in a queue for a car park in central Belfast. Buses from Mayo and Galway were pulling in at Great Victoria Street, and there were car registrations from as far away as Waterford and Kerry. Overhead a buzzard soared over St Anne's Cathedral, banked over the quays towards the City Hall, and reappeared over the vast flat roof of Castlecourt, quartering the heart of the city for prey. For the first time in a quarter of a century such a creature, wild as the wind, could hunt undisturbed: the helicopters had abandoned the sky.

The 1974 loyalist strike only succeeded because, except for blackspots, the provincial economy was still booming. Then came the OPEC oil crisis and resultant dislocation throughout the world. Several large multinationals closed their branches in Northern Ireland, and synthetic fibre production— dependent on cheap oil—contracted sharply. Meanwhile traditional industries such as shipbuilding continued to decline, and the region has become exceptionally dependent on public sector employment. Nevertheless Northern Ireland has come through the recession of the early 1990s in far better shape than many economists predicted.

No country or province should be judged by the worst moments in its history. How many would have predicted in 1945 that Germany would become a bastion of democracy with one of the strongest economies in the world? Ten years ago no prominent figure or pundit predicted the demolition of the Berlin Wall and the break-up of the Soviet empire. Week by week we read of acts of violence here, but too many people have a vested interest in peace for Northern Ireland to slide into bloodletting on the scale perpetrated in Bosnia. There are many positive signs: the reclamation and reopening of the Erne-Shannon waterway (as Seán Rafferty put it, making it possible to travel from Enniskillen to New York by boat); some of the best public housing in Europe; the revitalisation of the city centres in Belfast and Derry; developments along the lower Lagan, including a concert hall; the success of power-sharing in Dungannon and other local authorities; Belfast City Council no longer the bear garden it was before; the opening of interpretative centres at Navan Fort and Benburb; as rich a life-style for the middle classes as anywhere in the United Kingdom; and a growing realisation that the natural beauty of so much of Northern Ireland is an asset beyond price.

Partition is likely to remain a central political issue for years to come. John Major probably spoke from the heart when he stated Britain's lost interest in Northern Ireland in December 1993. At the same time Dublin governments, after decades of rhetoric against partition, contemplate with alarm the prospect of taking responsibility for one of the most dependent and subsidised economies in the world.

Suggestions for Further Reading

Arthur, Paul, and Keith Jeffery, *Northern Ireland since 1968,* Oxford 1988.
Bardon, Jonathan, *Belfast: an Illustrated History,* Belfast 1982.
—— *A History of Ulster,* Belfast 1992.

Flackes, W. D., and Sydney Elliott, *Northern Ireland: a Political Directory, 1968–1993,* Belfast 1994.

Harkness, David, *Northern Ireland since 1920,* Dublin 1983.

Harris, R., C. Jefferson, and J. Spencer (eds.), *The Northern Ireland Economy: a Comparative Study in the Economic Development of a Peripheral Region,* London and New York 1990.

Laffan, Michael, *The Partition of Ireland, 1911–1925,* Dundalk 1983.

McCutcheon, W., *The Industrial Archaeology of Northern Ireland,* Belfast 1980.

Mallory, J., and T. McNeill, *The Archaeology of Ulster: from Colonisation to Plantation,* Belfast 1991.

Purdie, Bob, *Politics in the Streets: the Origins of the Civil Rights Movement in Northern Ireland,* Belfast 1990.

Robinson, Philip, *The Plantation of Ulster: British Settlement in an Irish Landscape, 1600–1670,* Dublin and New York 1984.

4 The Two Economies of Ireland: An Analysis

John Bradley

How far back in time need one go in order to understand an economy? Is the world around us the inevitable consequence of a linear history, with recent events overshadowing those of the remote past, or have remote events so constrained subsequent choices that we must seek them out, examine and remake them? The Japanese economist and scholar Michio Morishima went back beyond the year 200 in his quest to understand why Japan 'succeeded', and devoted almost half his book to periods earlier than the nineteenth century, covering the post-1945 reforms in a short final chapter. Such a long horizon may be necessary if, following Max Weber, one believes that a nation's 'ethos' is predetermined and that only economic structures compatible with this ethos are likely to evolve and prosper.

In this short essay it is not possible to delve too deeply into the search for the Irish 'ethos'. Professor Joe Lee has already done so in his magisterial *Ireland, 1912–1985,* with profoundly pessimistic and unflattering conclusions. Instead, I first wish to discuss some crucial turning points in the evolution of our island economy over the last two hundred years—events that almost certainly tipped the balance and, by excluding alternatives, dominated subsequent history. Some, like the Great Famine, were apocalyptic, even by world standards. Others were of more local consequence, such as partition or the fall of Stormont. The recent ceasefires can yet be assigned only a potential importance, conditional on their duration.

Having scanned two centuries of history, I then narrow the focus to the most recent three decades, examining lost years since the onset of civil strife in the North in 1969. The damage done to the North, and to a lesser extent to the South, is only now beginning to be understood and addressed. Although economists of nationalist and unionist hues are likely to interpret the socio-economic record of recent decades with differing degrees of emphasis, the facts tend to speak for themselves and invoke the desirability of stronger, more imaginative and generous cross-border links on the island.

I conclude by addressing more controversial matters, exploring three interrelated post-ceasefire economic scenarios that differ in their assumptions concerning future North-South policy interactions and institutions. The first is the case of peaceful but separate development, or the economic status quo ante. The second is the case of North-South co-ordinated development, where limited forms of political-economic co-operation are put in place. Finally, I attempt to conceptualise the case of a single island economy, borrowing and extending a term used in a more restricted context by Sir George Quigley, chairman of the Ulster Bank, in his seminal address to the Confederation of Irish Industry (now IBEC) in 1992.

Economic Turning Points

Ireland was on the move in the second half of the eighteenth century. Under a devolved parliament, however imperfect its structures, economic and social advances were being made at a time when the early effects of the industrial revolution in Britain were beginning to spill over into adjoining countries. Whatever else it did, the Act of Union in 1800 fundamentally changed the terms on which Ireland would relate to the global superpower on its doorstep and ushered in an era of what has been called 'dependence' or 'capitalist colonisation'. After the Union, policy-making adjusted to control from London, and there was to be no protection from the full rigours of competition with the British economic giant.

To claim that all economic progress stopped after the Union is grossly simplistic, and a more balanced view is given in Cormac Ó Gráda's recent economic history of Ireland. However, Ireland's industrialisation was never to emulate Britain's generalised economic and technological leap forward. Rather, it was to involve specific sectors (brewing, linen, shipbuilding), and selected locations (mainly Dublin and Belfast), and bypassed much of the rest. The calamity of the Great Famine in the late 1840s, the causes of which had been building up for decades, tore asunder the fragile economic fabric of the island. By decimating the population, through death and emigration, it prevented the emergence of a dynamic home market for local industry. By bearing most heavily on the more agricultural south, it further accentuated separation from the north. Even today the Famine remains an event that, above all others, we use to define ourselves and our potentialities.

It was almost historically inevitable that the issue of partition should have arisen in the first two decades of this century, a time when the economy of the north-east of Ireland, centred on Belfast, was at its zenith. A subsequent irony was that the very northern industries that required insider access to the British market—mainly linen, shipbuilding, and associated heavy engineering— were the ones that suffered most in the aftermath of partition, except during the extraordinary circumstances of the Second World War. The sundering of the engineering and industrial North from the agricultural and food-processing South destroyed any possibility of building intra-island synergies. The centrifugal bonds of ethnicity were simply too strong for the centripetal forces of economic rationality. North-South trade diminished, sources of supply adjusted, and economic planning on the island accommodated to partition, even if political rhetoric did not.

The events leading up to the fall of Stormont in 1972, bringing to an end self-government for Northern Ireland within the United Kingdom, may not appear to have been driven by economics but had, in fact, many of their deeper roots in disparities of inter-community development, both real and imagined. The partial exclusion of the Catholic community from Northern Ireland's governance had serious consequences for economic policy-making. In particular, most of the pre-1969 economic growth had been concentrated east of the Bann, since a passive industrial policy led naturally to firms seeking to benefit from the agglomeration economies of the greater Belfast area. Even within Belfast, segmented labour markets reinforced divisions between the two main communities. But just as the almost contemporary entry of the South into the EEC in 1973 brought in its train a wide-ranging reform and liberalisation of many aspects of life, so too did the imposition of direct rule impose British standards of social services and equity on the North. However, given the low state of economic development in the North relative to Britain, parity of treatment created a massive dependence on financial transfers from Britain (the 'subvention'), which amounts today to a total annual injection of almost 25 per cent of Northern GDP.

Is there to be a happy ending to our history of discord? The recent ceasefires have an economic importance that parallels their immediate humanitarian consequences. They show every sign of marking a watershed in North-South relations and have coincided with a resurgence of business-driven cross-border interaction and collaboration. The fragmentation of the island economy, which had roots in the extraordinary late nineteenth-century success of the north-east region, no longer has any logic or justification. The challenge to policy-makers today will be to design political solutions that will permit the long-suppressed natural benefits of the island economy to emerge.

The Lost Years: Economic Consequences of Violence

Politics and economics were interrelated at the foundation of Northern Ireland, since the spatial distribution of the two main communities on the island was mirrored by a similar spatial division in economic orientation and specialisation: a largely agricultural South and a more industrialised North. In looking to the future it is essential to understand the more recent dramatic origins of the present-day economic problems of Northern Ireland, particularly the change that came about during the last three decades, and to compare these with the problems of the South.

Four interrelated issues stand out for the Northern economy: the decline of manufacturing, the massive expansion of the public sector, problems of high long-term unemployment, and chronic regional trade deficits. Parallel issues in the South concern the rise of foreign-owned high-technology manufacturing, difficulties experienced in striking a balance between the roles of public and private sectors, the continued role of emigration combined with the emergence of long-term unemployment, and a successful recovery from the chronic fiscal and trade imbalances of the 1980s.

The high level of Northern industrialisation relative to the more agricultural South was significant in two respects, both as a visible sign of economic superiority and increasing the likelihood of Northern self-sufficiency within the United Kingdom. As fig. 1 shows, even as late as 1960 there were still more people employed in manufacturing in the North than in the South, in spite of the latter's larger population. During the 1970s and early 1980s this position changed dramatically, for a variety of reasons: the decline of older 'sunset' industries in the United Kingdom and elsewhere (see fig. 2); wider economic troubles in the slow-growing UK economy, the consequences of which were exacerbated by the continuing very close links between the North and Britain; restricted scope for regional fiscal and development policies compared with the more autonomous South; and the inability of the North to win a sizeable share of American direct investment.

Fig. 1: Size of manufacturing sectors and employment, 1960 and 1990

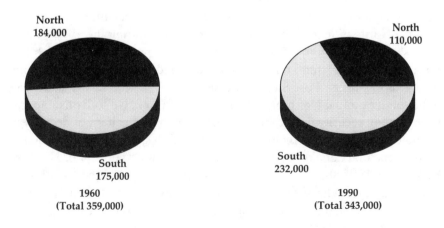

North
184,000

South
175,000

1960
(Total 359,000)

North
110,000

South
232,000

1990
(Total 343,000)

Fig. 2: Employment in manufacturing, 1963–89 (base: 1963 = 1.0)

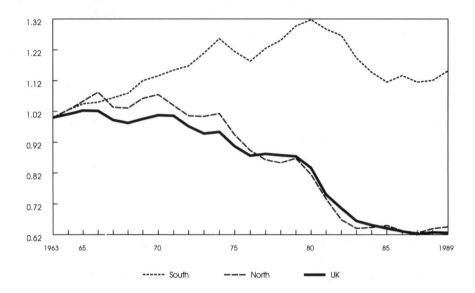

The Southern story is very different. After tariff barriers were dismantled in the 1960s there was a shake-out of inefficient indigenous firms that were unable to adjust to world competition and whose survival had depended on protection. Within the indigenous sector the progressive rationalisation of food processing through mergers and take-overs led to scale efficiencies and increased exports. Finally the South captured a large share of internationally mobile—mainly American—high-technology investment, attracted by generous financial incentives and the high level of human capital. Fig. 3 shows the results in terms of employment, where the rise in importance of the largely foreign-owned high-technology sector is quite dramatic.

As the Northern manufacturing sector contracted during the 1970s, much of the slack was taken up by the expansion of the public sector, which had knock-on benefits for market services and small inward-looking manufacturing firms. Post-Stormont decisions to provide social and other public services to the North on the basis of 'need' relative to British norms, and escalating security expenditure, broke the previous pattern of decades of moderate Northern public sector deficits. The North shifted into a situation of chronic structural deficits, amounting today to about 25 per cent of Northern GDP (fig. 4). If Northern policy-makers remain indifferent to the size of these deficits and regard the subvention as an enduring aspect of their economy, then Northern Ireland risks becoming trapped in a Mezzogiorno-like problem of permanent dependence.

Fig. 3: Manufacturing employment by sector, Republic of Ireland, 1960–90

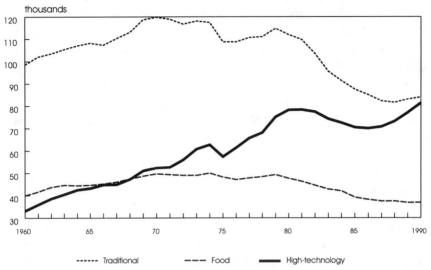

Fig. 4: Northern Ireland subvention as percentage of GDP, 1967–91

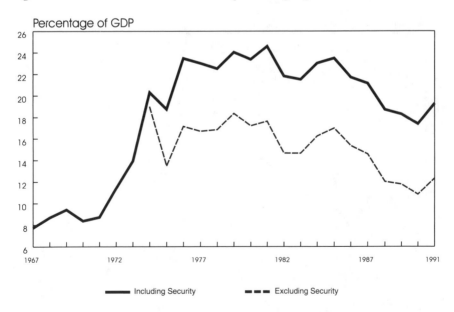

The situation in the South has uneasy parallels with the North. Economic growth during the 1960s, and entry into the EEC in the 1970s, brought with it pressure for a bigger public sector role. This pressure culminated in the late

1970s in an explosive growth of public spending, which was followed after the second OPEC-induced world recession by an unsustainable rise in the public debt. The necessity to tackle the fiscal crisis by a combination of tax increases and expenditure cuts caused the South's recession to be long and deep but produced the basis for a healthier period of high growth, which has lasted to the present day. This period provided salutary lessons for the South that are relevant to the North, in that it illustrates how a small economy can achieve fundamental change, even with a limited range of policy instruments.

The deterioration of the Northern labour market from the late 1970s and throughout the 1980s was replicated in the South, where the overshooting of employment creation after the fiscal expansions of the late 1970s merely delayed the inevitable retribution. In both regions a serious problem of structural or long-term unemployment has emerged (fig. 5). Economic studies in the South indicate that unemployment rose initially as a result of world recession, higher taxes, and population growth pressure. Sociological studies show that a key characteristic of long-term unemployment is low skill levels and that working-class marginalisation arises from the rapid and uneven nature of class transformation in Ireland and changing patterns of emigration.

Fig. 5: Long-term unemployment (>1 year), 1971–93

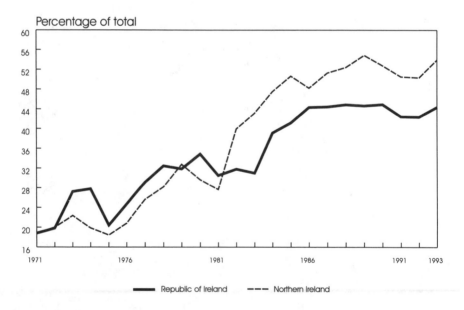

These Southern factors clearly operated in the North as well but were overlaid by 'community' and 'location' issues whose interpretation has been an area of great controversy in Northern socio-economic research. The fact that a

Catholic male is almost two-and-a-half times more likely to be unemployed than his non-Catholic counterpart is not necessarily associated with past or present discrimination but certainly should direct attention to a serious Northern problem of complex origins that has been at the heart of the civil unrest.

The Northern public sector deficit, as manifested in the need for ever-larger subventions, served to sustain a high level of public and private consumption, public investment, and imports. A corollary was the emergence of a chronic trade deficit, now believed to amount to between 20 and 25 per cent of regional GDP (fig. 6). Ironically, the South currently enjoys a trade surplus with the North of some £400 million, a case of beneficial spill-over from the Northern subvention. The South had embarked on a similar expansion of public expenditure in the late 1970s and early 1980s but without the benefit of free external finance. The subsequent economic costs of restructuring were massive but were eased in the latter part of the 1980s by a boom in the world economy.

Fig. 6: Net trade balances, 1961–93

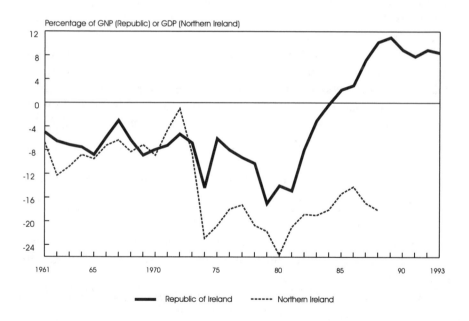

Given the massive injection provided by the subvention, the financing of the trade deficit was not a problem for the North. However, the existence of the trade deficit may also be linked to an underlying problem with regional competitiveness, associated with such factors as the sectoral coverage of Northern manufacturing, the continued concentration on the British market, and close links between British and Northern wages and costs. The fact that the South emerged from a similar case of twin deficits during the 1980s may hold interesting lessons for future Northern transformation.

The picture of the Northern economy that emerges is one where economic prosperity is underwritten to a large degree by the British taxpayer. The size of the public sector, and the role played by transfers to people and companies, appears to have engendered a culture of dependence that goes considerably further than its Southern counterpart. Northern attitudes to this dependence take different forms. For nationalists it requires in effect that their political aspirations be worked out in the short to medium term within the context of the United Kingdom. Unionists go further: dependence for them is both a birthright from their UK citizenship and a bulwark against any possibility of a united Ireland, given the inability and/or unwillingness of the Southern taxpayer to take over the present subvention and thus sustain the higher Northern standard of living.

If Northern Ireland had continued to function under the financial constraints that applied under Stormont before the imposition of direct rule, it is quite likely that the standards of living in both regions of Ireland would have converged during the 1970s and 1980s, to a level below that of Britain and, *a fortiori,* below that of the main EU members. We can only guess at the nature of the pressures that might have emerged in Northern Ireland either for greater policy independence along Southern lines or for a negotiated form of full integration into the United Kingdom that may have differed from the imposed direct rule. We call these 'lost years', because the postponed problems are only now being addressed.

Economic Prospects: Alternative Peaceful Scenarios

Since violence was a central negative factor influencing the economy of the North since 1970, the prospects for a rapid acceleration of growth in the aftermath of peace could indeed be very great as the benefits of the improved infrastructure and human resources, previously unrealised, are exploited by the private sector.

To explore possible implications of a permanent peace, it will be necessary to hypothesise a range of North-South economic policy and institutional configurations. Such configurations carry with them profound political implications, the treatment of which goes far beyond this essay. Nevertheless it is difficult to see how one can seek to identify the principles and key strategies that should inform economic policy responses to the peace process without carrying out such *ex ante* thought experiments, however provocative they may appear.

I have identified three broad alternatives for the future economic evolution of the two regions of Ireland in a period of permanent peace: separate development, co-ordinated development, and a single island economy. If the Northern violence were to resume, the first alternative, 'separate development', would very likely be the only feasible option, continuing the previous historical pattern of minimalist North-South interaction.

Separate development is essentially the institutional situation that prevailed before the ceasefires, with only modest North-South economic interaction and no formal policy co-ordination. It is the conceptual background for many studies of the costs of the Northern violence to the two Irish regions and to Britain, and for economic forecasts prepared before the ceasefires.

Two different costs associated with violence can be considered under this heading, with their mirror images of potential benefits of peace as these costs are reduced or vanish altogether. First, there are the obvious costs, in terms of extra security expenditure, together with human injury and material damage, business disruption, and the like. Second, there are the hidden costs, such as previous growth potential not realised, failure to attract foreign direct investment, stunted tourism growth, and so on. The former costs are not negligible and were estimated by DKM (in 1989 prices) at about £365 per capita annually in the North and £225 per capita in the South. However, they are probably overshadowed by the second type of costs, which represent a more direct loss to the island rather than a diversion of public expenditure away from productive activities.

Under the 'separate development' alternative it is important to correct some misunderstandings about the costs of violence and the consequential benefits of peace. Not all of the accelerated decline of Northern manufacturing during the 1970s was caused by violence, since the composition of Northern manufacturing was such that a serious shake-out was inevitable in any event. However, the inability of the North to substitute 'sunrise' for 'sunset' industries is probably largely attributable to the violence, as comparison with Scotland and the Republic shows.

Nor can the rise in the Northern subvention be regarded as a 'cost' of violence, in this case one to be borne by the British taxpayer. Even if Stormont had survived to the present day, it is difficult to see how a massive rise in net transfers from the other British regions to the North could have been avoided. An important aspect of future UK government policy towards the North must be to send clear signals about the future of the subvention, and in his speech to the Institute of Directors in Belfast on 21 October 1994 the

Prime Minister, John Major, gave such assurance, stating that 'the government will take full account of Northern Ireland's special needs in setting future levels of public expenditure for the province.' This may mean that any savings in expenditure on security are likely to be recycled to other areas, designed to boost activity in the private sector in addition to augmenting deserving areas of the already large public sector. Nevertheless it may eventually appear desirable to reduce the role played by the subvention and encourage the growth of private sector activity. If not, there is a risk that the North will be locked into a semi-permanent dependence that, however comfortable in the short term, can hardly be healthy.

Any restructuring of the subvention would be of as much interest and concern to the South as it would be to the North. At present the Northern economy is dominated by its trade, investment and other links with Britain. The Southern economy, on the other hand, has diversified away from a similar dominance during the last three decades and is now more internationally oriented. However, the Southern trade surplus with the North, at about £400 million, is an important by-product of the subvention that sustains Southern jobs.

The crucial issue for the future is whether the previous pattern of separate economic development will continue to be thought to be the best choice for the future, or whether these weak links can be developed to become an additional force for mutually reinforcing growth in the island economy. Enhanced policy co-operation and a vibrant Northern manufacturing sector with strong inter-firm and intra-firm links with its Southern counterpart may be exactly what will be needed to push the economy of this island towards faster sustained growth and prosperity.

Co-ordinated development assumes an increased level of co-operation in areas such as tourism, cross-border infrastructure and industrial policy to attract foreign investment and encourage the growth of indigenous industry and services. The use of the term 'single island economy' by Sir George Quigley in his CII address should probably be thought of as a case of 'co-ordinated development' in our terms. Co-ordinated development is increasingly seen by the business community, North and South, as a logical and efficient way of exploiting the strengths of the island's human and physical resources. Such arrangements are envisaged in the Framework Document, albeit somewhat tentatively. However, under co-ordinated development the fiscal and monetary arrangements in the North would continue to be set within the United Kingdom, and thus the process stops short of the notion of island EMU. The Framework document is silent on these matters, presumably because they touch on issues of great political sensitivity, both between these two islands and for Britain's wider relationship with the EU.

The principle of subsidiarity would indicate that future North-South policy co-ordination would deal with matters that are best resolved at a local level. Examples include matters that intrinsically concern the island as a unit, such as the promotion of tourism, planning of physical infrastructure, promoting mutually beneficial business linkages, etc. However, it is more difficult to see such co-operation extending easily to potentially competitive areas such as the attraction of foreign industry to locate North or South, or the encouragement of harmonisation in the wide range of social and educational policies on the island. Indeed, the absence of fiscal and monetary harmonisation introduces a potentially serious North-South complication, particularly if the United Kingdom deviates from evolving European consensus on economic and social harmonisation.

Just as the Single European Market and EMU contain an internal logic of further integration, so too a process of North-South co-ordinated development is likely to lead inexorably to suggestions for further harmonisation and policy convergence. Even within the United Kingdom, strains have already emerged because of the higher level of grants offered by the North to attract foreign industry where other British firms feel threatened. The controversy over the Howlon plant is one where the debate has actually led to British textile manufacturers challenging the level of Northern aid in the European Court. Given such intra-UK disputes, it is doubtful if a process of North-South co-ordination could succeed unless all the policy cards were on the table, at least in the longer term.

Under co-ordinated development there is no reason to believe that the existing subvention financing of the North would be called into question. Indeed this option would appear so attractive as a means of copperfastening peace that a wide range of direct and indirect benefits could flow to the North, with beneficial spill-overs to the South: American and EU direct aid; island-wide initiatives in the area of industrial promotion; cross-border initiatives to bring the border counties into the economic mainstream; a re-think of island regional policy; and the evolution of an enlarged and more demanding domestic market to encourage greater innovation by indigenous industry. There can be few limits to where co-operation might lead, and ultimately the economic fragmentation of this island, however logical it may have appeared in the 1920s, might be reversed, as a single island economy evolves under whatever political structures are freely chosen.

In my concept of a single island economy I envisage a situation of increased co-operation, over an appropriate time-scale, leading to a virtually complete harmonisation of economic and social policies and institutions, where it is found that their absence imposes costs on the island. No exact analogue of this scenario exists elsewhere, although useful insights can be obtained from the Benelux experience, suitably modified for the Irish situation. Clearly, this notion of a 'single island economy' goes far beyond that raised by Sir George Quigley in his CII address. It is a deeper concept because of doubts that the more restricted 'economic' concept could come about without the kind of political movement whose logic would require and facilitate an ever-increasing level of economic policy harmonisation.

In the light of the present acrimonious debate on European integration taking place in Britain, it is doubtful if the above logic of Irish policy integration will find complete favour. But it is not difficult to show that the present policy integration within the UK is not without its problems for the Northern economy. A considerable part of Northern industrial policy is aimed at offsetting the comparative advantage of the South, arising mainly from the ability to set a low rate of corporation tax, and compensating for the greater Northern peripherality within the United Kingdom with subsidies that are often higher than their British counterparts. Research by the Northern Ireland Economic Research Centre and others has shown that blanket subsidy-based Northern industrial policies are very inefficient.

Since the major stumbling block to island policy harmonisation is the size of the present Northern subvention, we must ask what would be a reasonable period over which the subvention could be reduced to the level, say, of the Southern exchequer borrowing requirement, given favourable world economic developments and appropriate transitional aid.

Analysis by the Cadogan Group purports to show that the subvention is a permanent feature of the Northern economy. However, a problem with this kind of static analysis is that is fails utterly to take into account the fact that an island political settlement would be likely to release major economic forces that would work towards the regeneration of private sector activity in the North and permit North-South synergies to emerge as businesses benefited from a larger, truly single market of five-and-a-quarter million consumers. Indeed the implicit Cadogan assumption that the North is never likely to return to balance between regional expenditure and taxation is either a damning vote of no confidence in the future of the Northern economy or a political attempt to deflect attention away from real economic issues and potentials of North-South co-operation.

Peace Dividends

Five to ten years of peaceful growth will lead to a complete transformation of the Northern economy, in ways that we should not prejudge and that are likely to have entirely beneficial spill-over effects for the South. There will be peace dividends under all three of the above alternative strategies. Unfortunately, prior attitudes to all three, be they those of unionists or nationalists, are likely to be self-fulfilling. Thus we must expect that the emergence of an optimal level of North-South economic policy co-ordination will be highly constrained by existing political, economic and cultural attitudes.

Under all three alternatives, the peace dividend is likely to have four main elements, which are interrelated in a way that will require later detailed quantitative analysis. First, the inevitable restructuring of the balance between the public and private sectors in the North, not all of which is security-related, is likely to be at worst a zero-sum game if budgetary savings are recycled as promised by the British Prime Minister. Second, tourism growth seems poised to take off as the synergies between the two previously isolated parts of the island are about to be realised. Third, a recovery in high-technology inward direct investment in the North is very likely and could be accelerated and mutually beneficial if the South is actively generous in making its successful experience and contacts available to the North. Finally, the recent dramatic surge in North-South business contacts and the deepening IBEC-CBI (NI) initiatives hold out the prospect of developments and strengthening in the indigenous industrial and service sectors that have eluded both regions over the past thirty years.

Even negative aspects of the island economy may come to be looked at with more optimism. It cannot have escaped attention that since the scale and characteristics of Northern and Southern unemployment have much in common, perhaps the underlying causes and eventual solutions have much in common as well. In the North unemployment has a regional dimension that coincides partially with the community divide. Policy in the South appears to have been more successful in addressing regional imbalances, particularly through the dispersal of foreign plants throughout the country; Northern policies appear to have been less successful in removing regional blackspots. Future island policy must balance the need for economic efficiency against the desirability of spatial equity.

A crucial issue for the future is whether the present modest 'arm's length' North-South links can be developed to become an additional driving force for mutually reinforcing and beneficial growth in our island economy. Given the complexities, uncertainties and sensitivities involved, there can be only modest optimism at this stage. In reflecting on the economics of the island, I had in mind the admonitions of Charles Haughey, to economists in general and to Sir Charles Carter and Professor Louden Ryan in particular, after their presentations to the New Ireland Forum on 21 September 1983. Mr Haughey complained that economists 'could not formulate for us in this Forum a prospect of an all-Ireland economic entity capable of developing its own inherent dynamic for progress provided the political structures are right.' In these more peaceful and hopeful times the exploration can be more imaginative and free-ranging, the questions can be franker, and the answers need not be so pessimistic.

Selected Background Reading

Bradley, John, Nuala O'Donnell, and Niamh Sheridan (eds.), *The Two Economies of Ireland: Public Policy, Growth and Employment (Proceedings of the Second International Fund for Ireland Joint ESRI-NIERC Conference, 23 March 1995)* (in press).

Breen, Richard, Damian Hannan, David Rottman, and Christopher Whelan, *Understanding Contemporary Ireland*, Dublin: Gill & Macmillan 1990.

Lee, Joseph, *Ireland, 1912–1985: Politics and Society*, Cambridge: Cambridge University Press 1989.

Lessnoff, Michael, *The Spirit of Capitalism and the Protestant Ethic: an Enquiry into the Weber Thesis*, Aldershot: Edward Elgar 1994.

Morishima, Michio, *Why Has Japan 'Succeeded'?: Western Technology and the Japanese Ethos*, Cambridge: Cambridge University Press 1982.

Munck, Ronnie, *The Irish Economy: Results and Prospects*, London: Pluto Press 1993.

Ó Gráda, Cormac, *Ireland: a New Economic History, 1780–1939*, Oxford: Clarendon Press 1994.

Whyte, John, *Interpreting Northern Ireland*, Oxford: Clarendon Press 1990.

Wilson, Tom, *Conflict and Consent*, London: Basil Blackwell 1989.

5 Economic Geography: How Ireland's Wealth is Dispersed

Jim Walsh

The study of the spatial structure of an economy is concerned with an analysis of the factors that influence the location of economic activity and the types of interactions that occur between activities at different locations. The range of factors that are of importance include natural and human resource endowments, the availability of capital and know-how, access to markets, linkages or barriers to interaction with other regional economies, and a wide gamut of public policies. The relative importance of any of these factors can vary over time, and so also can the externally determined role of a regional economy such as Ireland's within the larger global system of which it is a small but strategically located component between the two largest economic blocs—North America and the European Union.

There are two approaches that can be adopted in an analysis of the spatial structure of an economic system. One is to view it as a 'jigsaw', which suggests high levels of regional distinctiveness and separateness and units that are frequently defined on the basis of political boundaries that have no real economic meaning. An alternative perspective can be described as a 'Russian dolls' model, which emphasises the nesting of locations in hierarchical relationships (e.g. rural areas and villages nested around towns; national or regional capitals such as Dublin or Belfast nested around European and global centres such as London).

This chapter provides a sketch of the factors that have influenced the spatial organisation of the economy of the island of Ireland. Four themes are considered: (*a*) external economic and political relations and how in the past these have shaped, and continue to shape, the internal economic geography of the island; (*b*) internal influences on the spatial organisation of the economy; (*c*) previous proposals to alter the spatial structure in the context of a divided Ireland; and (*d*) spatial strategies for an all-Ireland economy.

External Economic Relationships

Two distinct regional economies emerged in Ireland in the nineteenth century. A specialised and export-oriented industrial region developed in the north-east, centred on Belfast, along the lines of similar regions elsewhere in the United Kingdom. This region was based initially on the mechanised linen industry, from which an engineering industry and thence a major shipbuilding industry developed.

The rest of the island of Ireland experienced a process of de-industrialisation in the nineteenth century, due partly to the centralisation of the linen industry in Belfast following the introduction of mechanised production in the 1820s but mainly to the introduction of free trade after the 1800 Act of Union. Free trade had a devastating impact in particular on the substantial woollen and cotton industries that had grown up in Ireland in the eighteenth century, because of their exposure to competition with the corresponding British industries, which by this time were far more advanced. As a result, the nineteenth-century Irish economy (outside the north-east) became mainly oriented towards supplying agricultural products and labour to industrial Britain.

The contrasting patterns of sectoral development between the north-east and the remainder of the island had a major influence on the evolution of the settlement pattern and the location of transport infrastructure. Belfast became the principal economic centre of the island, with its population expanding by more than 500 per cent between 1841 and 1911, by which time it had reached almost 390,000; over the same period Dublin had increased much more slowly, from about 273,000 to just under 305,000. Furthermore, the economic impulses that contributed to the growth of Belfast were diffused throughout an extensive hinterland, with the railway network playing a considerable role in this process. In the north-west, Derry, helped by rail and port services, also emerged as an industrial city.

The experience of Dublin throughout the nineteenth century demonstrates most clearly the way in which the development of a regional economy can be disrupted by changes in external political relations. With a population of about 180,000 in 1800, Dublin was the second-largest city in Ireland or Britain. Following the Act of Union, Dublin lost its administrative and financial roles. Its industrialisation was for the most part connected with food processing, mainly from cereals grown throughout its hinterland. While it lost to Belfast its position of pre-eminence within the island urban system, it remained the key urban centre outside the north-east. Its centrality was greatly enhanced by the railway system, which evolved in a predominantly radial pattern. Outside Dublin, Cork was the only regional centre to experience modest growth, which was linked to a narrow industrial base and a range of retail, administrative, professional, legal, financial and educational services. Thus by the 1920s, when the island was partitioned into two political entities, a spatial framework had already been established that was to significantly shape the pattern of regional development in the twentieth century. Furthermore, the failure of the economy throughout much of rural Ireland to provide sustenance for the population resulted in a massive exodus to North America and Britain. Many of the descendants of these early emigrants have maintained a close interest in political and economic development in Ireland and continue to be able to influence both US government policy and US private and corporate investors.

Following partition, the two economies remained closely linked to the UK until the 1970s, after which the Republic developed stronger links with continental Europe. However, the nature and impacts of the links were quite different. Northern Ireland benefited considerably from its close ties to a strong UK economy. The benefits took the form of unrestricted access to a large market, substantial financial transfers that helped to modernise its economic sectors, and considerable investment in physical infrastructure, giving it a much better-quality road network. From the late 1940s a number of branch plants of UK firms were attracted to the North as part of a strategy of alleviating the weaker regional economies in the UK. One negative aspect of the relationship that has developed between the North and the UK has been a strong dependence on UK public finances, with, perhaps, insufficient commitment to local policy and strategy formulation.

The economic relations between the Republic and the UK have been different. After a short period of free trade up to the early 1930s there followed almost a quarter of a century during which various restrictions were introduced to inhibit trade and protect manufacturing. The limitations associated with the linkage to the UK were all too obvious by the mid-1950s. New policies were required to promote export-led growth to new markets. An industrialisation programme based on the attraction of foreign investment was embarked upon. After an initial slow start, the flow of foreign investment began to increase as the 1960s progressed, buoyed first by the Anglo-Irish Free Trade Area Agreement of 1965 and then impending entry to the EEC. Foreign firms were responsible for the bulk of the 20 per cent growth in manufacturing employment that occurred in the 1970s. In 1973, foreign firms accounted for 22 per cent of total manufacturing employment, the bulk of it from the UK and the United States.

Following accession to the EEC in 1973, the experience of the island economies began to diverge. There was a considerable increase in the volume of manufacturing investment attracted to the South from the United States and to a lesser extent the UK, Germany, and Japan, which reflected the critical role the Republic had acquired as a stepping stone for overseas investors seeking access to the EEC market. Gradually the level of economic dependence on the UK was reduced as a greater share of exports was destined for continental Europe.

In Northern Ireland, by contrast, the level of economic activity since the early 1970s has been affected by an ailing UK economy and, more importantly, by the level of civil unrest, which acted as a major deterrent to overseas investment. Thus by the early 1990s the economy of the North had lost much of its source of strength, while in the South new external relationships had been forged that provided it with a highly competitive economy.

Internal Influences on the Spatial Structure of the Economy

Several endogenous factors influence the spatial structure of the island economy. For land-based activities such as agriculture or forestry there are major sources of differentiation related to land quality and size of farms. These differences, allied to historical patterns of regional specialisation in agriculture and a distinctive east-west pattern of innovation diffusion, have resulted in a contrast between the east and south of the Republic and its western and north-western parts. A less pronounced pattern of regional differentiation emerged in the North. Inter-regional differences in the performance of the agricultural sector were accentuated under the EC Common Agricultural Policy, with an increasing division opening up between the more competitive medium-sized to large dairying and cereal farms of the south and east and the smaller farms of the west and north-west, which have tended to concentrate on lower-productivity enterprises such as young cattle and sheep rearing. Increasing numbers of farmers have become dependent on direct income subsidies, which are expected to rise to 40 per cent of total farm income by 1996.

Tourism has become a major component of the rural economy, especially in the otherwise poorer regions of the south-west and west in the Republic. Its development in Northern Ireland has been greatly hindered by the 'Troubles', which deterred visitors from the South and overseas. Given the quality of its natural and human-made tourist attractions, it is likely that under more peaceful conditions there will be an upsurge in tourism both in rural and urban areas.

Industrial location policy has been a major influence on regional development. The industrialisation that occurred under the protectionist policies of the 1930s and 1940s was highly concentrated in the main urban centres and particularly in Dublin and the surrounding counties. Thus, the share of total manufacturing employment located in Dublin city and county rose from 36 per cent in 1926 to 47 per cent (almost twice Dublin's share of the national population) in 1961. Much of the remainder was concentrated in the surrounding counties and in the cities of Cork, Waterford, and Limerick.

The high level of concentration of employment growth in the Dublin region was related to the fact that Dublin constituted the main market for the new industries (which were almost entirely focused on the domestic market), that Dublin was also the main port through which industrial raw materials were imported, and that, as the hub of the national transport network, Dublin provided the best base for supplying the national market. Inter-regional economic linkages remained poorly developed.

Likewise in Northern Ireland the geographical pattern of industrial development in the early postwar period remained highly concentrated on the greater Belfast region: some 75 per cent of new firms established between 1945 and 1959 were located within fifty kilometres of Belfast city centre.

An additional factor that was common to the systems of public administration in both parts of the island was a high level of centralisation of power and control over resources into Dublin and Belfast. By the 1960s the processes referred to above had contributed to significant disparities in economic development and welfare between the highly urbanised and the more rural regions. These contrasts were manifested in very high levels of migration from rural areas, particularly in the 1950s. Approximately one-seventh of the population of the Republic left between 1951 and 1961.

The contemporary regional situation has been summarised by Horner (1993). Two 'city-regions' (Dublin and Belfast) and five 'proto-cities' (Cork, Limerick, Derry, Galway, and Waterford) have been identified. The remainder of the island, consisting of small-town and rural Ireland, is divided into three regions: the east and south, the west and north-west, and Northern Ireland.

Since the two economies have tended to function almost independently for most of the past seventy years, the proposals that have been made in relation to their spatial structures are considered separately.

Proposals to Alter the Spatial Structure—the Republic

For most of the first three decades after the achievement of political independence there were no policies or strategies to influence the locational aspects of economic development. It was not until the Undeveloped Areas Act, 1952, that the first recognition was given to the fact that the poorer western counties required special assistance. This approach, based on designation of certain areas, has been maintained to the present. It is guided by the 'jigsaw' perspective, which tends to emphasise the special problems of these areas with little attention to the linkages with other regions. In fact it was not until the late 1960s that any detailed analyses were undertaken of key components of the spatial structure of the economy. In the meantime a vigorous debate had been initiated on the locational policy to be pursued with respect to the new foreign firms. While the Government, for political reasons, favoured maximum dispersal, particularly to rural regions, a strong case was articulated for the pursuit of a concentrated growth centre approach, on the grounds that a limited number of industrial centres would represent a more efficient allocation of public investment on infrastructure and would provide a more attractive operating environment for incoming firms.

The debate on growth centres versus dispersal culminated with the completion of the Buchanan Report in 1968, which recommended a new policy orientation for urban settlement based on a hierarchy of growth centres. It proposed that over a twenty-year period 75 per cent of new industrial employment should be concentrated in nine centres: Dublin, two 'national growth centres' at Cork and Limerick that would grow to a sufficient size to enable them to compete effectively with Dublin, and six 'regional growth centres', at Waterford, Galway, Athlone, Sligo, Dundalk, and Drogheda. Four 'local centres' would also receive preferential treatment. In addition, it was proposed that roads of motorway standard be constructed between Dublin and Northern Ireland and from Dublin towards Cork and Limerick.

In 1968 the Government was also presented with a major study on the future of the hospital system, which recommended a strategy of locating regional and general hospitals at twelve centres, most of which coincided with Buchanan's centres. Earlier the *Investment in Education* report (1965) had recommended a new tier of third-level colleges at most of the places that were to be recommended as growth centres. Thus by the late 1960s there appeared to be a widely shared view among Government advisers that there was a case for intervention to alter the spatial structure of the urban system so that a more efficient spatial allocation of public resources could be achieved.

The main thrust of the Buchanan strategy met with strong opposition, which led the Government to opt for an eclectic mixture of limited concentration and a continuation of dispersal strategy which it had supported throughout the 1960s. A reduced commitment to growth centres than was envisaged by Buchanan was evident in the first five-year industrial plan published by the IDA in 1972. This plan, and its successor for 1978–82, became in effect the principal element of the Government's strategy for regional development.

In the short term, the Government and IDA strategy was successful in achieving a politically more acceptable distribution of manufacturing. Through the provision of advance factories and fully serviced industrial sites and the flexibility to vary investment grants, the IDA was able to achieve a wide dispersal of new inward investment. By the end of the 1970s Dublin's share of the manufacturing sector was greatly reduced, through a combination of severe losses in traditional sectors and the discriminatory application of the IDA strategy, which did not provide assistance to new firms setting up in or around the capital. High levels of job losses in traditional sectors also exceeded the levels of new employment created in the cities of Cork, Limerick, and Waterford. By contrast, there was a high level of growth in manufacturing employment in many rural and small urban areas, especially in the west and midlands.

The level of success achieved in dispersing new manufacturing employment, along with the substantial gains in farm incomes under CAP price supports, was accompanied by a modest level of convergence of regional per capita incomes and, significantly, a considerable reduction in the number of rural areas experiencing population decline. However, it is not at all clear whether these short-term benefits were achieved without some opportunity costs. Furthermore, the question of systematically restructuring the urban system over the medium to long term had been avoided. The services sector, which was about to take off as the major growth area for employment, was almost totally neglected in policy documents. In particular, the complex relationships between private sector and/or institutional investment, property development, office employment and location were largely ignored, so that a disproportionate share of accommodation for services was provided in Dublin (much of it on a speculative basis), while much less was provided in other cities until special financial measures were introduced in the mid-1980s.

In the early 1980s serious questions were raised about the wisdom of industrial policy—notably by the Telesis Review Group—which led to a refocusing on more competitive sectors, such as electronics, data-processing equipment, pharmaceuticals, and internationally traded services such as financing, software development, and telemarketing. This sectoral refocusing has also had locational implications. There is now a much higher level of international competition for inward investment, and the types of projects that are now attracted to Ireland are less footloose than previously. A number of key locational requirements have emerged; these include high accessibility, especially to international airports, a supply of highly skilled graduates, specialist support services from research centres such as universities and other private suppliers, and physically attractive and well-serviced industrial and business parks. There are very few centres that can provide this range of services. The evidence in regard to the spatial aspects of demographic trends for the late 1980s suggests that for the most part it is only the larger urban centres that are continuing to grow. Analyses of the migration patterns of third-level graduates also confirm the attractiveness of Dublin as the main employment location: approximately 60 per cent of primary degree graduates obtaining employment in Ireland do so in Dublin.

Proposals to Alter the Spatial Structure—Northern Ireland

As in the Republic, for most of the postwar period there has been an almost exclusive reliance on industrial policy as a means of adjusting the spatial distribution of economic activity. It was not until 1964 that the economic disparities between the Belfast region and the remainder of the North were officially acknowledged. The Matthew Report proposed curtailing the expansion of Belfast by imposing a 'stop line' and simultaneously the identification of six 'key' centres west of the Bann. The growth centre concept was reaffirmed in two subsequent reports and pursued with some vigour in the late 1960s, especially in relation to Londonderry. However, circumstances changed in the 1970s. The combination of a significant decline in traditional industries, increasing unemployment and mounting civil unrest brought about a major rethink in industrial location policy. The twenty-year regional physical development strategy published in 1977 involved a reduced commitment to growth centres and more emphasis on the dispersal of industries; in this respect the strategy was quite similar to the eclectic approach adopted in the South.

Throughout the 1980s more attention was focused on Belfast and Derry as the severity of their economic and political problems increased. There was also a significant shift in policy towards supporting small indigenous enterprises, which appears to have been most successful in the smaller towns and rural areas.

While there has been considerable renewal of the physical fabric of Belfast and Derry, their economic bases have not been sufficiently diversified to enable them to become competitive centres. In contrast to Dublin, Belfast has not developed a significant traded services sector. There are probably several reasons for this, including the very poor performance of the Northern economy over the past twenty-five years, the role of the city as a regional capital, and the relocation of political decision-making to London after the fall of Stormont. However, the indications already are that with the arrival of a more peaceful regime there will be renewed international interest in investing in the city.

Spatial Strategies for an All-Ireland Economy

This section considers some options in relation to the organisation of the spatial structure of an all-island economy. An 'island economy' can be fostered in the short term through a series of co-operative ventures such as joint marketing of the island for tourism, joint participation in international trade fairs, the provision of energy supplies, and improving information in relation to industries and services in both parts of the island so as to encourage import substitution. However, there is also a need to consider the factors that are likely to influence the overall growth and competitiveness of the island economy over the medium to long term.

One of the most striking findings of a recent European review of urban functions and urbanisation trends was a renaissance in the growth of those cities that had adopted entrepreneurial strategies. The establishment of an International Financial Services Centre in Dublin is part of a trend to encourage private enterprise to redevelop a formerly derelict or redundant part of the city landscape. However, in a recent classification of European financial centres Dublin is identified as a potential third-order centre, while Belfast is much further down the hierarchy as a fifth-order centre. The slower than expected growth of the Dublin financial centre is a salutary reminder of its relatively modest position in the European urban system. This has to be borne in mind when considering proposals to adjust the present structure of Ireland's urban hierarchy.

There has recently been a revival of interest in regional and spatial economic planning in Ireland. The economic rationale for a spatial policy is based on the notion of 'market failure'. There are several types of market failure that may lead to sub-optimal spatial arrangements of economic activity. These include imperfections in the mobility of labour and capital, the creation of external economies and diseconomies, the availability of information, and the quality and quantity of physical infrastructure and human resources.

At present there is no clearly articulated policy for spatial development, North or South. However, recent trends suggest a return to a tendency towards greater concentration. Given the recent improvements in telecommunications and transport infrastructure, it is no longer appropriate to revert to the same arguments that were used in favour of concentration in the 1960s. Looser geographical structures involving linkages between firms that may be located at some distance from each other are not only feasible, they are also capable of generating external economies while at the same time achieving a more equitable spatial distribution of welfare.

Much of the spatial and regional economic intervention strategies of the past three decades has been guided by a 'constant returns' orientation, which has attached little importance to the creation of synergistic and innovative milieus. If progress is to be made in narrowing the differential in development indicators between Ireland and the core regions of the EU, some changes in policy instruments are required, which will also include an explicit consideration of the factors that influence the geographical organisation of the economy and society. It is against this background that it is appropriate to consider briefly a recent proposal to promote an economic corridor between Dublin and Belfast.

A study of the feasibility of developing an economic corridor has been prepared by Coopers & Lybrand/Indecon (1994) for the CBI (NI) and IBEC. The corridor concept is predicated on the prior existence of vibrant growth centres that have a high potential for interaction over the intervening space. Following a review of the literature on successful corridors, the report identifies several important requirements, such as good transport infra-structure and excellent support facilities, clusters of dynamic and mutually interacting export-oriented manufacturing and service firms, access to government agencies and institutions, and the availability of venture capital. The socio-economic profile of the proposed corridor was then examined; this led the consultants to the conclusion that, with appropriate actions, an economic corridor could be developed. However, careful analysis of the characteristics of the area suggests that this conclusion may be overoptimistic.

The data presented in the report confirms that, far from being dynamic growth poles with a strong potential for increased interaction, the two cities have business sectors that have been developed independently so that there are very few complementarities and there is no tradition of inter-city economic linkages. One index of inter-city interaction is the volume of telephone traffic: the amount of traffic between Dublin and Belfast is only about two-fifths of the amount on the Dublin-Cork route. This is due in part to the political situation, especially over the past twenty-five years; more fundamentally it is also an outcome of the industrial strategies in both parts of the island, which has not succeeded in fostering strong local linkages. The report does not examine the wider implications of its proposals for the spatial organisation of the economy in the remainder of the island.

Looking to the future geography of economic development on the island one must consider the scope for intervention, institutional arrangements, and prioritisation of actions over a time-scale.

There are a number of areas where public intervention is required, including the upgrading of infrastructure (especially in the South), improving the effectiveness of education and training systems (more so in the North), eliminating gaps in information, which at present are very large, and identifying potential for linkages and joint actions on export-related activities. Mechanisms to ensure greater co-operation and co-ordination in the private and public spheres of the economy are required in the short term, while over the medium term the types of cross-border institutions envisaged in *Frameworks for the Future* (1995) should be considered. Progress towards the development of an 'island economy' perspective is likely to be slow unless it is possible to demonstrate that real economic benefits can be realised. To initiate a process that might lead to the goal of a total welfare-maximising spatial structure for the 'island economy', considerably more research is required into the locational dynamics and inter-regional linkages of the economy, with particular reference to the role of the larger cites and also the role of smaller centres and rural space. While at present the linkages between Dublin and Belfast are very weak by comparison with those between Dublin and Cork, this situation could change over the medium term, given the much larger size of Belfast over Cork and the shorter distance separating it from Dublin. Over the medium to long term, businesses that have traditionally catered for the market in the Republic may start thinking of Belfast rather than Cork as the second city. New opportunities may also emerge among the western regions, with Derry providing a focus for developing the north-west. Over the next decade Ireland should seek to learn from the positive integration measures that have been under way in the European Union over the past decade; these include the establishment of the internal market and the accompanying reform of the Structural Funds to take account of the regional implications of a more competitive market.

Concluding Remarks

Throughout this chapter the emphasis has been on articulating the need for a perspective on the spatial organisation of the economy. The economic rationale for intervention in relation to the spatial arrangement of economic activities is to overcome spatially induced instances of market failure. To identify and remedy the market failures it is necessary to pay particular attention to the changing significance of Ireland and places within it as an economic space in the context of a more integrated European space economy. The historical experience has shown that the relative position of different regions can change substantially over time. Detailed analysis and a strategic approach to spatial planning are required to ensure that the total welfare of the population of the island of Ireland is maximised.

References

Albrechts, L., and E. Syngedouw, 'The challenges for regional policy under a flexible regime of accumulation' in L. Albrechts et al. (eds.), *Regional Policy at the Crossroads: European Perspectives,* London: Jessica Kingsley 1989, 67–89.

Bradley, J., N. O'Donnell, and N. Sheridan, 'Infrastructure, Human Resources and Competitive Advantage: Ireland, North and South' (paper to Conference on the Two Economies of Ireland: Public Policy, Growth and Employment), Dublin: Economic and Social Research Institute 1995.

Breathnach, P., 'The demise of growth centre policy: the case of the Republic of Ireland' in R. Hudson and J. Lewis (eds.), *Regional Planning in Europe,* London: Pion 1982.

Buchanan and Partners, *Regional Studies in Ireland,* Dublin: Foras Forbartha 1968.

Bull, P., et al., 'Government-assisted manufacturing activity in a peripheral region of the United Kingdom: Northern Ireland, 1945–1979' in L. Collins (ed.), *Industrial Decline and Regeneration,* Edinburgh: Department of Geography, University of Edinburgh 1982, 39–64.

Collins, B., 'The Irish in Britain, 1780–1921' in B. Graham and L. Proudfoot (eds.), *An Historical Geography of Ireland,* London: Academic Press 1993, 366–98.

Commission of the European Communities, *Urbanization and the Functions of Cities in the European Community,* Brussels: EC 1992.

Coopers & Lybrand/Indecon, *A Corridor of Opportunity: Study of the Feasibility of Developing a Belfast-Dublin Economic Corridor,* Belfast and Dublin: Confederation of British Industry (NI) and Irish Business and Employers' Confederation 1994.

Fitzgerald Report: Outline of the Future Hospital System, Dublin: Stationery Office 1968.

Gillmor, D., *Economic Activities in the Republic of Ireland,* Dublin: Gill and Macmillan 1985.

Hart, M., 'Belfast's economic millstone?: the role of the manufacturing sector since 1973' in P. Doherty (ed.), *Geographical Perspectives on the Belfast Region* (Special Publication no. 5), Dublin: Geographical Society of Ireland 1990, 37–53.

Hart, M., R. Scott, R. Keegan, and G. Gudgin, *Job Creation in Small Firms,* Belfast: Northern Ireland Economic Council 1993.

Hoare, A., 'Problem region and regional problem' in F. Boal and J. Douglas (eds.), *Integration and Division: Geographical Perspectives on the Northern Ireland Problem,* London: Academic Press 1982, 195–224.

Horner, A., J. Walsh, and J. Williams, *Population in Ireland: a Census Atlas,* Dublin: Department of Geography, University College 1987.

Houston, C., and W. Smyth, 'The Irish diaspora to the New World, 1720–1920' in B. Graham and L. Proudfoot (eds.), *An Historical Geography of Ireland,* London: Academic Press 1993, 338–65.

MacLaran, A., *Dublin,* London: Belhaven 1993.

National Economic and Social Council, *New Approaches to Rural Development,* Dublin: Stationery Office 1994.

Northern Ireland Economic Council, *The Implications of Peripherality for Northern Ireland* (Report no. 111), Belfast: NIEC 1993.

O'Malley, E., *Industry and Economic Development,* Dublin: Gill and Macmillan 1989.

Operational Programme for Transport, 1994–1999, Dublin: Stationery Office 1994.

Porter, M., *The Competitive Advantage of Nations,* London: Macmillan 1990.

Ross, M., *Personal Incomes by Region in 1977* (Report no. 51), Dublin: National Economic and Social Council 1980.

Royle, S., 'Industrialization, urbanization and urban society in post-Famine Ireland, c. 1850–1921' in B. Graham and L. Proudfoot (eds.), *An Historical Geography of Ireland,* London: Academic Press 1993, 258–92.

Telesis Consultancy Group, *A Review of Industrial Policy,* Dublin: National Economic and Social Council 1982.

Walsh, J., 'Dublin: region-state relation' in A. Horner and A. Parker (eds.), *Geographical Perspectives on the Dublin Region* (Special Publication no. 2). Dublin: Geographical Society of Ireland 1987, 82–95.

Walsh, J., and D. Gillmor, 'Rural Ireland and the Common Agricultural Policy' in R. King (ed.), *Ireland, Europe and the Single Market* (Special Publication no. 6), Dublin: Geographical Society of Ireland 1993, 84–100.

Part 3

Policy Frameworks

(i) EU

(ii) UK/Ireland

6 The European Union: The Island's Common Cause

Peter Brennan

The views expressed are the personal opinions of the author.

The European Union is entering a potentially difficult period. There are a number of economically significant problems that will have to be tackled by the turn of the century. Popular support throughout Europe is at a low ebb. There is no clear political vision about the future. Upwards of ten more countries want to join the EU. Against this background, EU governments are about to embark on a lengthy negotiation to amend further the Union's Treaties. Diversity of approach and disharmony between political groups and member-states is likely to be a feature of the forthcoming Intergovernmental Conference that begins its work in 1996.

It will be critical for the development of the island economy that the strategies chosen reflect our respective best interests and that the combined influence of the Irish and UK governments and Northern Ireland political representatives are brought to bear to ensure that the island is at the core of the negotiations.

One of the most important decisions to be taken is, without doubt, when to proceed to the third phase of economic and monetary union. By 1 January 1997 a simple majority of member-states (8 out of 15) can decide to move to the third and final stage of EMU, including a single currency, and set a date for such a move. If no date is set, as now seems probable, stage 3 will begin automatically on 1 January 1999 and will comprise those countries that comply with the Maastricht economic convergence criteria.

It is not widely appreciated that, strictly speaking, Ireland (and other member-states) must proceed to stage 3 if it complies with the essentially monetary criteria as prescribed by the Treaty on European Union. On the other hand, and UK including Northern Ireland has a choice, as an 'opt in' is available. That said, there is little likelihood of Ireland being coerced into joining EMU against the wishes of the Government.

The critical question is whether Ireland and the UK will join together and, if this does not happen, what the implications are for the island economy. While the wider costs and benefits of EMU have been well documented elsewhere, no strategic government policy exists—nor is one envisaged as far as I am aware—on what would be best for the two economies, North and South.

I raise this issue at the outset, as much of the co-operation and business development that is planned could suffer if the wrong choices are made about the move to EMU. In short, the competitive equilibrium of the island could be adversely affected if one of our economies operated outside the monetary and economic disciplines that will be required of full EMU members and one operated inside it. Put more bluntly, economic tensions resulting from one part of the island not having to comply with EU rules and disciplines would put the other part at an unnecessary and potentially damaging competitive disadvantage.

This example serves to illustrate the appropriateness of having a common approach to some EU policies.

The challenge of competitiveness will be very familiar to most companies on the island. At European level, the European Commission's 1993 White Paper on Growth, Competitiveness and Employment highlighted the fact that the EU has become a high-cost, low-growth and over-regulated economy when measured against other comparable regions in the world. The document was supposed to provide the framework for governmental action to offset this competitive deficit. So far, there is little evidence that anything has been done in this area.

The task of generating enough investment to create sufficient jobs to reduce our collective dole queues is quite daunting. The problem of unemployment is the number one economic priority in Europe at present. Reducing unemployment on the island should be facilitated, to a very significant extent, by the peace process. Industry invests when the economic and political climate is generally positive. Such an environment exists at present, and we must hope that it continues.

At a practical level, are there lessons to be learnt from the different experiences and approaches taken to job creation on both islands? Could the Irish Government and the Northern Ireland authorities share their experiences about local, community and rural development? Could Ireland experiment with the Training and Enterprise Councils (TECs) that are now widely established throughout the UK? What scope is there for encouraging the services sector as a rich source of new jobs? Could youth placement programmes such as IBEC's European Orientation Programme be resourced on an all-island basis? To my mind, EU assistance should be refocused to investigate the best practices available in order to minimise the levels of unemployment on the island and to give our school-leavers more meaningful careers.

The approach of the Irish and UK governments to the question of future European integration will be central to the development of inter-relationships on the island. This is a fact, with or without any Framework Document. The Irish Government's position on the European Union will be articulated in its forthcoming White Paper on Foreign Policy; it would be reasonable to presume at this stage that a pro-European approach will remain the Government's policy. The attitude of the UK to Europe can be readily discerned from various statements by the Prime Minister, John Major. Popular opinion in Ireland shows an electorate very supportive of EU membership, positive in attitude to further enlargement, and reasonably comfortable about moves to ever-closer union. The attitude in the UK is in marked contrast.

In 1996 the two governments will join their European partners in a series of negotiations that will amend, perhaps quite fundamentally, the EU's Treaties. While there may be much communality of policy about Northern Ireland, it may be stretching reality to suggest that both governments share the same vision on the future development of the European Union. For example, the UK's social policy opt-out is already of concern to Irish employers, as, over time, it could give the UK a competitive edge in an uncommon market; fortunately, so far just one EU Directive is covered by this arrangement.

If a 'hard core' of countries decides to move ahead after the 1996 IGC and the UK decides not to follow the majority, an uneven application of EU rules on the island could well result, at a time when efforts and resources are being devoted to capitalising on the peace process. Depending on the relationship eventually agreed by the UK with its EU partners, it is not beyond the bounds of possibility that the Irish and UK governments could find themselves at opposite ends of the European equation. In such a scenario, which I fervently believe must not be allowed to happen, formal and informal barriers to business would inevitably appear.

While no sample surveys exist, the people of Northern Ireland may associate more with the broad economic objectives of the Union than many other regions in the UK. As decisions taken in Brussels have an impact in a very practical way in Northern Ireland—be they in the areas of the Common Agricultural Policy or EU funding—it would be instructive to find out how the electorate on the island view their shared European agenda.

Brussels favours regional development. Brussels supports cross-border co-operation. Brussels is also in favour of co-operation where this contributes to the economic well-being of those involved. How best can this political good will, shared by all members of the European Union, be optimised so that every opportunity is taken to boost the level of economic activity on the island?

We already have one such example. The Irish Business and Employers' Confederation and the Confederation of British Industry in Northern Ireland set up a Joint Business Council in 1991, with the aim of taking a number of practical initiatives at European level to promote their joint mission, i.e. to develop and maximise North-South trade and to make Irish industry more efficient vis-à-vis international competition.

Many initiatives have already been completed. For example, in January 1993 the Joint Business Council agreed a common approach to EU Structural and Cohesion Fund spending. Their document provided a comprehensive breakdown of measures to strengthen the infrastructure, industrial base and human resources on the island.

Specifically, IBEC and the CBI argued that EU, government and private sector investment should try to achieve the following objectives over the period to 1999:

1. To maximise the level of trade between the two parts of the island in order to increase employment, particularly in the border regions.

2. To improve the quality and efficiency of the transport infrastructure, and by so doing to reduce transport costs towards the EU average.

3. To raise the level of R&D in industry.

4. To invest in energy facilities in order to provide the necessary integration with European energy networks and to reduce costs.

5. To improve the productivity of industrial employees, particularly in their first year of work, through effective pre-employment training.

6. To improve standards of education and training to the highest in the EU.

7. To raise the level of international marketing competence of small firms.

8. To expand tourism and rural development, especially in border regions.

The results of the subsequent negotiations that led to the conclusion of Ireland's Community Support Framework and the Northern Ireland Single Programme Document are illustrated on the following page. A good number of the recommendations were accepted.

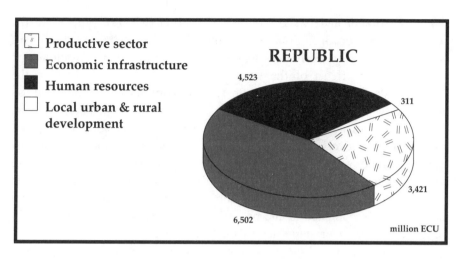

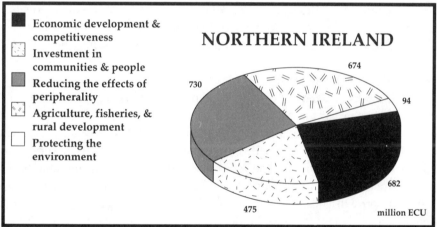

(Note: 1 ECU ≈ £0.82.)

The potential for the development of genuine cross-border projects has also been recognised by the Chambers of Commerce of Ireland and the Northern Ireland Chambers of Commerce and Industry, their Chamber-Link project being a good example. Sectoral organisations in the clothing and construction industries are also seeking to work more closely together on practical cross-border projects. Local authorities are taking their first tentative steps to identify common and mutually beneficial investment projects.

The EU's Community Initiatives to promote cross-border activities and to promote peace and reconciliation are apt in this context. The sceptics might argue that cross-border projects achieve very little; but the first Interreg programme was very effective, according to an evaluation study, and made a significant contribution to assisting in the development of cross-border networks.

Interreg II will underwrite around 262 million ECUs of projects in the period to 1999. The Operational Programme that has been approved provides the rationale for why the EU assists such measures: the EU is conscious that the centralising effects of the single European market will work to the economic detriment of frontier zones, especially those handicapped by peripherality and by poor infrastructure and socio-economic performance. The island of Ireland fits into this category. We are also considered as regions that suffer from levels of unemployment and levels of income per head that are considerably worse than the EU average. High dependence on agriculture is also a common characteristic of both economies. In deciding to allocate EU funds, due account was taken of the substantial economic costs—direct and indirect—of the violence of the past twenty-five years; an amount of £470 million a year has been suggested by the Commission.

The areas that are eligible for funding include the whole of Northern Ireland apart from Belfast, and the border counties of Cavan, Donegal, Leitrim, Louth, Monaghan, and Sligo. Provided there is a demonstrable and high degree of cross-border co-operation, EU co-financing may be extended outside these areas up to a limit of 10 per cent of total investment. Project selection is already under way.

On the other hand, the new Community Initiative for peace and reconciliation in Northern Ireland and the border counties of Ireland is not expected to become operational until the end of 1995. The initiative will contribute 300 million ECUs in the period 1995–97 towards a very wide variety of projects whose central focus must relate to the consolidation of the peace process. Particular priority will be given to the measures to boost economic growth and employment, local development and urban and rural regeneration, increased cross-border development arising from the peace process, the promotion of reconciliation, and projects aimed at improving and promoting competitiveness.

There are many practical examples that demonstrate clearly that the island's EU interests are very similar—some would say almost identical. How then can we capture this common agenda and capitalise on the genuine good will that exists throughout Europe to assist in cross-border co-operation and to co-finance projects that will facilitate peace and reconciliation?

Without wishing to delve too much into the political agenda, I feel that a serious examination could be made of one particular section of the Framework Document that has received scant attention until now: the paragraphs (26 and 28 in particular) on EU matters. The document proposes that common arrangements need to be developed in relation to EU issues. Specifically, there is a suggestion that there should be an agreed approach for the whole island in respect of the challenges and opportunities arising at EU level. Joint action as regards policy formulation, implementation, management and monitoring of all EU programmes and initiatives on a cross-border or island-wide basis is also mooted.

My preliminary impression is that these recommendations, if implemented, would have profound implications for the way in which our respective governments and communities respond to EU policies.

Leaving aside the delicate question of whether and how the suggested institutional set-up might best be put in place, I feel there is considerable merit in adopting an island approach to (some) EU funding programmes. A single approach to infrastructural projects co-financed by the Structural Funds has merit, as the IBEC-CBI joint initiative has already shown; given the EU requirement to have partners from several member-states, there is an obvious case for a joint approach in areas such as R&D, education and training, and environmental protection.

At present the Irish and UK attitudes to many EU policies are quite different in terms of substance and direction. As both governments prepare for what will almost certainly be very difficult negotiations to amend the Maastricht treaty, it appears to me that it would be very useful to commission an audit on the impact of current EU policies on Ireland and Northern Ireland, jointly and separately, and the potential consequences for the island as a whole if all concerned pursued a common agenda on key European policy issues.

By the turn of the century—a few short years hence—the EU will be a much more competitive market. Enlargement of the Union to the low-cost and loosely regulated economies of eastern and central Europe appears to be an inevitability. Further reform of the CAP will be under way. EMU will probably have been completed in many (but not all) member-states. A new EU budget will also be in place. The Internal Market will be more of a reality than it is today. Europe will have completed (and voted on) a wide-ranging and popular debate about its future. There will be tight controls on EU funding programmes. If, in the next century, ever-closer union, to borrow a phrase from the Maastricht treaty, becomes by consent the political aim of the majority in Europe, will this island economy, in ever-closer union, wish to opt in or out of such an arrangement?

To conclude, I suggest that a much wider debate needs to take place, North and South, about the strategic vision for both economies in a more challenging and competitive European market. In short, the EU dimension to the peace process is a crucial factor which cannot be ignored. To promote the debate, I would recommend the following:

1. A common strategic approach to priority European issues should be agreed at the earliest possible date.

2. A 'competitiveness audit' of the island economy vis-à-vis other European countries and regions should be completed.

3. Long-term planning for common infrastructural projects should begin, some of which may be funded by the EU.

4. Cross-border institution-building between business representative organisations and public bodies should be given a much higher priority.

5. An island approach to minimising our common long-term unemployment problem should be explored.

6. A much higher proportion of the EU funding than is currently available for cross-border initiatives—as much as 50 per cent—should be allocated to projects that have a proven beneficial impact on both sides of the border.

The Irish Business Bureau and the Northern Ireland Centre in Europe already co-operate in sharing information and advice on EU affairs. We do so in a pragmatic way for the mutual benefit of the organisations we represent. Much more can and should be done between us.

7   The European Union: A Better Life on the Border

Gerry McAlinden

The sixty-five European border regions are described in Jacques Delors's *L'Unité d'un Homme* (1994) as 'the real life places of the European experience.' The border regions on the island of Ireland have been a painful reminder of the conflict and hostility, suspicion and economic stagnation that typified the experience of many such regions in Europe in the past. European union, if it is to mean anything at all, is as much about changing for the better the reality and prospects of life for the communities sharing the geography of the border between Northern Ireland and the Republic as it is about European political and monetary union.

In this chapter I will give an overview of the impact of European union on cross-border development and co-operation based on a number of different cases of local cross-border actions. The approach I have taken draws on the local economic development experience as distinct from wider development programmes implemented by the two member-states with EU support. I shall trace the emergence of new models of co-operative economic management, local in character and potentially more responsive to the needs of border areas than some current, more broadly strategic approaches.

European Regional Policy and Border Regions

Cross-border co-operation and the development of border regions are key elements of the strategic objective of economic and social cohesion, which in itself is a pillar of the Single European Act of 1985. The lack of public investment in peripheral border regions throughout Europe was identified as a significant obstacle to that objective. Early efforts to compensate for the centralising tendencies of state spending patterns resulted in the European Commission setting up the Non-Quota Border Regions Programme. This was project-driven and provided a valuable and visible source of support and solidarity for hitherto neglected areas. Typical projects assisted were tourism, transport or environment-related.

In the reform of the Structural Funds in 1988 the European Commission provided for a special initiative aimed at reducing the negative effect of borders on local economies and increasing the potential for co-operation and cross-border linkages. Interreg was approved as a Community Initiative in 1990, and the Joint Programme for Northern Ireland and the Republic was agreed the following year with a total EU contribution of 76 million ECUs for the period 1991–93. The programme focused on tourism, agriculture, fisheries and forestry, human resources, the environment, and regional development.

Interreg I, as it is known, has now been wound up and is the subject of an evaluation that throws up a number of interesting findings and recommend-ations. The evaluation report records that the programme provided a major impetus to cross-border co-operation, which will offer many lessons for future joint actions. The most clearly successful example of cross-border co-operation cited relates to the experiences of a state and a semi-state body in the forestry sector (Northern Ireland Forestry Service and Coillte), which moved from ad hoc co-operation, through tentative linkages and exchanges to the regular provision of joint training programmes.

A further example of the catalytic role of Interreg is identified in the emergence of joint 'management' structures, involving state bodies and agencies and local representatives from both sides of the border to oversee the exploitation of the major infrastructural projects financed under the programme. The Joint Co-ordinating Committee for the Shannon-Erne Waterway was set up to oversee and provide for the tourism development potential made possible by the completion of the Ballyconnell Canal. As an international tourism product, this project in its first operative season exceeded every target set, including its ability to attract further investment. As a direct result of the canal a £4 million cruiser base is to be established in Fermanagh and a £15 million hotel has been built in Ballyconnell. Significant investment has also occurred in all the villages along the route.

'Back-to-Back' or 'Shoulder-to-Shoulder'

It seems clear that Interreg may have uncovered and stimulated, but not altogether tapped, a significant dynamic for cross-border co-operative development in the willingness of local groups from the private, local government and non-profit sectors to undertake joint co-operative ventures. There are a number of reasons for this. In the first instance, the design and management of Interreg I represented a new opportunity, and a new challenge, for government departments to work on a more regular basis with their counterparts across the border than hitherto. The information needs of potential participants were found wanting. Programme priorities were not always shared, differences in administrative traditions intervened, and, as a result, cross-border partners, obliged to apply separately to their respective national authorities, were frequently treated differently. In a number of cases, initiatives intended as joint actions had to be implemented 'back-to-back', sometimes over different periods, because of the lack of co-ordination at central administration level.

A second factor acting against cross-border co-operation projects (as distinct from projects simply located in border regions) making little or no planned impact at a cross-border level is that the European Commission guidelines for Interreg itself do not differentiate between the two priorities articulated in its aims and objectives. Consequently, the development of a golf course in, say, Letterkenny, or co-financing selective financial assistance projects in Craigavon, can be presented as contributing to the aims of the programme just as directly as the formation of the Joint Co-ordinating Committee for the Shannon-Erne Waterway, although such investments have no *cross-border* impact.

Cross-Border Partnerships

Interreg I is only the beginning of the developing story of cross-border co-operation on the island of Ireland. The pattern of co-operation varies along the border region, rooted in the mutual benefit of local communities, as in Strabane-Leitrim Partnership, the Central Border Area Network (Armagh, Dungannon, Omagh and Fermanagh along with Cavan, Leitrim, Donegal, Monaghan and Sligo), the North-West Region (involving Derry, Donegal, Strabane, and Limavady) or the East Border Region (Newry and Mourne, Down District, Louth, and Monaghan). (The CBI-IBEC Joint Council is on an island-wide basis as distinct from locally cross-border.) Other partnerships are driven by business organisations such as the Gap of the North Association of Chambers of Commerce (Newry, Armagh, Dundalk, and Monaghan) and ECOM (which brings together the Chambers of Commerce of Londonderry and Letterkenny).

What all these ventures have in common is that they have come about largely as a result of EU regional policy (including rural development and human resources development). Structural Fund support has not simply put the focus on cross-border co-operation but has given a real impetus to locally driven solutions to local development problems by promoting a 'bottom-up' growth model as distinct from, yet complementing, the conventional 'top-down' approach to economic development. However, it must be acknowledged that the locally based approach is still in its embryonic form. The next step to self-sustaining development is critical. It is premature in the learning curve to identify ready examples of success. Nevertheless, these are significant instances of good practice and promising beginnings.

Local enterprise and human resources development are common themes for cross-border partnerships. One such example is the long-standing relationship between the Louth County Enterprise Board, Dundalk Employment Partnership, and Newry and Mourne Enterprise Agency. This group, with EU support under the Sprint initiative, recently completed a feasibility study for a border technology park to accommodate innovative business projects seeded and grown in the border region. The objective of the initiative is to create a catalyst for advanced technological industrial innovation and to encourage the clustering of high-technology small firms in the border region, which has a significant proportion of highly qualified but unemployed graduates. It will build on the improved transport and telecommunications (ISDN) networks that have opened up development possibilities in the region and seek to attract further technologically advanced inward investment. In time these partnerships must move to new forms of co-operative management, perhaps based on such forms as European economic interest groupings (EEIGs).

Inter-Regional Partnerships

In some instances the cross-border partnership has become the springboard to wider interregional links involving different regions of the European Union. The best-known example of this is ERNACT, which brings together Derry City Council and Donegal (joint leaders) with Ålborg (Denmark), Kortrijk, (Belgium), Zeeland (Netherlands), and Galway. ERNACT has been working in relation to the use of advanced communications and information technology, with the objective of improving services to local citizens. The project is being taken by many as an early prototype of the new 'information superhighway' concept and has excited much interest in Commission and other circles. The Donegal-Derry hub partnership has served to provide a centre of gravity for the network.

Local Ownership—Local Options

One of the most innovative features of the regional development plan submitted to the European Commission by the Northern Ireland authorities in 1993 was the inclusion of a modest measure that would permit local authorities, acting in partnership with other social and economic participants in the local economy, to formulate local strategies based on an analysis of local strengths and weaknesses, focusing on those needs not met by statutory or private agencies. The measure, which builds on a recent extension of the powers of local authorities in the region by using locally generated funds to 'lever down' EU Structural Funds, provides the opportunity for local area partnerships (comprising private sector interests, statutory agencies and the community and voluntary sector as well as local authorities) to implement agreed strategies for local development over the next five years. For many, the learning curve will be steep and not without risks; but the palpable sense of ownership and local commitment to the plans suggests that the extended powers are unlikely to be readily retracted and that local management of micro-economies will be a feature of regional development for some time to come. Many see in the initiative the further consolidation of the peace process by putting the focus on shared social and economic goals at local level.

Plans in general reflect local conditions and needs: some prioritise local labour market strategies, tackling long-term unemployment and job creation; others build on natural advantage, as in the development and promotion of local (or shared) tourism projects. A few seek to exploit new technologies as a means of encouraging industrial development—all of them in the context of integrated strategic development plans.

It is clear that many of the Northern local authority areas adjoining the border share development problems or opportunities and have long recognised the need for co-operative action. In some instances locally established cross-border groups, such as the bodies mentioned above, have been seeking to jointly pursue priorities, frequently without the means of achieving their ends. We can expect that as local economic development becomes a core issue for local government on both sides of the border, despite being bounded by administrative and budgetary differences, it will, in the medium term, add to the momentum for local cross-border co-operation.

That is not to say that there will be a *'champ libre'* for cross-border development at local level. Many difficulties remain. Locally, the appetite for cross-border co-operation varies depending upon the political chemistry of the area. There is no blueprint and certainly no agreed theory of cross-border action other than enlightened, co-operative self-interest. While a number of areas have pressed ahead in the formation of cross-border groupings on the basis of their assumed geographical and cultural homogeneity (e.g. the East Border Region, which groups the Newry and Mourne district and Down district in Northern Ireland with Louth and Monaghan), others have been more tentative in coming together.

Some cross-border partnerships have been driven by the imperative of their economic ambitions, as in the North-West Region Cross-Border Partnership, for long perceived to be on the periphery in terms of regional development on both sides of the border and for that reason inclined over the years to depend on local co-operative initiative. The North-West Area Strategy puts forward an integrated development plan that emphasises co-operative development in infrastructure, industrial development, research and development, tourism, rural development, and the application of information technology for regional development.

A further model is the Central Border Areas Network, mentioned above. This came about largely through awareness of the potential for EU support. It is a much wider association, and, although it is still in the formative stage, there are signs that the preferred approach will be more pragmatically driven. Co-operation will focus on such areas of common interest as rural regeneration, energy, transport, technology, education and training, and tourism, in the form of cross-border actions and programmes. Support for such developments will in the first instance focus on concrete projects meeting a shared need or realising a common opportunity. There is no commitment to developing a continuing co-operative development strategy, although in some cases these may emerge from the repeated experience of working together on successive and successful projects.

Future Prospects

The Interreg II programme for Northern Ireland and the Republic for the period 1994–99 was approved in March 1995. The programme has an EU Structural Funds allocation of 157 million ECUs (twice as large as the previous programme) and a total value of 262 million ECUs. The key themes in the new programme are regional development (which attracts 27 per cent of the EU allocation), human resources (9 per cent), infrastructure (34 per cent), agriculture, fisheries, and forestry (9 per cent), and the environment (21 per cent). Interreg II will provide a significant stimulus for cross-border development up to the end of this century, involving a wide range of bodies from every sector.

The new programme differs from its predecessor in several respects, but most notably by proposing to make available, more or less on a pilot basis, single packages of funding to cross-border partnerships that have a record in co-operative activity, with or without EU support. The shift to greater decentralisation in decision-making should allow established groups to submit for approval integrated development strategies with local cross-border management structures, releasing a new dynamic in the management of cross-border micro-economies. What seems clear at this stage is that programme managers will be keen to promote genuine cross-border activity rather than 'stand-alone' projects in one or other jurisdiction.

Both member-state administrations, as well as the local beneficiaries, will have to come to terms with new forms of financial management and accountability. Policy-makers and managers from both sides of the border will be looking to Europe for possible examples of cross-border co-operation. The Euregio (Netherlands-German) border region has experienced jointly managed programmes, albeit on a small scale, over a number of years. There are other examples along the Spanish-Portuguese border, where, after a slow, almost reluctant, start, local communities have developed local forms of cross-border partnership in the context of wider international agreements.

More flexible forms of funding for cross-border partnerships are also likely to feature in the delivery of the Special Support Programme for Peace and Reconciliation in Northern Ireland and the Border Counties, otherwise known as the 'Delors package' (in acknowledgment of the former president's very real personal commitment to the peace process). The overriding theme of the special initiative is reconciliation between the two communities in Northern Ireland and between the two parts of the island. Cross-border development is one of the five priority areas for action and will attract at least 15 per cent of the total package, worth 300 million ECUs. Local development is envisaged as a natural area for co-operation.

The gradual removal of existing barriers, including physical barriers such as impassable border roads and inadequate infrastructure, will lead to more evenly spread economic development in border regions. One of the difficulties facing programme managers will be finding adequate indicators for measuring the impact of measures in terms of their contribution to the goal of reconciliation. This will require sensitive handling at both regional and local level to overcome the scepticism and the antagonisms that have intensified in some border areas over the last twenty-five years. However, experience has shown that the common interest can coalesce around identifiable projects breaking down barriers through the process and experience of working together.

The impact of the European Union on the border regions of the island of Ireland goes far beyond the direct financial flows to the regions, although these in themselves cannot be considered negligible. The local interest generated by the first Interreg initiative, the consultation and debates that have preceded the submission of national and regional development plans to Brussels, the growing evidence that these programmes can change for the better the quality of life for those living in border regions and the increasing transparency of the monitoring and evaluation process have all led to a much greater awareness of local potential and consciousness of the need for local leadership and action. We are witnessing not only a quantitative increase in investment in border regions but also a qualitative change in the process of growth. Self-reliance and partnerships for mutual interest are replacing the apathy, inertia and sense of exclusion born of suspicion with a dynamic for growth as border communities from east to west on the island of Ireland assert the economic potential of the periphery and take ownership of their future.

The views expressed are those of the author and not necessarily of the Northern Ireland Centre in Europe.

The author expresses his warm acknowledgments to Gerry Burns, chief executive, Fermanagh District Council; Margaret Andrews, chief executive, Newry and Mourne Enterprise Agency; and to his colleagues Colm McClements and John Kennedy.

8   Fiscal Realities: The Degrees of Difference

John Simpson

Two contrasting statements illustrate the diverse issues affecting economic management and the scope for economic co-operation on the island of Ireland.

First some reassurance: both parts of the island are within the European Union and can benefit from the evolution of the European single market. The frontiers for trade, payments and movement to find work anywhere in the EU have, in the main, disappeared. Although the United Kingdom is reluctant to remove internal border checks within the EU, there is the equivalent of a Schengen agreement between Ireland and the UK.

Second, a recognition of the degree of difference that remains: the Republic of Ireland is a self-governing state that, within the constraints of the EU and international obligations, manages its own economic policies, determines its own balance of taxation and public sector spending, and must take account of its own exchange rate, interest rates, and anti-inflation policies. In Northern Ireland the same statements cannot be made. The United Kingdom government determines the main economic policies, the balance of taxation and public sector spending, and influences the other economic variables.

In short the Republic is an independent state within the EU; Northern Ireland is a region with some modest degrees of devolution in a fairly centralised United Kingdom framework. Consequently, while trade and payments respond to market forces, co-operation in the judgments about, and the mechanisms to pursue, economic policy-making across the border on the island are much more complex to be able to rely simply on good will and local initiatives in North-South relations.

To extend and maximise the gains from cross-border co-operation, this chapter explores how the existing economic framework might be improved within the constraints of the wider political setting involving the United Kingdom and Ireland as well as the European Union.

The Economies Compared

While there are differences in recent economic performance between North and South, largely as a direct and indirect consequence of the costs and perceptions of violence in Northern Ireland, the main economic determinants affecting development are remarkably similar.

Both parts of the island have experienced, for many years, levels of unemployment that are higher than those in Great Britain or, on average, in the EU. Both are accepted as Objective 1 regions of the EU (i.e. regions qualifying for the highest level of financial assistance), although both are close to the limits of the economic performance indicators that determine this status, in terms of GDP per person.

The island of Ireland is geographically peripheral to the main EU markets, lacks significant supplies of indigenous sources of energy, lacks major advantages in the ready availability of materials for heavy industry, and depends extensively on the production of temperate foodstuffs, many of which tend to exceed supply within the EU.

Employment trends, with one exception, have been similar. Farm employment continues to decrease and is now less than 7 per cent of all employment in Northern Ireland and less than 14 per cent in the Republic. Employment in most services, public and private, has increased rapidly in the last couple of decades. The exception has been the recent evolution of output in manufacturing industry and its effects on employment. Whereas manufacturing output in Northern Ireland over the past twenty-five years has increased slightly, this has not been enough to prevent a 40 per cent fall in manufacturing employment. In contrast, in the South output has more than doubled, and manufacturing employment is now significantly higher, although the increase occurred mainly in the 1970s and tended to be reversed slightly in the 1980s.

The demographic trends also differ from those in many parts of Europe. The birth rate is falling but, North and South, is still much higher than in other European countries. Northern Ireland now has the highest birth rate of all regions in the EU. Both areas have, therefore, potentially an increasing domestic labour supply that, to some extent, tends to be offset by migration at different stages of the economic cycle. Because of past emigration, the proportion of elderly people in the population is lower than in many other European countries.

There is still a difference in average living standards, North and South. However, the gap has closed dramatically in the last thirty years. Measured in terms used by the EU, Northern Ireland GDP per head was 75 per cent of the EU average in 1989–91; the Republic was 68 per cent. In the early 1960s this gap was much wider. The impact of improved economic management, economic restructuring, EU membership and EU support has allowed the Republic to close the gap with Northern Ireland.

Differences

The main cross-border differences of significance for economic progress are:

(1) Monetary:

- lack of a common currency, imposing transaction costs on payments;
- an exchange rate that is variable, adding a degree of uncertainty to trade;
- a 'green pound' exchange rate that varies (of importance for farming);
- divergences in levels and structure of interest rates;
- differences in the availability and use of specialist financial institutions;

(2) Fiscal:

- some differences in the structure and rates of VAT;
- differences in excise duties;
- differences in personal income tax rates;
- differences in corporate tax rates;
- special tax provision in the Republic affecting the cost of bank borrowing in defined circumstances;

(3) Government expenditure:

- usually higher levels of per capita spending on public services in Northern Ireland than in the Republic;
- some differences in support mechanisms for sectors of industry or farming;

(4) External finance to assist government finances:

- different levels and types of external support for government spending;
- major differences in the need for, and scale of, public sector borrowing.

The main determinants of fiscal policy in the two areas contrast sharply. The Government of the Republic has consistently faced the difficult decisions of an independent state where the public sector balance of revenue, expenditure and borrowing has been a continuous constraint. While for a period in the 1980s the level of borrowing reached unsustainable levels and there was a concern that this might have major monetary and inflationary implications, in general over the last forty years economic and monetary management has been successful, by European comparisons, even though difficult problems remain, particularly high rates of unemployment.

Much of the informed debate has had to take account of the consequences of changing levels of exchequer borrowing, external borrowing, and the cost of servicing the national debt as a big item affecting expenditure.

In Northern Ireland there has been no comparable set of variables. The essence of public sector management has mainly related to determining expenditure levels. Once public sector expenditure guidelines were set and accepted by the UK Treasury, there was no problem in securing revenue. Indeed the Treasury mechanisms ensured that revenue was allocated to match approved expenditure, not vice versa. This is met by a transfer, usually termed a subvention, from the UK Treasury that has increased in relative size over the last twenty-five years.

An outcome of these financial arrangements is that, with limited exceptions, Northern Ireland has no major public sector borrowing requirement or debt outstanding. Where the Republic has borrowed to finance the public sector, Northern Ireland has received a non-repayable subvention, whether for capital or current expenditure. Not being required to repay borrowing, because grants are received instead, makes public sector management easier.

This feature has an often misunderstood effect on the scale of the subvention from the UK Treasury. When UK government expenditure rises more than revenue, the UK borrowing requirement rises, as it did in 1992–94. Since Northern Ireland usually enjoys parallel changes in expenditure, a rise in the UK borrowing requirement tends to be reflected in a rise in the subvention. Thus the subvention may vary without this being a measure of changes in the underlying strength, or weakness, of the Northern Ireland economy. For example, when the UK government's borrowing requirement rose in 1993, exceptionally, to £50 billion, this might indirectly be linked to a rise of nearly £1.5 billion in the subvention to Northern Ireland.

The subvention is, of course, a continuing reflection of fiscal redistribution within the United Kingdom that is not measurable for different regions within Great Britain, because there are no separate regional public sector accounts. It is automatically measured for Northern Ireland because of the institutional arrangements.

Financial Support

A North-South comparison that is frequently the source of contrasting interpretations is the degree of dependence of governments in both areas on external sources of financial support. The most conspicuous components of external support are, in the Republic, the flow of funds from the EU and, in Northern Ireland, the flows of funds (over and above the attribution of tax raised in Northern Ireland) from the UK Treasury and from the EU. These financial flows are large, both North and South.

For the Republic, EU funding support has been a relatively recent and growing phenomenon. In the 1970s, after accession to the EC, the first major financial support came from the working of the Common Agricultural Policies. Then, emerging in the 1970s but expanding in the 1980s and 1990s, the Structural Funds (including the European Regional Development Fund and the European Social Fund) increased in size. Various targeted Community initiatives (such as Interreg and Leader) have added to the flow of funds, and more recently these have been further supplemented by the EU Cohesion Fund, from which the Republic, but not Northern Ireland, qualifies for support.

EU support for economic and social development in the Republic is expected to provide approximately £1 billion a year for the rest of this decade, to which must be added what may be even larger sums in the form of guarantee payments under the Common Agriculture Policies. In the early years of the 1990s the total is averaging over IR£2 billion a year.

The changing scale of the support, excluding any borrowing, from the EU is illustrated in table 1.

Table 1: Gross and net receipts from EU budget, Republic of Ireland, 1978–93

Year	Receipts (IR£M)	Contributions to EU budget (IR£M)	Net receipts (IR£M)
1978	410	46	364
1981	507	105	402
1984	867	203	664
1987	1,100	255	845
1990	1,741	283	1,458
1993	2,245	453	1,792

Source: Department of Foreign Affairs, Dublin.

While the net receipts from the EU are large in absolute terms, the relative impact can be illustrated in terms of the equivalent proportionate addition to total government revenue. In 1993, receipts of IR£2,245 billion represented

22 per cent of Government revenue and 7 per cent of GDP. It was the equivalent of the whole interest bill on the outstanding national debt.

The flow of funds from the EU to Northern Ireland is absolutely and proportionately much smaller than the net receipts by the Republic. The flow is also less precisely measured, since much of the impact of expenditure on CAP intervention cannot be precisely identified by a particular point of benefit within the UK.

Apportioning the CAP expenditure according to the scale of agricultural production, estimates can be made of the impact of EU funding in Northern Ireland. These are summarised in table 2.

Table 2: Gross and net receipts from EU budget, Northern Ireland, 1978/79–1992/93

Year	Receipts (£M)	Contribution to EU budget (£M)	Net receipts (£M)
1978/79	44	24	20
1981/82	86	50	36
1984/85	162	68	95
1987/88	212	92	121
1990/91	254	108	146
1992/93	354	115e	239e

Source: Department of Finance, plus 6.18 per cent of UK intervention spending through CAP.

EU support is much smaller in Northern Ireland than it is in the Republic, whether measured in proportion to the total population, total Government spending, or GDP. While in 1993 EU support, before the deduction of contributions to the EU budget, was equivalent to 22 per cent of total Government revenue in the Republic, in Northern Ireland in 1992/93 the ratio was nearer to 5 per cent.

In population terms, Northern Ireland has about 45 per cent of the population of the Republic; EU support has rarely exceeded 20 per cent and has recently been nearer to 18 per cent of that in the Republic.

If account is taken of the net contribution from both areas to the EU budget, the contribution from Northern Ireland is a larger proportion of its gross receipts. In 1990/91 Northern Ireland made a payment of nearly 40 per cent of the net receipts; the Republic made a payment equivalent to only 16 per cent of gross receipts in the comparable year. The reason for this difference in financial flows from the EU budget lies principally in the way in which the allocation of EU funds is determined. The European Commission makes indicative allocations that, implicitly, recognise the balance of needs and alternative resources available in countries and regions. In this calculation, Northern Ireland's position as a region with major fiscal support from the UK is taken into account. When the UK subvention is added, Northern Ireland is seen to have a proportionately higher degree of support than the Republic.

The UK Subvention to Northern Ireland

The usual method of measuring the UK subvention to support public sector spending in Northern Ireland is to use the total of the grant in aid provided by the Treasury and add the cost of the Northern Ireland Office, the courts service, and the support for the National Insurance Fund (which equalises the resources and expenditure of the separate Northern Ireland and Great Britain funds). In 1993/94 this gave the following estimated outcome:

Grant in aid	£2,392 million
NIO	£923 million
Courts	£39 million
National Insurance	£40 million
Total	£3,390 million

These sums are made available in addition to the attribution of all local taxes.

The scale of the subvention can be illustrated by comparing the total with the published total of public sector spending. The two concepts are not directly comparable, but as a broad measure, in 1993/94 the subvention was equal to 51 per cent of expenditure of £7,600 million.

The concept of the subvention attracts debate. Because of the extra costs incurred as a consequence of twenty-five years of violence and the economic distortions, the subvention can be argued to be an overstatement of the dependence of Northern Ireland on the UK Treasury. In 1969/70 the subvention amounted to only 16 per cent of total central government spending.

Since 1969 two big changes have taken place. First, on a UK-wide basis, the role of the public sector has increased. Second, large sums have been spent in Northern Ireland offsetting the violence in many different ways. Removing the effects of violence from the equation is difficult, but if the assumption is made that the cumulative effect must be at least £1,000 million a year, then the underlying subvention in 1993/94 would have been nearer to 36 per cent of all public sector spending, after deducting £1 billion from both totals.

Another perspective by which the subvention can be assessed suggests that it is used to overstate a picture of dependence. Since the subvention is a residual, calculated after expenditure has been agreed and local revenue deducted, and since expenditure is agreed on the basis of concepts of parity of treatment and parity of effect between different parts of the UK, the subvention is simply a mathematical measure of fiscal redistribution in a centralised economy. Northern Ireland, in that sense, obtains no special favours. Also, to some extent the subvention is an artefact influenced by wider policy questions, including the PSBR, and an unfair measure of dependence.

Nevertheless, in answer to the simplistic question 'To what extent is government spending in Northern Ireland higher than government revenue raised in Northern Ireland?' the conventional calculation of the subvention is appropriate.

Table 3: The UK subvention to Northern Ireland

Year	Amount (£M)	As percentage of public spending
1969/70	73	16
1978/79	945	43
1981/82	1,024	32
1984/85	1,413	35
1987/88	1,554	32
1990/91	1,975	34
1993/94	3,390	51

The subvention has varied over the past twenty-five years. The broad trends are illustrated in table 3. This table, however, is subject to the distorting effects of variations in the UK budget relationship between government revenue and expenditure, as expressed in the PSBR. A significant part, but not all, of the increase in the proportion of government expenditure financed by the subvention in 1993/94 may be a consequence of a large rise in the PSBR.

If 1990/91 is taken as a more representative year, and if about £800 million is deducted from the subvention and government spending as a crude estimate of the cost of violence and the net loss of local potential tax revenue, then the underlying subvention would be 20 per cent.

Fiscal Support Compared

Adding together the net effect of EU funding and the scale of the subvention makes possible a North-South comparison of the degree of external financial support.

Table 4: Official financial inflows compared (gross receipts), Northern Ireland and Republic, 1978/79–1992/93

Year	NI (£M)	Rep. (£M)	Rep./NI (%)
1978/79	989	410	41
1981/82	1,110	406	37
1984/85	1,575	711	45
1987/88	1,766	999	57
1990/91	2,229	1,619	73
1992/93	3,744	1,932	52

Note: Figures for Republic are for calendar years, converted to sterling.

Two features are conspicuous. First, Northern Ireland is proportionately more dependent on external finance to maintain current levels of government spending. After a major increase in the scale of this support at an early stage of the politically linked civil disruption, it now tends to be between 35 and 51 per cent of total public spending. Second, the Republic receives a smaller level of external support, but, from almost nothing in the early 1970s, the level of support has grown and is growing rapidly. From the equivalent of less than 9 per cent of exchequer spending for much of the 1980s the ratio increased to 17 per cent in 1990 and 22 per cent in 1993.

Although the comparison is unrefined and subject to a number of qualifications, as a crude measure of the significance of these different levels of funding it is interesting to compare public expenditure per capita, North and South, and estimate the degree to which this is made possible by the differing levels of external finance received.

In 1990/91 public sector spending in Northern Ireland was £5,872 million—about £3,690 per capita. In 1990 exchequer spending and borrowing in the Republic was IR£9,606 million—about IR£2,740 per capita, equivalent to £2,550 sterling. The latter figures include the amounts needed to pay interest on the national debt, which is an element that is not within the Northern Ireland framework.

On these figures, public sector spending was some 30 per cent lower in the Republic than in Northern Ireland. More than half of this gap can be directly attributed to the differing levels of external support. However, a part of the difference is not explained by extra support and may be attributed to other factors, one of which may be a combination of slightly higher living standards and a more robust tax base in Northern Ireland.

Cross-Border Developments

If inter-government co-operation on a North-South basis develops there will be an interest in identifying those aspects of economic management where both economies can gain if changes are made. Changes in monetary relationships are not likely to fall within this remit unless both the UK and the Republic join a European monetary union with a single currency. That question rests with national governments. The outcome could be critical, since, of all the economic variables, an unstable North-South exchange rate relationship would be a deterrent to further economic integration.

Differences in the level of funding for government expenditure are likely to remain. Even on an optimistic forecast for EU transfers, government spending in Northern Ireland is likely to remain higher than in the Republic. There would, however, be areas of expenditure where economies of scale suggest a sharing of provision, whether current or capital, such as university specialisms, public infrastructure, or some public services. There is also scope for co-operation between North and South to avoid distortions in schemes aimed at stimulating business. In particular, the differing mixtures of tax and expenditure incentives for outside investors cause adverse comment in Northern Ireland, given the effects on inward investment projects that are able to choose between the two areas. The UK government may need to be persuaded to allow Northern Ireland manufacturers to enjoy a similar tax regime to that in the Republic.

Part of the theme for cross-border co-operation may focus on the role of the EU in facilitating harmonisation on the island. One particular plea to the EU may be for an extension of the Cohesion Fund regulations to allow trans-European networks to be planned and financed on an integrated basis, including a degree of integration from Ireland to England.

While many features of the two economies will remain distinctive, because of the interaction between a region of one national government and another independent government, there is scope for significant cross-border development to promote economic change in infrastructure, incentives to investors, shared public sector services, and securing better cohesion within the EU. The practical benefits will not be secured unless there is an appreciation of the limits to economic integration as well as the scale of the opportunities. North-South co-operation is, by constitutional arrangements, constrained but also offers the potential for significant benefits.

The monetary and fiscal aspects of the border on the island of Ireland will remain one of the complex and difficult elements of cross-border co-operation for many years.

Part 4

Working Together

9   Agriculture and Food: Island of Ireland?

Bill Hodges and Eugene Regan

'Border crossings' neatly encapsulates the means by which fortunes have been made North and South since the division of Ireland in the 1920s, most notably in the livestock sector. Cattle dealers and farmers have never been slow to take advantage of different trading opportunities 'across the border'; if the border had not existed, the farmers of Ireland would surely have invented it. Long before the United Kingdom and the Republic joined the European Community, the movement of animals and produce across the border, both legally and illegally, had contributed greatly to the wealth of individual farmers and processors, but not necessarily to the economies of both parts of the island.

We discuss in this chapter how changes in Europe demand a different response, and the necessity for agriculture on the island to come to terms with these changes.

Today the pressure to reduce agricultural support prices within Europe is substantial. The system of 'intervention' in the European Union under which guaranteed prices are paid for farm produce has largely disappeared. The drive towards value-added convenience foods has an unstoppable momentum. As an island off Great Britain and further off continental Europe, Ireland has a potential new image born of the 'peace process'.

Can, therefore, a country of parts, no greater than Denmark, effectively mount a challenge in the late twentieth century to become a major participant in the European food market other than with a unified approach? Commercial advantage should be the driving force rather than political expediency, and the potential generated by the current peace process must not be lost.

The agriculture sectors in both parts of the island are production-led, largely for historical reasons. Both need to become market-led in the changed circumstances in the European market. The dairy sector requires greater rationalisation and consolidation island-wide and needs to reduce its dependence on commodity-type products. The beef and lamb sectors desperately need an attitudinal change to market demand as well as further structural adjustments to size and scale. The pork sector has been restructured but has yet to realise its potential by penetrating markets with financial success. Poultry is limited in its expansion by the high cost of its imported grain, though it remains the shining example of what can be done in a market-led, support-free sector. Fish and mushrooms give cause for optimism of what is possible on an island-wide basis.

Identity of Interests

From the time of the entry of the United Kingdom and the Republic of Ireland into the EC in 1973 it became readily apparent that when it comes to agricultural matters the interests of Northern and Southern farmers were essentially identical. The application of the Common Agricultural Policy meant that the key decisions relating to market support measures and structural aids were made in Brussels, not in London, Dublin, or Belfast. In European farm organisations such as COPA, farmer representatives from Northern Ireland and the Republic found themselves essentially pursuing the same type of policies. This identity of interest arises from the simple fact that farmers north and south live on the same island with similar climatic and soil conditions and a similar type of agriculture, based largely on grassland. Furthermore, agriculture is more important to the island of Ireland than to most other regions of the EU, making a contribution to GNP of 8.2 per cent in the Republic and 4.2 per cent in Northern Ireland, compared with an average 2.8 per cent in the rest of the EU. The identity of interests in agricultural matters is reinforced by the fact that over 70 per cent of agricultural output in both the Republic and Northern Ireland is sold on export markets, with Great Britain a critically important market for both.

The views of Northern Ireland farmers on the CAP diverged significantly at times from that of the British government. While Northern Ireland's agricultural sector was mainly export-oriented, Britain by and large was an importer of agricultural produce and accordingly was more interested in a cheap food policy. For example, Northern Ireland farmers in the 1970s sought price increases through changes in the 'green pound' (the official currency used to convert ECU-denominated farms prices into national currency), but the British government resisted such a policy approach, on the grounds that it would be inflationary. This has been demonstrated in *Agriculture in Northern Ireland and the Republic of Ireland* (1981) by Professor Séamus Sheahy, James O'Brien, and Séamus McClelland, in which the authors state that 'agriculture in the North was handicapped by being part of the UK which operated to slow down increases in prices received by farmers by delaying green pound increases.'

The consequence in the early years of EU membership was that 'the incomes of Southern farmers raced ahead of those in the North. Allowing for inflation which was more or less the same in both regions, Southern incomes increased in real terms by 44 per cent while Northern incomes fell by 20 per cent' (if one compares the three-year average 1969–71 and the period 1977–79).

Furthermore, as Michael Drake, agricultural correspondent of the *Belfast Telegraph,* pointed out in a recent article, 'over the years Ulster farmers have had good reason to look on Dublin as affording better protection to agriculture than London, particularly when it comes to subsidies or grants from Brussels. It is no secret many benefits to agriculture came to the province on the back of aid to the South.'

The best example of this is the special milk quota reserve agreed for the Republic, largely due to the walk-out by the Taoiseach, Garret FitzGerald, in the European summit of 1984. The UK government was at first opposed to a special extra quota for the Republic, but when it became apparent that other member states were willing to make major concessions, given the vital importance of the milk sector to the Republic's economy, the UK government lifted its reserve. If, however, the milk sector was of vital interest to the Republic, it was equally of vital importance to the economy of Northern Ireland. Accordingly, the United Kingdom government was forced to apply for extra milk quotas for Northern Ireland dairy farmers, which resulted in the securing of an extra 65,000 tonnes.

Commercial Reality

The fact that the island of Ireland is a single source of raw material supply for the agri-food industry north and south presents a new commercial reality that transcends borders and political divisions. Significant exports of pigs from Northern Ireland to processors in the Republic have highlighted weaknesses in the Northern Ireland pig-meat processing sector and resulted in the establishment of an industry task force to review and to map out a strategy for the development of that industry. A significant trade in live sheep takes place between Northern Ireland and the Republic. Traditionally there have been significant cross-border movements, both legal and illegal, of live cattle. Veterinary restrictions arising from BSE, which hopefully will be temporary, inhibit trade in live cattle at the present time. Since 1 March 1995, with the dismantling of the Northern Ireland Milk Marketing Board. there is a new commercial opportunity for trade in liquid milk between North and South. There is already evidence that significant volumes of milk are being purchased by milk processors in the South, which in turn will give rise to changes in the structure of the milk processing sector in Northern Ireland, where Golden Vale and Waterford Co-Op are already major participants, and at the same time there are opportunities in the Republic's liquid milk market for Northern milk producers such as Strathroy.

In beef the situation is more complex. In the early 1980s distortions in the beef market were caused mainly by monetary compensatory amounts, the meat industry employment subsidy (MIES) in Northern Ireland, and the UK variable premium on the slaughter of animals in Northern Ireland, which made it more attractive to operate in Northern Ireland. Significant investments were made by Southern meat plants in Northern Ireland; by the early eighties over 60 per cent of the Northern Ireland beef industry was owned by Southern meat companies.

With the change in UK policy towards the green pound, the ending of the MIES scheme, and the establishment of a claw-back on the variable premium in subsidies on beef exported from Northern Ireland, there was no longer any major incentive for Southern operators to concentrate their activities in Northern Ireland. With further restructuring in the beef processing sector, the involvement of Southern operators in the Northern beef industry is now more limited.

With the ending of 'intervention' in the beef sector and the pressure to reduce trade in live animals to continental Europe and non-EU countries, the creation of a level playing field in terms of EU and national subsidies creates the potential for a co-operative effort in the future development of this sector while recognising the competitive pressures between the different participants in both parts of the island.

Investment from the South has also taken place in the Northern Ireland pig-meat sector in the case of Unipork and Denny's; and a thriving mushroom industry in Northern Ireland is essentially based on an all-Ireland production system through a Southern-owned processing and marketing operation.

The new commercial reality resulting from the free movement of the basic raw material across the border and southern investment in the agri-food sector in Northern Ireland in order to secure raw material supplies and increase market size have created a new dimension that will reinforce the need for a common approach in many areas of policy affecting the food sector.

Pressure for Change

Pressure for change in society is usually either political, social, or economic. In this chapter we are looking at the economic imperative for change in the agricultural and food sector on the island of Ireland.

The pressure for change in the agricultural sector, as already touched on, has by and large been dictated by the CAP and the continuous reform of that policy. Its structure over the past twenty years has been dominated by market price support measures, be they by means of public or private intervention or export refunds. The preoccupation of farm organisations, agri-food representative bodies and member-state governments has been with the manner in which these price supports operated as their implementation dictated developments in the market.

A sea change has now taken place in the structure of the CAP, with greater emphasis on direct income support to farmers and less interference with price formation in the market. The idea is that in future, prices should approximate more to world market levels. In addition, the new GATT agreement provides for a definitive quantifiable control on the volume and financing of exports to non-EU countries over the next five years.

Milk and beef production in Europe is now controlled more effectively than at any other time since entry into the EU. The milk quota system has not only been successful in controlling milk production but has also contributed significantly to stabilising beef production, because fewer cows are required to produce milk up to the quota limitation. In addition, the new premium system applied in the beef sector, particularly in the case of suckler cows, will help to stabilise production in the coming years. This curtailment of production will lead to more concentration on servicing the EU food market with beef and dairy products from the island of Ireland rather than 'third-country' commodity market outlets.

The new shape of the CAP means that agricultural surpluses, particularly in beef and dairy products, from the island of Ireland will no longer be accommodated by the EU intervention system, or for that matter by the traditional heavy subsidisation of exports. The logical consequence, therefore, is that the future development of agriculture on the island of Ireland must be export-led, with a much greater emphasis on securing a solid foothold in the European market.

In this new situation in which Europe is the target market for both Northern and Southern producers, it makes little commercial sense for the two parts of Ireland to be selling essentially the same products, produced in many cases by the same companies, and to be promoting and marketing these products separately. The perception of Ireland in Europe is of one small island selling its agricultural produce on essentially the same criteria, i.e. a grass-fed product in a clean, green island, with a pollution-free environment and a high animal health status.

While the success of the Irish food sector in Europe will largely depend on the skills, enterprise and professionalism of the individual exporters, North and South, we believe this must be underpinned by a marketing and promotion strategy that creates a quality image of Irish food throughout Europe. This can be done in tandem with the tourist programmes in which both parts of Ireland are currently fully co-operating. The alternative is that Irish exporters remain principally commodity exporters, with a consequent loss of added value and of food sector employment, North and South.

Two Key Questions

Professor Alan Matthews of Trinity College. Dublin, in his review *Agriculture and Natural Resources in Ireland and Europe: a Shared Challenge* (1992), outlined very succinctly the scope for economic co-operation between North and South in the agricultural sphere.

'1. Cases where the policies pursued in one part of the island have spill-over effects on the economy of the other. Examples include price support arrangements and plant, animal and fish disease control.

'2. Cases where sharing resources, co-ordinating programmes or organising schemes in common would avoid duplication and permit the exploitation of any economics of scale. Examples include agricultural research and education facilities, the marketing of food products and undertaking cross-border schemes.

'3. Cases where additional resources could be attracted specifically through joint action and a common approach. The availability of funding from the EC's research programmes, the EC's structural funds or other funding sources such as the international fund for Ireland is often conditional on joint applications of this kind.'

The question is, can we go further than mere co-operation in certain fields of activity? Is there a case to be made for a common approach on two fundamental issues: firstly, whether it is in the interest of farmers and the agri-food sectors, North and South, that the island of Ireland should be considered as a single unit under the CAP, and, secondly, whether there should be a single organisation for the promotion and marketing of food from the island of Ireland in the EU market?

The Island of Ireland under CAP

Michael Drake highlighted a distortion in the application of the CAP to the island of Ireland. He wrote in his recent *Belfast Telegraph* article: 'If a cross border structure were in place at present farmers in Northern Ireland would probably have parity with their Southern counterparts over beef de-seasonalisation payments. As it stands these are not being paid here while they are in the South. As a consequence of the de-seasonalisation premium livestock farmers in the Irish Republic are 15p/kilo better off than their Northern Ireland counterparts. Northern meat plants are also deprived of necessary raw material because they cannot afford to pay extra money for it. The irony of it all is that for some twenty years or more one third of the animals required for production have come from the Irish Republic.'

The Irish Farmers' Association and the Ulster Farmers' Union have put forward one idea for resolving the problem in their submission on agriculture and rural development to the Forum for Peace and Reconciliation in March 1995. They proposed that if cattle slaughterings in either Northern Ireland or the Republic in the months of September, October and November are more than 40 per cent of total slaughterings for the year, the whole island should qualify for the de-seasonalisation premium (paid to even out cattle supplies throughout the year). Their submission points out that if both Northern and Southern figures were taken together to determine eligibility, the whole island would not meet the necessary 40 per cent criteria. On an island-of-Ireland basis the combined figure for 1994 would be 38 per cent. The organisations propose that to maintain the de-seasonalisation premium in the longer term, the present 40 per cent qualifying criterion for slaughtering during those months should be reduced by the EU to 35 per cent.

Treating the island of Ireland as a single unit for the purpose of this de-seasonalisation premium would add a new dimension to negotiations with the European Commission. The application of this premium in Northern Ireland and its retention in the Republic is most likely to be best safeguarded by a joint proposal for the island of Ireland to be considered as a single unit, with a 35 per cent eligibility criterion.

In the dairy sector the transfer of milk quotas between member-states is at present prohibited. While measures would have to be adopted to protect certain less favoured areas—and some such measures have already been adopted in regard to the west of Ireland—there appears to be a powerful economic argument for allowing the trade in milk quotas between North and South.

One of the accompanying CAP reform measures—the farmer retirement scheme—does not apply in Northern Ireland, as the UK government considers that there is a satisfactory age structure in UK agriculture overall. However, in their submission to the Forum for Peace and Reconciliation the IFA and UFU state that Northern Ireland farmers have a very similar age profile to farmers in the Republic. If the island of Ireland was considered as one unit, the application of the EU retirement scheme would apply to Northern Ireland as well as to the Republic.

While the establishment of the island of Ireland as a single unit for CAP purposes could give rise to political argument, we believe that this should not be the case. Where there is a strong economic justification for the island of Ireland to be considered as a single unit under CAP, and where the benefits to farmers in the North and South can be clearly demonstrated, a pragmatic approach should be adopted by the British and Irish governments in pursuing such a policy with the European Commission.

Single Currency

The establishment of a single currency outlined in the Maastricht treaty has now become a political imperative for the European Union in its efforts to consolidate the single European market. The creation of a single currency is in fact also critical to a proper reform of the CAP. Successive reforms in the past have been defeated by currency turmoil. Measures have been adopted in the agricultural sector to deal with currency fluctuations, such as monetary compensatory amounts, the switch-over mechanism, and now the new agri-monetary rules. The switch-over mechanism alone is estimated to have increased agricultural prices in the EU by the order of 20 per cent and added 5 to 6 billion ECU to the cost of the EU agricultural budget. The reforms carried out under the former Irish Commissioner Ray MacSharry, which are seen by some observers as the definitive reform of the CAP, may again be defeated by currency fluctuations within the EU. The new agri-monetary rules provide that if one or more of the currencies of the strong currency countries appreciate by more than 5 per cent, their green rates may be reduced by half of the appreciation. This in turn would give rise to an increase in reform and accompanying aids. In addition, for products not covered by the reforms, national aids may be introduced to compensate farmers that would be part-financed by the EU. The increase in reform aids and the part-financing of national aids could cost the Union 1 billion ECU. The Commission has succeeded in partially revising this policy by restricting compensation to farmers who have actually suffered losses as a result of currency instability, thereby limiting to some extent the EU's budgetary exposure. However, it is evident that a rational and cost-effective CAP is critically dependent upon the establishment of a single European currency.

At present the Irish Government is fully committed to the single currency and to Ireland's participation at the earliest opportunity. On the other hand, the United Kingdom has an opt-out in the Maastricht treaty from participation in the single currency. It would be most undesirable and damaging to the agricultural sectors North and South if after years of breaking down barriers and distortions to trade between both parts of the island new barriers were to be created by the Republic and the United Kingdom following different routes to a single European currency.

Food from the Island of Ireland

Given the change in the structure of the CAP referred to earlier and the fact that the comfort of intervention supports are no longer available to the food industry, the future development of that industry is vitally dependent on greater penetration of the European food market. In his summing up to the Forum for Peace and Reconciliation on the agricultural debate, Professor Séamus Sheahy stated: 'I think a lot has been achieved across the border under the present regulations. It is clear also … if we can get new agreed arrangements there is a lot more again that can be achieved, because the road ahead is … a road of marketing and … global competition. It's not going to hit us tomorrow but in ten years our farmers, our commercial farmers are going to have to play and compete with the commercial farmers of the other great producing countries of the world, so we have a breathing space. The CAP in the past and all the intervention in the intervention era was a great distraction from marketing and from efficiency. That's now past.'

An island of Ireland promotional and marketing body can play a vital role in underpinning the marketing and sales efforts of individual companies throughout the European Union; in addition, by being in touch with the market and providing the necessary feedback to individual enterprises, such a body could have a very positive effect in directing investment programmes towards relevant value-added products.

In the past the Irish Livestock and Meat Board (CBF) and the Northern Ireland Livestock Marketing Commission (LMC) played a very important role in enhancing the image of Irish beef in the European market. At the same time their promotion in the market and encouragement of investment in vacuum-packed beef has eventually paid dividends, which is acknowledged by the entire meat industry in Ireland, North and South.

The shortcomings, however, of a piecemeal approach to the promotion of food from Ireland has been acknowledged with the establishment of An Bord Bia, the new Irish Food Board.

The fact remains that producers North and South are endeavouring to sell essentially the same type of food products to the same market and to promote these products with limited financial resources. In the new post-GATT and CAP reform situation there is an overwhelming argument for the establishment of a single promotion and marketing body for the whole island of Ireland, which would initially be jointly financed by the Irish and British governments and by the European Union. The establishment of such a body would enable the agricultural and food sectors North and South to pool resources in pursuing the marketing goal of a major share of the European food market for Irish exporters. Such an approach, we believe, makes commercial sense.

One immediate practical benefit of such a joint approach to the marketing and promotion of Irish beef from the island of Ireland can best be illustrated by the current application of the European Union's beef promotion programme—regulation 2067/92. This programme provides financial support for the generic promotion of beef and therefore cannot be 'biased in favour of any trademark nor confer advantage on products from a particular member state.' It is ironic that under the terms of this regulation the marketing of Scottish beef can be subsidised but the marketing of Irish beef cannot. The fact is, however, that if beef from the Republic and Northern Ireland was promoted under this scheme the promotion of 'Irish beef' would then be eligible for aid, as Irish beef would then be seen as coming from two regions of the EU rather than from one member-state.

While there are sensitivities in the consumer mind in some member-states towards UK and Northern Ireland beef, as a hangover from the BSE scare, Northern Ireland beef can nevertheless be exported to most member-states under normal EU veterinary rules. In those markets where such sensitivities do not exist there is scope for a common joint programme for the marketing of Irish beef under this measure.

The establishment of a single organisation for the marketing and promotion of Irish food would have the additional benefit of providing a feedback to individual enterprises, the industrial development authorities and other government bodies on the appropriate investment policies in this indigenous sector. Up to the present time national investment programmes for the food sector have been adopted in the Republic and Northern Ireland with little cognisance being taken of investment programmes in the other part of the island. Given the common pool for raw material sourcing, it no longer makes sense for investment programmes to be adopted that are premised on securing a disproportionate amount of raw material from the other part of the island and that do not take full account of the processing capacity in each area.

Finally, the establishment of such an island-of-Ireland marketing promotion body would focus minds on the veterinary, animal health, animal welfare and environmental issues that are critical to the enhancement of the image of Irish food from the island of Ireland.

Conclusion

There is no choice for both parts of the island but to move to a food-based, market-led environment. Size and scale point to the necessity for co-operation. The economic case for the island to be treated by the European Union as one unit under the CAP is substantial. A level playing field in production terms throughout the island as a whole is economically and commercially sensible. Given equality of EU supports and the need to promote one image, 'Food from Ireland' is commercially pragmatic while allowing for competition between companies, both north-south and east-west. Gaining a greater market share in Great Britain and in key parts of the continental European market is a common aim. Barriers to equality of production and marketing opportunities must be opposed and the best use of common resources encouraged. Ultimately the commercial reality of how much better we can do things together must take pre-eminence over preoccupations with a wider political agenda and objectives.

10 Manufacturing: Two Plus Two Makes More than Four

Geoff MacEnroe and William Poole

In this chapter an attempt is made to carry out a dispassionate analysis of the manufacturing sectors in the Republic of Ireland and Northern Ireland, to examine the potential for increased North-South co-operation, and to outline the main benefits that would accrue to the manufacturing sectors North and South.

It is universally accepted that the economies of Northern Ireland and the Republic have historically been poorly integrated. Both economies have developed separately following partition in 1921, and the two markets have developed separately without sufficient attention being given to developing cross-border trade. Both regions have also developed separate approaches to developing export markets. In 1993 total trade between the Republic and Northern Ireland, based on import and export statistics provided by the Central Statistics Office, was IR£1,127 million. In 1993 the Republic's imports from Northern Ireland represented 2.8 per cent of the Republic's total imports, and the Republic's exports to Northern Ireland represented 3.6 per cent of the Republic's total exports.

It is noteworthy that total North-South trade has been static in the years 1989–93. It is also noteworthy that in 1981 North-South trade showed a balance of IR£2 million in favour of Northern Ireland, but since then there has been a growing trade balance in favour of the South. In 1992 the trade balance in favour of the South was IR£357 million. Given the relative sizes of the two economies in GDP and population terms, one would expect the balance of trade to be in favour of Northern Ireland.

It is concluded that there is considerable scope for increasing trade in both directions, and, given the size and structures of the two economies, there is greater scope for Northern Ireland companies to increase exports to the Republic than for increasing trade in the other direction.

External Trade

The lack of achievement by companies in developing North-South trade is emphasised when the performance of the Republic's and Northern Ireland's external trade are examined. The Republic's total exports have grown from IR£4,083 million in 1980 to an estimated IR£22.4 billion in 1994. Exports of Irish goods now account for 58 per cent of Gross Domestic Product, compared with approximately 20 per cent in the UK and 10 per cent in the United States. In 1994 export growth in the Republic ran well ahead of the 7 per cent growth in world trade and also ran ahead of the growth of imports in the main export markets.

In the Republic in 1992, manufactured goods accounted for 71.6 per cent of total exports, compared with 45.1 per cent in 1972. In 1972 the EU (excluding the UK) accounted for 17.5 per cent of exports but in 1993 accounted for 39.8 per cent of total exports. Today, two out of every three employed in manufacturing industry in the Republic work in exporting firms.

The growth of trade in indigenous manufactured goods in recent years has consistently exceeded that of the Republic's total trade. The Republic's industry has shown an impressive capacity to meet a rising demand for sub-contract work from multinational companies abroad and in Ireland. Sales on the home market, now worth IR£10 billion, represent almost half of the Republic's industrial output.

A comprehensive survey of export performance of the Northern Ireland manufacturing sector indicates that in 1991 total exports (external sales or sales made outside Northern Ireland) were valued at Stg£4,216, of which 54.5 per cent went to Great Britain and 19.4 per cent to the rest of the EU (excluding the UK). In the same year, exports of manufactured goods to the Republic valued at Stg£446 million represented 10.6 per cent of Northern Ireland's total exports of manufactured products. In 1991, manufactured goods with an estimated value of Stg£6,488 million were sold by Northern Ireland firms, of which Stg£2,272 million or 35 per cent was sold in the home market.

In table 1 the destination of export and external sales for Northern Ireland and the Republic are compared. The Republic has reduced its dependence on the British market and has developed continental European markets. Northern Ireland is still highly dependent on the British market and has achieved much slower growth in other markets.

Table 1: Destination of exports and external sales, 1991 and 1993 (%)

	North (1991)	South (1993)
Great Britain	54.5	24.9
Republic of Ireland	10.6	—
Northern Ireland	—	3.6
Rest of EU	19.4	39.8
Rest of world	15.5	31.7
Total	100.0	100.0

The Manufacturing Base, North and South

To make predictions about the potential for expanding North-South trade and for developing a single market for the manufacturing sector on the island of Ireland, it is necessary to understand the size and composition of the manufacturing base in both parts of the island. The evolution of the two economies and in particular the manufacturing base on the island over the past thirty years has been significant. In the thirty-year period 1960–90 aggregate Northern and Southern manufacturing employment declined from 359,000 to 296,427. In 1960 employment in manufacturing in Northern Ireland (184,000) exceeded manufacturing employment in the South (175,000). Thirty years later the position had been reversed. In 1990, manufacturing employment in the South had grown to 194,177, while manufacturing employment in the North had declined to 102,250. In other words, between 1960 and 1990 manufacturing employment increased by 11 per cent in the South but decreased by 44 per cent in the North.

The Manufacturing Base, Northern Ireland

Two features have characterised economic developments in Northern Ireland during the past forty years: the decline of employment in manufacturing industry, and the expansion of the public sector. Manufacturing employment fell from 195,000 in 1950, 36 per cent of total employment, to 100,970, or 18 per cent of total employment, in 1993.

The decline in manufacturing employment was caused by a number of factors, including a disproportionate concentration of employment in traditional industries and inward investment having taken the form of branch plants with external head offices, resulting in their being particularly vulnerable to closures. While the 'Troubles' were one of a number of factors contributing to job losses in manufacturing, they were the main factor responsible for a loss of multinational confidence in Northern Ireland. In the period 1966–71, multinationals established fifty-one new manufacturing plants in the North and created 11,600 new manufacturing jobs. Between 1972 and 1976, multinationals established only fifteen new plants, creating only 900 new jobs.

In 1990 there were just over 200 externally owned manufacturing plants in Northern Ireland, employing approximately 49,000 people. Externally owned plants now account for approximately 40 per cent of overall manufacturing employment in Northern Ireland. In the South, 763 externally owned manufacturing plants accounted for 45 per cent of manufacturing employment.

Despite the decline in manufacturing, total employment in Northern Ireland has remained stable, because of the expansion in public expenditure and public sector employment. There has also been a growth of employment in private services generated by growing public sector employment.

The main manufacturing sectors in Northern Ireland, in terms of employment size, are engineering, including shipbuilding and aircraft manufacture, employing 29,280; food, drink, and tobacco, employing 19,800; the clothing and footwear industries, employing 14,950; and the textile industry, employing 10,140. These four sectors in 1993 accounted for 73 per cent of total manufacturing employment. Other industries in Northern Ireland include paper, paper products, printing and publishing (employing 6,380), timber and wooden furniture (5,310), rubber and plastics (4,344), and chemicals (4,030). Four sectors—food, drink, and tobacco; transport equipment; chemicals; and electrical engineering—account for three-quarters of all manufacturing exports from Northern Ireland.

Table 2: Employment by main sectors

	North (1993)	South (1990)	Total
Engineering	29,280	67,693	96,973
Food, drink, tobacco	19,800	42,891	62,691
Clothing, footwear	14,950	13,401	28,351
Textiles	10,130	10,627	20,757
Paper, printing	6,380	14,449	20,829
Timber, wooden furniture	5,310	7,580	12,980
Chemicals	4,030	13,587	17,617

The Manufacturing Base, Republic of Ireland

Since the 1960s, manufacturing employment in the South has remained stable, largely because of significant inward investment. Foreign investment grew rapidly over the period 1958–75, mainly in the engineering and textile sectors. In the 1970s and 1980s the emphasis of inward investment shifted to computers, chemicals, and pharmaceutical products. Over the last two decades, employment in externally owned (mainly American) manufacturing companies increased by over 30 per cent; this contrasts sharply with a fall of 50 per cent in employment in externally owned manufacturing plants in Northern Ireland.

Data from manufacturing firms taken from the Census of Industrial Production in 1990 shows that there were 4,602 manufacturing establishments in the Republic, directly employing 194,177 people. Indigenous industry employed 105,884 in the manufacturing sector, compared with 88,293 employed in non-indigenous industry. Total manufacturing output was IR£19.968 billion, of which 45 per cent was produced by indigenous industry. Manufactured exports of indigenous industry were IR£3.02 billion, representing 24 per cent of total manufactured exports.

Almost 60 per cent of indigenous firms in the Republic are engaged in export activity. Indigenous exports have a reliance on one market, with some 40 per cent of indigenous exports going to the UK.

The main manufacturing industries in the Republic, in terms of employment size, are metals and engineering, employing 67,693; food, drink, and tobacco, employing 42,891; chemicals (including synthetic fibres), employing 13,587; paper, paper products, printing, and publishing, employing 14,449; and clothing, footwear, and leather, employing 13,401. Employment in other manufacturing industries include the textile industry (10,627), manufacture of non-metallic mineral products (11,117), and timber and wooden furniture (7,580). Four sectors—engineering and metals; food, drink, and tobacco; clothing and footwear; and textiles—account for 69 per cent of manufacturing industry, compared with 73 per cent in Northern Ireland. In the Republic, food products account by value for 24 per cent of total export trade. The four next-largest categories of exports are computers, chemicals, electronic equipment, and pharmaceuticals.

In some respects the structure of manufacturing industry North and South is complementary. The engineering sector in the South has a higher proportion of light engineering and computer manufacture, while in the North there is a higher proportion of heavy engineering. Production of chemicals and pharmaceuticals is much more significant in the South. Textiles and clothing, traditionally very important in the North, still occupy a much more important position in the North than in the South.

Trade Between Northern Ireland and the Republic

An analysis of the current level of North-South trade by sectors is also necessary before drawing conclusions on the potential for further developing cross-border trade in manufactured goods. Table 3 shows the performance of trade between Northern Ireland and the Republic in 1992, based on export and import statistics produced by the Central Statistics Office. North-South trade in the food, drink and tobacco sector represented 39 per cent of total cross-border trade. Trade in the more general category of manufactured goods represented 49 per cent of total cross-border trade.

No attempt has been made to predict the likely growth in cross-border trade over the next five years within each particular sector. Many factors will have an influence on what level of growth is achievable, including:

- the extent to which each market, Northern Ireland and the Republic, is currently supplied by domestic production and by imported products;

- the extent to which the market has a demand for products not currently produced in either part of the island;

- the extent to which new production capacity and products will come on stream as a result of new investment from the indigenous sector and from new inward investment.

The degree to which local production can increase market share in either part of the island will also be determined by the competitiveness of each industry sector in competing with existing imported products or with new products that may be launched in both markets.

Both Northern Ireland and the Republic are two of the most open economies in Europe. In general, both regions produce what they do not consume and consume what is not produced locally. Any company planning to develop cross-border sales will almost inevitably meet competition from outside the island of Ireland. It is also generally true that, because of the comparatively small size of both markets, most companies will not be competitive by purely selling on the island-of-Ireland market. To be competitive, companies located on the island must also put resources into developing markets outside the island far sooner than is the case for companies manufacturing in larger markets.

Table 3: Trade in manufactured goods between Republic and Northern Ireland by main categories, 1992

	IR£000		
	South to North	North to South	Total N-S trade
Meat & meat preparations	85,962	47,748	133,710
Cereals & cereal preparations	38,954	14,439	53,393
Dairy products	55,053	28,406	83,459
Other food & food preparations	88,002	38,956	126,958
Beverages	44,617	30,143	74,760
Crude materials	29,559	10,949	40,508
Pharmaceuticals	3,747	1,595	5,342
Fertilisers	6,145	32,117	38,262
Chemicals	32,960	14,974	47,934
Paper & paperboard manufacturers	19,669	31,384	98,987
Textiles	30,296	31,339	61,635
Non-metallic mineral manufacturers	24,063	23,605	47,668
Metals & metal manufacturers	35,902	12,185	48,087
Industrial machinery	31,670	15,103	46,773
Data-processing machines & parts	13,329	3,822	17,151
Electrical machinery	8,517	5,004	13,521
Road vehicles	43,278	10,922	54,200
Furniture	19,800	5,565	25,365
Clothing	54,131	20,253	74,384
Miscellaneous manufactured articles	21,157	45,637	66,794
Total trade	825,053	468,168	1,293,221

Food and Beverages

Cross-border growth in trade in food products, beverages and agricultural products will depend on the size of the grocery markets, North and South, and on the extent to which agricultural products and food ingredients can be sold into the food and drinks processing sectors on both sides of the border.

Table 4: Size of the grocery market (Ir£ billion)

	North	South	Total
Grocery market	1.3	4.3	5.6

The potential for supplying the grocery markets on a cross-border basis is limited by the size of the individual grocery markets and by the growth of domestic consumption. The Republic's grocery market is worth IR£4.3 billion, compared with the grocery market in Northern Ireland valued at Stg£1.3 billion. Potential new suppliers of food products will have to meet demanding standards set by buyers in the major supermarkets. Buyers North and South expect prospective suppliers to have an understanding of the local grocery market and the products already stocked.

Potential new suppliers are often expected to outline the business development opportunities of their product from the retailer's point of view and offer buying terms that will affect the level of market share and produce volume sales. Suppliers are also often expected to be in a position to provide a minimum 99 per cent service level. However, despite stringent conditions, supermarket buyers are always interested in looking at products that are unique or slightly different. They are also interested in promotional and marketing support with unique ideas for increasing sales.

Only a limited number of small and medium-sized food companies will be successful in having their products listed by the major retail outlets, where shelf space is already at a premium. While there are fewer opportunities for companies to supply ingredients to food producers that are expanding their sales in export markets, international food markets are not limited by size of population as on the island of Ireland. It makes considerable sense for the exporters of food products to source food raw materials on an island-of-Ireland basis and exploit the 'green' image of Ireland in a world market that is becoming increasingly conscious of the environment.

Industrial Products

The Republic's sub-contracting industry has grown dramatically over the last twenty years, with local companies supplying the large number of foreign manufacturing firms that have been set up and that require high-quality components. The range of services being offered by sub-contractors North and South has also expanded, and an increasing number of companies that once produced only their own finished product now have expertise and facilities to offer to industry on the island of Ireland. In Northern Ireland the traditional industries of aircraft manufacture, shipbuilding and textile machinery have provided a wide range of engineering skills. Engineering companies on both sides of the border are supplying world-renowned companies on and off the island, meeting the highest specifications on a competitive basis through building effective partnerships with purchasers.

The opportunities that already exist for sub-supply companies North and South to supply this market on a cross-border basis have largely been neglected. If the combined capacity of sub-contracting industry on the island of Ireland was promoted by the industrial promotion agencies North and South when foreign multinationals are being persuaded to invest on the island of Ireland, this would help to maximise the future size of the sub-contract market.

Buyers in industry in the South (excluding the food sector) spend close to IR£7 billion a year on materials. Less than one-third of this business goes to local suppliers. Even though much of this purchasing relates to products that are not manufactured on the island, there are significant opportunities for sub-contractors North and South to develop this business. It has been estimated that at present less than 25 per cent of industrial sub-supply business, North and South, is placed with Irish firms. It is also estimated that over IR£1,000 million in new business in the area of sub-supply to industry on the island of Ireland is available to be won by competitive Irish suppliers.

The absence of an automated foundry on the island to supply castings to the engineering industry was identified at a North-South meeting of companies under the IBEC-CBI North-South Business Development Programme, with companies North and South importing castings from Great Britain, Germany, and Portugal. Since then a new foundry has been set up that has started to supply engineering castings on an all-Ireland basis. Over the past three years the aerospace industry in Northern Ireland has made a concerted effort to explore areas of synergy and co-operation with the aerospace industry in the South, which has included some Southern suppliers being awarded 'preferred supplier' status. While many new sub-supply linkages have already been established on a North-South basis, there remains huge potential for developing this business, particularly in the Republic with a larger manufacturing and foreign-owned sector.

The Public Sector Market

Combined public sector expenditure on goods and services on the island of Ireland is valued at about IR£4.3 billion a year. The public sector accounts for 35 per cent of total employment in Northern Ireland (24 per cent in the Republic). The market in the South represents 75 per cent of the public sector market on the island. Considerable differences between the Republic and

Northern Ireland in public procurement structures and systems make it difficult for companies that have been supplying one market to quickly develop business across the border. In the South the total market is fragmented among numerous organisations, and with decentralisation of procurement it is a more difficult market to access compared with the North, where purchasing is more centralised.

Table 5: Public sector expenditure, 1991

	(IR£ billion)		
	North	South	Total
Expenditure on goods and services	1.07	3.22	4.29

North-South co-operation to open up the public sector procurement markets to companies on an island basis is going beyond the spirit of European directives in this area. Guides to public procurement on both sides of the border have been published, including lists of key buyers. Through co-operation between the Irish Export Board, the IBEC-CBI North-South Business Development Programme and public sector buyers North and South, a series of 'meet-the-buyer' workshops have been organised in Dublin and Belfast, aimed at promoting increasing cross-border competition for public sector business. The Irish Trade Board operates a public procurement intelligence service on Minitel, which provides notification of public tenders, North and South, and a similar tendering service has been launched in Northern Ireland.

The recent launch of a new Suppliers' Charter by the Government Purchasing Service (GPS) for Northern Ireland is also a welcome development. An objective of the charter is to ensure that small and medium-sized enterprises are given maximum encouragement and opportunity to compete for public sector contracts in Northern Ireland.

Although some companies on both sides of the border, when questioned about supplying the public sector across the border, considered that they had been discriminated against because of their location, there is already a clearly established trend on both sides of the border towards greater openness and competition in public procurement. With greater opportunities for suppliers, companies manufacturing on the island will be able to increase their share of the public sector markets over the next five years.

Specific initiatives to expand public sector purchasing on a North-South basis should be made a priority of governments North and South. New initiatives in this area should also include formal procedures for dealing with complaints.

Barriers to Developing North-South Trade

While it may be accepted that there are substantial benefits to be gained by everyone on the island from developing cross-border trade and North-South economic co-operation, there are real and perceived barriers that have discouraged these developments. Before the border customs posts were removed following the completion of the single European market at the end of 1992, long delays for trucks at the border inhibited the development of trade. The poor quality of the road and railway systems connecting the two parts of the island was also a major deterrent. Fluctuating exchange rates between the two currencies and different VAT and excise duties have created uncertainties and price disparities.

Perhaps of greatest importance has been the psychological barrier caused by lack of communication between people living on both sides of the border. As a result of the 'Troubles' in Northern Ireland, many business people in the South were reluctant to travel to Northern Ireland. Business people in Northern Ireland were unsure of how they or their products would be received if they attempted to do business in the Republic. An IBEC-CBI survey has shown that a very high proportion of companies already trading across the border had experienced no barriers in developing cross-border trade.

A major reason why cross-border trade is low is that many companies did not target the market across the border. The fact that so many companies and business people did not have a reason to cross the border and that cross-border communications had been absent for so long led to a lack of market information, including information on the structure of industry and potential customers in the other part of the island. Many companies that could have been trading were unaware of the opportunities.

Today, many of the most significant barriers have now been removed or are in the course of being removed. Border custom posts no longer exist, and the transport infrastructure connecting the two parts of the island is being upgraded. Joint cross-border trade development programmes implemented by the Irish Trade Board, the Industrial Development Board for Northern Ireland, the Small Business Agency in Northern Ireland (LEDU) and the joint business initiative of the Irish Business and Employers' Confederation and the Confederation of British Industry in Northern Ireland have produced a wide range of sectoral information on the two markets. In addition, programmes implemented by these organisations over the past three years, which have provided opportunities for manufacturers to meet buyers on a North-South basis, have been both well attended and enthusiastically received by companies. More companies are now giving serious consideration to developing trading links across the border.

The Case for Further North-South Economic Co-operation

If there is to be significant growth in cross-border trade between now and the year 2000, food and manufactured goods, which accounted for 88 per cent of cross-border trade in 1992, are the sectors where further significant growth will need to be achieved. A pattern of trading across the border has already been established by companies within these sectors.

Developing trade across the border is an opportunity for companies to extend the traditional home market before developing new markets, which are more difficult to service. Northern Ireland companies have the potential to add an additional 1,200,000 households (2.2 times the Northern Ireland market) by entering the Republic market. The industrial base in the South, based on a comparison of manufacturing employment, is approximately 1.8 times the size of that in Northern Ireland. The public sector market on the island is four times the size of the public sector market in Northern Ireland.

For many manufacturers the market across the border is important as a test market. Southern exporters in many sectors can gain experience in Northern Ireland, meeting their key British competitors before approaching the British market. Northern Ireland companies supplying the industrial market have a base of over eight hundred multinational manufacturing companies to target in the South.

Developing exports across the border will force companies to be competitive, which will also enable them to become competitive in international markets. Given the relatively small size of the combined 'home' market, the future for manufacturing firms on the island lies in their ability to compete and to develop markets in the European and international market. A feasibility study to examine the potential of developing a Dublin–Belfast economic corridor, commissioned by IBEC and the CBI, pointed out that one of the features of many successful corridors is their outward-looking international focus. The study stated that corridors provide not just linkages between firms in the corridor but also a basis for developing international markets. The principle also holds in the context of developing linkages between firms throughout the island of Ireland.

Provisional statistics for the first eight months of 1994 show that the Republic's imports from Northern Ireland increased by 22 per cent. It has been estimated that total exports from the Republic to Northern Ireland increased by over 11 per cent in 1994. If these growth rates could be maintained, in five years North-South trade would have doubled and the trade balance in favour of the Republic would be eliminated.

The main case against developing cross-border trade is that it will also develop competition on the island that will result in the displacement of local suppliers. With imports representing such a high proportion of what is purchased and consumed, North and South, the development of trading linkages is more likely to result in import substitution. Provided the process results in developing import substitution rather than displacement, manufacturers in both regions will benefit.

On an island the size of Ireland (300 miles long by 200 miles wide) no town or company is a significant distance from any other for developing contact. Although there are already some concentrations of industrial sectors or clusters (for example aircraft manufacture and related engineering sub-suppliers in Belfast and chemicals and pharmaceuticals in Cork), there still remains a great opportunity for developing increased sub-supply on a North-South basis. Planned improvements in the strategic road and rail infrastructure North and South will provide a better opportunity for increasing passenger traffic and trade between the two parts of Ireland. Before the end of 1996 it will be possible to travel by rail from Belfast or Dublin, have a full working day in either city, and return home within the same day. Advances in telecommunications will assist in the development of networking between companies on and off the island and also lead to the generation of new business opportunities.

Strategic plans on both sides of the border for generating economic growth should be co-ordinated in order to identify and maximise areas of common interest. Increased North-South trade, greater interaction between indigenous and foreign-owned companies and acquisitions and joint ventures on and off the island will all lead to economies of scale and greater international competitiveness. These developments will also lead to an expansion of the manufacturing base on the island. Future prosperity for this island will be closely linked to using the skills of a growing labour force, North and South.

There is still a great deal of work to be done if this vision of the future is to become a reality. Many psychological barriers have still to be removed and will only disappear over time. Developing cross-border trade in manufactured products is seen as an important element in maximising growth and prosperity and raising living standards on the island of Ireland. Support from the Community Initiative for Peace and Reconciliation, Interreg, US Initiatives for Ireland and the International Fund for Ireland will assist the process.

11 Internationally Traded Services: Joint Ventures Abroad?

Joyce Irwin and Colum MacDonnell

Both parts of the island of Ireland are witnessing and participating in the services revolution and enjoying—or, some would argue, suffering—the effects. The service industries now employ 60 per cent of the working population in the Republic and an even higher percentage in Northern Ireland; agricultural and manufacturing outputs continue to rise with a smaller work force. In this chapter we look at some of the implications of what has been described as the post-industrial society.

Problems of definition arise in any discussion of services because of their intangibility. Internationally, no agreement has yet been reached on what constitutes services, as distinct from manufacturing and agriculture. Products increasingly rely for their functioning on services, such as the software that drives a computer, and they also depend on services for their added-value characteristics such as design, research, distribution, and disposal. For the sake of simplicity let us assume that the term 'services' embraces all activities not defined as manufacturing or agriculture, with one exclusion: we have not given any serious consideration to international financial services.

It may be helpful to refer to some distinguishing characteristics of the service industries. The essential point about services is that they are labour-intensive rather than capital or equipment-intensive. They must therefore be regarded as a benign force in the employment context. They cannot benefit, as manufacturing does, from mass production methods; they enjoy economies of scope rather than of scale. Another feature is that they cannot be stored, being consumed as soon as they are created. Generally speaking, the provider of the service must be available at the time the service is consumed, which in part explains their employment intensity.

Let us take some examples to illustrate these principles. A modern Japanese car plant or an American petrochemical factory can have an enormous production capacity and get by with a handful of operational staff.

On the other hand, intensive care in a modern western hospital or a luxury hotel in the Far East has an enormous dependence on staff: both can have a ratio of staff members to patient or resident in excess of 1 to 1. It is obvious that, while the output of the automobile or petrochemical plant may be stored for a considerable time, the output of the hospital and hotel staff is consumed instantly. The location is another interesting question. While it may be obvious that the hotel service is delivered in the supplier's country to the buyer as tourist or visitor, the relatively modern phenomenon of moving patients from their normal habitat to a clinic in Switzerland, London, the United States or Dublin is now unremarkable. Specialised clinics in the UK and the Republic have long seen wealthy residents of other countries, with less developed diagnostic and treatment facilities, as a significant part of their market.

Services, like politics, could be described as the art of the possible. Their conception and delivery are bounded only by the imagination of the supplier and the regulatory environment in which they are provided. A surgeon can perform a remote operation while looking into a television screen, just as a bomb disposal expert can immobilise an explosive device by means of a remote-controlled robot. Witness the instant electronic movement of enormous capital funds that can destabilise a currency, as exporters appreciate only too well. The movements in global capital markets amount to fifty times the volume of the world's annual trade in goods and services.

On a less spectacular level, credit card counterfoils are shipped overnight from the United States to an island in the Caribbean for data entry and processing. Why? Because the operators on the Caribbean island are paid 30 to 40 per cent of the rate paid to their counterparts in the United States, with little difference in productivity. The components involved in the operation are rapid transport, the human skills for data entry, the computer's ability to process the information, and a telecommunications link to transmit the results instantly to the credit card company.

And this brings us to another point: the regulatory environment. While not yet fully achieved, we are on the threshold of a world market in services, in the wake of the relatively successful General Agreement on Trade in Services (GATS). At the time of writing, certain outstanding issues remain for settlement between the United States and the European Union, such as the audiovisual question. More recently we have witnessed moves by some EU member-states to limit the mobility of temporary workers; but, by and large, we can probably look forward to relatively free mobility of labour to execute contracts of services in the near future.

Our Record in International Services

How has Ireland been doing? Both the anecdotal and the more scientific evidence indicates a high degree of success in recent times. We rely on anecdotal evidence in the absence of the hard information that would be provided by reliable statistical values. Ireland is not alone in its deficiency of statistical evidence of international trade achievement in services. Commentators in the United States—that most statistical of economies— bemoan the lack of information in the foreign trade figures related to services, while the UK, which may derive as much as 25 per cent of its total foreign earnings from so-called invisibles, relies on surveys and estimates. We all use the residual or 'plug' figure remaining when visible or merchandise trade is deducted from the balance of payments flows. It has been estimated, however, that the Republic earns in the region of £800 million annually from exports of services, giving full-time employment to up to 16,000 people.

The Republic has been an excellent performer in areas such as educational services, medical care, hospital management, and exports of consultancy funded by the multilateral agencies. We have gained an impressive share of programmes such as TACIS and PHARE, funded by the European Commission. These programmes are aimed at providing technical assistance to the former Soviet Union and other Eastern European countries, respectively. Our success reflects the skills of our consultants in the private and state sectors as well as our ability to target relevant funds and to market ourselves to the task managers in the international agencies and responsible officials in the recipient countries.

Two outstanding examples of Northern Ireland involvement in international services are the Masstock successes in the Middle East, China, and East Africa, and the contracts won by Mivan Overseas Ltd in the Middle East. Their success in winning the refurbishment contract for the al-Aqsa Mosque and Dome of the Rock in Jerusalem, with Muir Associates of Dublin providing the design services, is a good example of cross-border co-operation by professionals in the construction sector. This project, incidentally, won the Construction Industry Federation International Construction Award in Ireland in 1993. To add that ESB International is at present undertaking contracts valued at £60 million in the Middle East and Europe and that the Telecom Éireann company TEIS is heavily involved in telephone exchange planning, installation and maintenance in the UK is simply to underline the island's enormous capability in the international technical consultancy field. NIE International, a specialist managed business unit of Northern Ireland Electricity PLC, has undertaken assignments in markets as far apart as Kenya and the Caribbean region. NICARE of Belfast, which specialises in health care consultancy, has carried out training and consultancy projects funded by the European Union in eastern Europe as well as directly funded contracts in western Europe, North America, the South Atlantic, Africa, and the Pacific Region.

So Have We Any Failures?

Some companies became overstretched, and some came to grief as a result of not being properly insured, but the majority have prospered in the international arena. The contribution that Irish companies, North and South, have made in overseas markets has been truly impressive. Obviously we have not had the ability to take on huge infrastructural projects, although our contractors and consultants feature as sub-consultants or sub-contractors, but we have shown a great ability to apply common sense and user technology, as distinct from manufacturer technology, to procurement problems facing project managers in the developing world.

Our successes have been much more significant than our failures. Irish consultants, North and South, are highly respected by the World Bank and the other multilateral agencies. If one were so unsporting as to criticise our performance it would be to fault our somewhat tentative approach, particularly at Government level, in the Republic. The time calls for bold initiatives. The 1993 report of the Task Force on Jobs in Services, under the chairmanship of the Department of the Taoiseach, indicates the steps that might be taken to move quickly. The Republic's fiscal regime does not reflect the genuine benefits to the economy that result from our internationally traded services activities. Consultants still pay the 38 per cent corporate tax rate on profits from overseas engagements, while their counterparts from Northern Ireland pay 25 per cent. When one considers depreciation and other allowances for machinery in the manufacturing sector in addition to the corporation tax rate of 10 per cent, we are surely witnessing an upside-down set of values. Internationally traded services pay the price of their invisibility: there are no huge factories or elaborate corporate headquarters or spectacular ribbon-cutting ceremonies with ministerial presence. They really are invisible, and that makes a full appreciation of their value difficult.

Where Are the Opportunities?

It has often been remarked that the neighbouring island represents one of the world's huge consumer markets where we share a common language, with a very similar commercial and banking system and tariff-free access. When we look at the merchandise trade, we may observe that the market is very important to our suppliers of goods—just as the Republic is Britain's sixth-biggest market in absolute terms. Services markets in Britain also offer huge possibilities for suppliers, North and South. We have free mobility of labour; we enjoy the access provided by the EU public procurement directives; but, above all, we have a network of contacts established during many years of virtual cohabitation in the construction, health and education fields. We enjoy similar systems of public administration. Our legal and accountancy systems are virtually identical.

The big difference that exists between the neighbouring islands, however, presents real opportunities for us to supply services: our human resources. Firstly, we have been investing heavily in education, while Britain has been heading in the other direction. Ireland, North and South, shares this dedication to education. Secondly, while the British population has a substantial proportion in the over-50s age bracket, Ireland has a preponderance of under-25s. Given that exports of services depend on well-educated and well-trained personnel, it must be obvious that we have here one of the vital prerequisites for successfully supplying the market. Unlike our competitors from Europe, English is our first language. If we add to this our complementarity in terms of population we begin to get a picture of great opportunity for Irish suppliers of services. The Irish population explosion—now slowing down—complements the British demographic implosion, and the opportunities thus revealed cry out to the observant marketeer. Services that require educated and well-trained personnel, a good command of English, good interpersonal skills and a younger age profile than the purchasers of services are those that we can supply in some depth and that the market is going to need and is willing to pay for. These services relate to people care, training, retraining, and the provision of sheltered housing.

If we look, for example, at the construction sector we see how Irish people, from each side of the border, have been heavily involved in the infrastructure, design and construction of buildings at professional and operative level. Irish people have had a huge impact in the sector, as a result of which networks and contacts abound. The security, management, cleaning and maintenance of buildings are all being contracted out to specialists in these fields, representing real opportunities for suppliers of these services.

Looking at the people caring area, the health care and nursing profession already provide excellent examples of Irish providers of nursing and medical staff to overseas markets using personnel recruited from Ireland, North and South. Both parts of the island have a well-deserved reputation in these fields.

While drawing attention to these areas where we have a particular strength, it would be a mistake to think that these are the only prospects. In truth they are almost limitless in a market driven by a combination of technology, the opening up of public procurement, and the privatisation of public services.

Looking further afield, the markets for services could be divided into those funded directly, such as the market for computer services in Europe or the so-called oil-fired markets of the Middle East, and those funded indirectly. The latter are financed on the one hand by the multilateral agencies, such as the World Bank Group, the UN Development Programme, and the European Development Fund, and, on the other, by the bilateral aid programmes of the developed countries. While Southern suppliers can access projects financed by the Irish Government's Overseas Development Co-Operation Programme, Northern companies can access the UK Overseas Development Aid programme.

The resources that both parts of the island can bring to those markets are quite considerable for our size. The North-South technical assistance and consultancy service data-base—which gives details of some eighty companies offering expertise in such diverse areas as aviation, banking, construction and civil engineering, management and finance, development of human resources, power supply, and transport—shows this clearly. Almost all the companies featured are experienced in working overseas and between them have covered all five continents. The data-base is the result of a combined effort by the IBEC, CBI, Irish Trade Board and Local Enterprise Development Unit (LEDU) and provides a most useful statement of national capability.

On the supply side it may be worth considering resources that will become available as a consequence of the normalisation of conditions in Northern Ireland, on the one hand, and more global forces, such as those referred to earlier and which apply to both parts of the island. There will undoubtedly be a decrease in security needs in Northern Ireland, releasing resources in the public and private sectors. Other services similarly affected will be the construction and repair of buildings and emergency hospital care. It is worth noting that while the construction sector accounts for 13 per cent of gross national product in the Republic, the Northern Ireland figure of 18 per cent reflects its relatively greater importance in that economy.

The single market means a reduced role in both jurisdictions for customs and excise personnel, many of whom are now engaged in the prevention of drugs trafficking but who could, in the short term, provide technical assistance in developing countries. If we take into account skilled engineers working for local government on roads and services and consider how this expertise might be applied in developing countries, it is not difficult to visualise a situation where personnel from both the private and public sectors could be gainfully and profitably employed in project design, project management and implementation, training, supervising, institution building and reform in Eastern Europe, Africa and the Middle East, right across the spectrum of sectors. Devco, which was established many years ago to provide technical assistance from public service organisations in the Republic to developing countries, can pinpoint opportunities and could provide an organisational framework.

It is interesting to speculate on the complementarity of skills and talents that each side would bring to the development of trade in services with third markets. At the risk of being accused of pursuing stereotypical thinking, we will argue that companies in the Republic have shown more propensity to get out and sell outside Ireland and Britain and have proved themselves good international marketeers. Companies in Northern Ireland, more oriented towards the British market, have the great virtues of solid achievement and a long tradition of excellence in areas such as engineering and shipbuilding. These talents, aided by the international contacts that both groups have built up, provide a formidable combination, making possible the development of a diversity of product and sector markets.

What Should We Be Doing?

The first task is *to create more awareness* of the possibilities and to get people thinking along the lines of providing services outside our own small island. It is necessary to accelerate the slowly dawning realisation that the service sector is more likely to address the unemployment question, North and South, than the traditional sectors of agriculture and manufacturing. A case in point is the recent announcement by the ISS group of Denmark of the establishment of an Irish subsidiary, with the twin goals of becoming market leader and employing 2,000 people in Ireland within five years. The company, reputed to be the world's largest employer, with 130,000 people employed in twenty-three countries, provides contract cleaning and other services to the hospital, airport, industrial and public sector markets.

Secondly, *information* on opportunities in the market needs to be provided. Both the Irish Trade Board and the British Department of Trade and Industry could design, and possibly jointly manage, a programme of sales and opportunity leads, especially addressing and encouraging the exporters of services in a North-South context. Looking at the institutional arrangements that might be put in place, we would consider that a project identification unit jointly funded and managed by both governments could provide the focal point for the identification and development of opportunities for exporters of services. These opportunities should include those in Britain as well as further afield.

Recognising that market prospecting can be a costly exercise, both governments could consider creating *a fund to help companies with their marketing programmes*. The benefits would be considerable when measured against the modest investment proposed here.

The financing of services exports is much more capital-intensive than is normally believed, because of delays in payment even by the multilateral agencies. This may require working capital equal to 60 or 70 per cent of annual turnover. Now it is well known that bank finance for the service sector is difficult to obtain. In sectors where the company assets are essentially the management and the other human resources employed, bankers are understandably reluctant to become heavily involved. Many exporters in the Republic cast envious eyes at the lines of credit made available by the British and other European governments to buyers in developing countries. Could our two governments agree on a *financing arrangement* that could fuel projects overseas jointly executed by contractors or consultants from both parts of the island?

The *insurance of contracts of service* against political or sovereign risk also needs to be looked at. As things stand, the situation is much easier for exporters from Northern Ireland than for those from the Republic. Here again we might suggest improving conditions up to the level currently provided by the British government for companies from both sides of the border collaborating in third-market contracts. While still on the financial aspect of the question, the availability of *bonds and securities* needs to be looked at. These have often proved an obstacle for exporters.

Looking at the *institutional arrangements* that might be put in place, we would consider that a project identification unit, jointly funded and managed by both governments could provide the focal point for the identification and development of opportunities for exporters of services North and South.

Companies on both sides should be encouraged to *seek partners*, even on a project basis, in the other jurisdiction. Apart from the additional resources thus identified, both sides might find the mix of costings advantageous and could conceivably find a way to enhance their tax planning if suitable conditions could be created.

There is also a need to *train managers and operatives* in the area of service management and provision generally, but specifically in researching markets, writing and costing proposals, project management, the application of information technology, consultancy and selling skills. A degree or postgraduate course or a module could be offered at third level, North and South, or indeed through the Open University, which has recently opened its doors in Dublin.

Our final point should probably be at the top of the action list. While the

North-South technical assistance directory is a highly commendable and useful work, there is need in addition for an *evaluation of our assets* or an analysis of our national resources that would capture the individual resources available and that might indicate gaps that should be filled. The latter might involve seeking technology transfer or partnerships from, say, the United States to enhance the package available in Ireland for exporting to the UK or the Continent. A typical example would be hospital administration software packages, where American companies may have a more developed program that could be incorporated in the Irish offer to manage a medical unit.

We need to think laterally to identify the asset and the opportunity that, combined, can become an internationally marketed service. If we take the linen industry alone, it is a reasonable assumption that considerable technological skills exist in Northern Ireland that constitute an exportable service, either as consultancy or technical assistance to a world that is constantly in search of exclusive fibres, yarns, and fabrics. Another major Northern industry, shipbuilding, has already given rise to Harland and Wolff Technical Service Ltd, established in 1989 to offer design and technical services to customers outside the shipyard. This expert company has reported on the privatisation, restructuring and long-term viability of the Polish shipyards at Gdańsk and Gdynia for the World Bank and others, to take just some examples.

Summary

It is widely recognised that the new world we see emerging daily, which some commentators have termed the information society, will not be able to depend on the old reliables of agriculture and manufacturing industry to provide gainful employment for all those who wish to enter the labour market. The services sector is employment-friendly and provides at least a partial answer to the quest for more jobs. Politicians and policy-makers should recognise this reality and should be encouraging and promoting the sector, because the reality is that over 60 per cent of those at work in both economies are already employed in providing a service of some kind, public or private, whether in the security forces, the construction industry, the distribution sector, or in professional services.

As an exporter of services, the island of Ireland has been successful. Our demography complements that of the UK and much of the developed world, which, allied to our high educational level, positions us to become suppliers of services to Britain and to the wider world.

While there is a similarity between the resources available on both sides of the border, there are differences in relation to market focus and achievement that should justify joint ventures between companies North and South in third markets. If these efforts were supported by the British and Irish governments by information and financial packages, substantial extra business could be achieved, with increased employment resulting.

A realistic evaluation of our exportable technology and technical assistance is called for, as well as a degree course in the management of service industries aimed at improving our marketing and the implementation of services contracts overseas.

Recent developments in Northern Ireland and the determination of both governments to secure and develop the peace process could be helped considerably by the development of international business jointly by companies in both parts of Ireland.

12 The Border Region: A Case Study

H. M. Robb

The European Economic and Social Committee studied the Irish border areas in 1984 and concluded: 'These areas … amongst the least economically and socially developed in Europe, have the additional disadvantage of being cut in half by a frontier that hampers normal economic development.'

The border extends for 343 kilometres, touching five county councils in the Republic and eight district councils in Northern Ireland. Sligo is treated as a border council, as is Down in the North, giving a total of fifteen border councils, with a population of 900,000, 17 per cent of the population of the island. That total includes 500,000 or 32 per cent of the population of Northern Ireland and 400,000 or 12 per cent of those living in the Republic.

As in other European border regions, economic development has suffered because the impact of the border has been to create underdeveloped basins on each side, cut off from one another and peripheral to the more dynamic national centres. Those results have been aggravated in the Irish border areas by poor infrastructure and the closure for security reasons in the early seventies of more than a hundred cross-border roads. (The reopening of these roads began in the autumn of 1994.)

Economic development has not been the sole casualty of the border. In *Prejudice and Tolerance in Ulster* (1972), a study of the nature of prejudice in a Northern Ireland border community, the anthropologist Rosemary Harris described how the border 'crystallised the opposition to each other of Catholic and Protestant, for in general Catholic and Nationalist opinion refused to recognise the border's validity, whilst Protestants regarded its maintenance as essential to their freedom. The border, close physically and omnipresent psychologically, brought into sharp contrast not only those actually separated by it but those separated because their opinions about it were opposed.'

As in other internal border regions, people on each side of the Irish border tend to live, so to speak, back-to-back, each group looking to its capital city as the centre of activity and patronage. In many parts of the border areas there

133

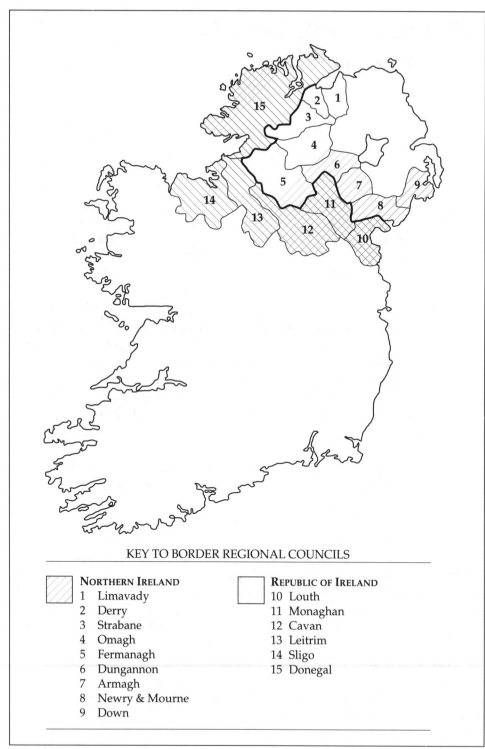

KEY TO BORDER REGIONAL COUNCILS

NORTHERN IRELAND
1 Limavady
2 Derry
3 Strabane
4 Omagh
5 Fermanagh
6 Dungannon
7 Armagh
8 Newry & Mourne
9 Down

REPUBLIC OF IRELAND
10 Louth
11 Monaghan
12 Cavan
13 Leitrim
14 Sligo
15 Donegal

Fig. 1 The Border Region on the Island of Ireland

are few links between people on opposite sides of the border. The general result, as the following examples suggest, is separate development of most activities on each side, with little interest being taken in what might be happening a few miles across the border.

- The proprietor of horse riding stables twenty miles from the border who planned on an expansion of his activities carried out market research in the middle of 1994 in neighbouring counties on his own side of the border but had not thought to examine possible markets and competition across the border.

- An agricultural officer spent two years planning a £30 million project to tackle pollution problems in a river that flows through his county and then across the border, without actively trying to secure co-operation from the relevant authorities on the other side.

- A small manufacturer of kitchen, bedroom and pub furniture three miles from the border who exports his products to the Far East and who supplies and installs them for customers in Germany and Italy had, in early 1995, never considered seeking business across the border.

Similar examples are to be found in other European border regions. The Irish border region is therefore not unique, but what the above cases suggest is its special nature compared with all other regions on the island of Ireland.

Economic Performance

In table 1, local and national statistics show the results of separate developments of the border areas for seventy-four years, combined as time passed with the increasing marginalisation of each side within its own area.

Table 1: The border region: selected statistics

	Northern Ireland		Republic	
	Nine border councils (%)	All (%)	Six border councils (%)	All (%)
Population change, 1981–91	+5.8	+2.9	–2	+2.3
Range across councils	–0.4/+8.7		–6.5/+1.2	
Unemployment, 1991	19.5	15.6	21.0	18.0
On register >2 years	39.0	34.0	31.0	27.0

High unemployment and a population fall on the southern side do not give the full economic story: on both sides there are notable examples of job creation. Indigenous companies in the border areas operating internationally include, for example, one of the largest clothing suppliers to Marks and Spencer, employing 2,800 in the north-west. World leaders in the manufacture of both veterinary medicines and small electric appliances are to be found in Newry. An American clothing manufacturer with 3,000 employees on both sides of the border in the north-west was attracted to the area by the vision and energy of an indigenous clothing manufacturer in Buncrana, County Donegal.

Monaghan has higher proportions of workers employed in manufacturing than any other county in Ireland and of Irish-owned manufacturing jobs. Activity in furniture, mushrooms and poultry is especially significant, supplementing low and declining farm incomes.

Despite the peripherality of the border areas, jobs grew at a faster rate on the northern side than in Northern Ireland as a whole in 1971–91. Against an overall total growth for the North of 9.8 per cent, seven of the nine district council areas recorded increases in total jobs in the range 18–24 per cent, and only Fermanagh, with 6 per cent, and Strabane, with 3 per cent, were below the overall total for the twenty-year period.

Other statistics also point to higher growth rates in rural areas. Hart and Gudgin in their study *Spatial Variations in New Firm Formation in Ireland, 1980–1990* state: 'The highest growth rates [of both gross and net new firm formation] are in the most rural and least industrialised regions of the country.' Of all the counties, Monaghan ranked second-highest, and four of the six border counties came within the first seven.

Decline in the Region

This background suggests grounds for optimism about future job creation through entrepreneurial activities in the border areas. There are, however, influences inimical to the emergence of entrepreneurial thinking: the many communities with traditions of high unemployment, and a dominant dependence culture; the lack of role models for youngsters in the more remote areas of local people who have made a success of entrepreneurship; and the cultural pressures on bright children to obtain qualifications in professions that offer no local employment.

Other negative influences include management weaknesses that, endemic in the 200,000 small and medium-sized enterprises on the island, are likely to be particularly acute in the more remote parts of the border areas. There are also problems of access to training.

Administrative Structures

Administrative structures differ markedly between Northern Ireland and the Republic. Northern Ireland district councils are not responsible for housing or roads but have an interest in tourism development. In 1993 they were, for the first time, empowered to spend up to 2 per cent of their rate income on economic development, increased to 5 per cent by the British Prime Minister when all district council chief executives visited Downing Street early in 1995.

County councils in the Republic have housing and roads responsibilities but are not involved in tourism. Two types of local entity have no Northern equivalent: county enterprise boards, which set objectives for promoting enterprise in a county, and the Border Region Authority, which co-ordinates some activities of the six border counties.

Since the mid-eighties two groupings of cross-border councils have emerged. In the north-west, Donegal and three Northern district councils, Derry, Limavady, and Strabane, have produced a joint economic plan. In the east, Monaghan and Louth work with two Northern councils, Newry and Mourne district and Down district, on possible joint ventures. A similar cross-border structure may well evolve in the mid-border areas.

Administrative arrangements for the EU funding initiative Interreg II have not yet been announced, but it is understood that such bodies may be empowered to operate as intermediaries between government departments and those who apply to Interreg.

EU Funds

Two EU initiatives have a particular focus on border regions. Interreg applies to all EU internal borders; the Initiative for Peace and Reconciliation covers Northern Ireland and the six border county council areas in the Republic. Both initiatives demonstrate the overarching influence of the European Union on the island.

Interreg is available to all of Northern Ireland except Belfast and to the six border county council areas. With matching funds, some £167 million will be provided in 1995–99. Interreg encourages cross-border co-operation throughout the EU. Priority is to be given to proposals made 'in co-operation with regional and local authorities in border areas and which include the establishment or development of shared institutional or administrative structures intended to widen and deepen cross-border organisations and voluntary bodies. Shared institutional or administrative structures should have the competence to implement jointly determined projects.'

Preferred projects will be based on 'a coherent regional strategy for the border areas concerned' for 'a single geographical unit with a clear statement of the development aims into which the aims of the operational programmes have been properly integrated' and will be seen 'to promote cross-border co-operation across as wide a number of fields as possible' (EU 'Explanatory Memorandum').

The EU Initiative for Peace and Reconciliation, which was approved at the Essen summit in December 1994, will provide some £234 million in 1995–97. The two governments will add £78 million in matching funds. Further funding may be provided in 1998–99. Up to 80 per cent of the fund is available for projects in Northern Ireland and not less than 20 per cent in the six border counties of the Republic, and at least 15 per cent of the overall amount will support cross-border activities.

Five priorities to be 'addressed in the context of the consolidation of the peace process' have been identified: 'employment, urban and rural regeneration, cross-border development, social inclusion, and productive investment and industrial development' (EU 'Draft Notice').

Each initiative will operate under a monitoring committee representing the two governments and the European Commission. Interreg began operation in early May. The approval and delivery mechanisms for the peace initiative were made known by mid-1995, with some funds starting to flow by early autumn.

Assessing the cross-border impact of Interreg in 1991–93 and of other funds may help the process of taking a view on the likely impact of the initiatives in 1995–99.

Most cross-border projects funded by Interreg were for infrastructure, notably the Shannon-Erne link, a 35-mile restored canal. Few cross-border projects were proposed by local groups, because most members then had neither the experience of running a group nor sufficient knowledge of their neighbours across the border to be able to readily identify possible joint activities. There are, however, some excellent examples of cross-border groups, such as Lisnaskea and Clones Enterprise Development and the Strabane-Lifford Development Commission, both established to enhance local assets for mutual benefit and to strengthen links between the neighbouring towns.

Many communities now have several years of formative experience in making and implementing decisions for their own development. That background is likely to encourage new entrants and to take the stronger groups into more sophisticated projects, including those of a cross-border nature.

Co-operation among business organisations is evident. The European

Economic Interest Group formed by the Londonderry and Letterkenny Chambers of Commerce has provided a meeting ground for cross-border interest groups, including those concerned with telecommunications, crafts, legal services, food, and clothing. Close links between the Enterprise Centre at Dundalk Regional Technical College and Newry Co-operative provide new frameworks for increasing regional co-operation. This background promises increased activity under Interreg II, especially in the new environment created by peace and alongside the EU Peace Initiative.

The impact of peace is apparent in the border areas. Local groups from north Monaghan and Dungannon district, for example, that before the August ceasefire had had no contact met frequently in subsequent months, and the two councils are considering a co-operative project to regenerate the Blackwater river. Such a project could lead to co-operation on a range of economic activities.

Possible projects include the development of local features to attract tourists, such as a mountain, Slieve Beagh, designated on the northern side as an area of outstanding beauty and shared by Fermanagh, Dungannon district, and Monaghan. Other features include many archaeological sites, white-water facilities on a tributary of the Blackwater, villages with historical associations, and, most ambitiously, the 55-mile Ulster Canal, which, if restored, would link the Shannon-Erne systems via Lough Neagh with the north Atlantic coast.

In parallel, a range of accommodation from youth hostels to luxury hotels, with a strong emphasis on bed-and-breakfast, has to be provided.

Alongside such developments there is much to be done towards job creation. This requires the active involvement of local third-level colleges and of the social partners. Local communities also need to be harnessed: their own processes of capacity-building and the development of co-operative projects will both build entrepreneurial skills in the area and create jobs.

In terms of regional development generally there is little new in any of these ideas: what is remarkable about them is the rapid emergence of border communities and councils that see the possibility for the first time of tackling such projects on a cross-border basis and that are preparing their plans with much enthusiasm.

Success Factors

Forms of support necessary to local groups, and for the identification of cross-border projects, include (*a*) three types of support from the two governments, (*b*) council support, (*c*) university support, (*d*) support from entities on both sides of the border, (*e*) support from the European Commission, and (*f*) support from the universities and the private sector. In detail these include:

Three types of support from the two governments:

- the adequate provision of information, advice and training on the various funds and on the demarcation lines among those funds that may support similar objectives;

- the creation of application review and decision mechanisms that are transparent, speedy, sympathetic to groups with good ideas but little experience, and all as close to the level of the applicant as is compatible with accountability and stewardship. (For the Peace Initiative, in particular, the development of the appropriate mechanisms is urgently required, and it is a matter of concern that review and decision problems aired as early as October 1994 had not, by late March, been resolved, given the great urgency to utilise the funding);

- the Chapter on Co-operation common to the Development Plans 1994–99 for both Northern Ireland and the Republic 'sets out the rationale for closer economic co-operation' and acknowledges common challenges, describes the high level of existing activities, and proposes enhanced co-operation across a large number of activities of mutual interest, not least under the stimulus of Interreg. It is not yet clear, however, that the two governments have identified the plans and resources necessary to implement the chapter, which is particularly relevant to the border areas.

For these purposes both governments must ensure that the various departments involved and any bodies to which powers are delegated have adequate resources. Personnel resources were clearly stretched under Interreg I, the volume of work involved having apparently been underestimated. Fortunately the two governments have decided to appoint one development officer to disseminate information on Interreg II. Whether one person can provide an adequate service to the 1.7 million people in the regions eligible for Interreg funding remains to be seen.

Council support: Some councils, such as Fermanagh, demonstrate what can be done by enlightened local measures to foster community development, tourism, and job creation. Similar local services are needed in all parts of the border areas and for cross-border activities.

University support: Some universities have provided both training and animation support (the latter in the form of trained facilitators working within communities in capacity-building and planning). Such support services will continue to be in demand, both on each side of the border and for cross-border projects.

Support from entities on both sides of the border: A further service required in the border areas is that of assisting in the identification and development of cross-border projects. The organisation Co-operation North has demonstrated since 1979 the benefits of such assistance from an entity that is equally based on both sides of the border. The Joint Chair in Cross-Border Business Enterprise at University College, Dublin, and the University of Ulster, has been able to provide similar support since its creation in late 1993. Such services will increasingly be needed for the more rapid development of future cross-border projects.

Support from the European Commission: It is difficult to access information on co-operative activities in other EU cross-border areas, and the Commission, it is hoped, will accept responsibility for disseminating such information.

Support from the universities and the private and public sectors: Support is needed for:

- the identification and removal of barriers to cross-border trade. Barriers include lack of information and understanding of markets on the other side of the border, and the problems for a business that has to deal with the legal and tax systems of two separate regimes.

- the taking of an active role towards the emerging technologies discussed in the 1994 EU white paper *Growth, Competitiveness, Employment,* including information and communication systems, the audiovisual sector, and biotechnology. These technologies pose a threat to those regions that fail to stay abreast of developments and a source of great opportunity for those that harness them. The white paper predicts that an additional two million jobs will be created in the audiovisual sector within the EU by 2000; the pro-rated figure for the border areas is 5,500.

These technologies are particularly significant for the border areas, because they can create the distance-independent jobs that can be performed as efficiently in remote locations as elsewhere.

Conclusions

It is likely that much less of the economic and social potential of the Republic and Northern Ireland has been realised in the border areas over the past seventy-four years than in all other parts of the island, because of the impact of the border. Indeed many believe that the consequent deprivation and social exclusion in the border areas have been a cause of the violence of the past twenty-five years.

Against that background, the combined effects of peace, the emerging technologies, the momentum among local communities to develop themselves and the very clear desire of people from both communities and from both sides of the border to work together, all suggest an unprecedented opportunity for social and economic regeneration.

With the benefit of the European single market and the positive discrimination of the EU funds in favour of co-operation, regeneration can surely be achieved without making any assumptions about political change. If that is allowed to happen, the history of the border areas in the next twenty-five years could differ dramatically for the better from that of 1968–94. Can there be a stronger argument for continued peace?

Part 5

Out of Work

13 A View from the North

Inez McCormack

In 1985 the Cambridge economist Bob Rowthorn described Northern Ireland as having a 'workhouse economy'. A large proportion of its population was unemployed, and those fortunate to have jobs were, as he put it, 'chiefly engaged in servicing or controlling each other—through the provision of health, education, retail distribution, construction, security and social services.' Chronically high levels of unemployment, and consequent deprivation, were mitigated by transfers from the British exchequer, a high proportion of which went towards welfare payments, and also by emigration. Nearly a decade later, in 1994, a leading Northern Ireland business figure described Northern Ireland as 'locked in an unrelieved downward economic spiral.'

These gloomy but realistic assessments of the Northern economy are thrown into sharp relief by the ceasefires of the autumn of 1994. There is a widespread acknowledgment that the peace needs to be underpinned by economic regeneration. In October 1994, hard on the heels of the cessation of violence, President Clinton announced his intention to host a trade and investment conference in the United States, saying that 'peace and prosperity depend upon one another.' The British Prime Minister, John Major, held an investment conference in Belfast on 13 December 1994, addressed by a senior member of the US administration and the deputy secretary-general of the European Union. The EU itself responded immediately to the cessation of violence with statements by the then president, Jacques Delors, following both republican and loyalist ceasefires. These were shortly followed by two important European initiatives: an announcement of some £240 million in extra funding and the setting up of a Task Force on Northern Ireland.

The European Commission's initiative recognised the need to seize the opportunity offered by the peace and the necessity to build confidence in it by making available funds that would have an immediate impact. How the money was to be used and how it was to be delivered quickly in order to make a visible change was the subject of a conference in Belfast in April 1995 sponsored by the North's three members of the European Parliament.

The EU Regional Policy Commissioner, Monika Wulf-Mathies, said that the funding initiative must be aimed at those groups that were most in need. She also emphasised the priority given to 'social inclusion' through developing and promoting community and cross-border co-operation. The Commission indicated that it would be co-ordinating its efforts with those of the US administration. This co-ordination at an international level should assist in bringing American investment to those most disadvantaged areas by improving their infrastructure.

The Commission recognised the need to address rural disadvantage, and in particular the problems of border areas. It is directing that some 20 per cent of the extra funding will go to border areas and that at least 15 per cent should be spent on cross-border schemes. This, of course, requires co-operation by both governments. The necessary integration of agencies North and South in the obvious areas of agriculture, tourism and arts and culture could be a blueprint for a more general integration of effort in relation to the two economies as a whole.

The ceasefires are only the first but indispensable element of a durable peace. The good will of the international community is another. However, as the president of the European Commission, Jacques Santer, remarked in Belfast, 'support from the international community, be it European, some American support, or a combination of both, may help to alleviate some of the economic difficulties, but it will take time to create the climate of trust which is needed to secure peace on the island once and for all.'

This statement indicates that the EU recognises the need for a short-term strategy as well as a long-term one that both take into account the realities of economic disadvantage and their unequal distribution in Northern Ireland. Sir George Quigley expressed part of the problem when he said that 'I think a minority have almost a vested interest in the troubles continuing.' In 1975 the Northern Ireland economy was subsidised to the tune of stg£1.2 billion; the subsidy from Britain and the EU currently stands at some stg£3.6 billion. In effect what this subsidy has done is to lock a proportion of the population into a position where their living standards have increased, while a growing proportion are locked out of the economy. There has been affluence and prosperity for a middle class, including a growing Catholic middle class; many others have been condemned to long-term unemployment. What is therefore required is a restructuring of the economy in order to ensure that the benefits of the peace are equalised.

This point was highlighted by President Clinton in his speech at the Washington Investment Conference that he hosted. This conference was significant in both composition and content. All elements of Northern society—economic, political, and community—were invited and participated. The conference recognised the centrality of targeting areas of economic disadvantage in order to maximise the potential of economic change to underpin the peace process.

At the time of writing, the North's official unemployment rate is 12 per cent, similar to that of France and therefore not exceptional by EU standards. But this figure hides a number of realities. Some 60 per cent of those unemployed have been out of work for at least a year; average household income is 14 per cent below that of the UK, and 20 per cent of household income in Northern Ireland comes from social security benefits, compared with 14 per cent in the UK as a whole. For those who are working, earnings are 90 per cent of UK levels. Since the salaries of those in the professions and the public services are in line with UK norms, this means that large numbers of workers are earning well below the UK average. Partly as a result of poor job prospects, a higher proportion of sixteen-year-olds remains in education; Northern Ireland school leavers obtain better A-level results than the rest of the UK, but the number who leave school with no GCE qualifications is double that of England (12 per cent as against 6 per cent).

Between the census years of 1971 and 1991 the male unemployment rate in Northern Ireland rose from 10 to 16 per cent. More importantly, however, the number of males recorded as economically inactive—i.e. out of the labour market altogether—more than trebled, from 5 to 16 per cent. Combining the figures for men of working age registered as unemployed with those economically inactive, the proportion of men without work doubled in the period from 15 to 33 per cent. Further, this precipitous increase was not experienced equally by the two religious communities. By 1991 the percentage of Catholic men of working age who did not have work was 43 per cent; the equivalent figure for Protestant men was 26 per cent. Averaging figures from the late eighties, the percentage of male Catholics without work in the 20–24 age group was 48 per cent, while for others it was 26 per cent.

These shocking figures show the failure of current economic policies to address needs *in both communities.* They also underline the view that what is desperately required is jobs *and justice*: the directing of greatest resources to where there is greatest need.

These figures are consistent with those from official sources from 1971 to the present, indicating that Catholics are significantly worse off than their Protestant counterparts on virtually every socio-economic indicator. In particular, throughout the last twenty-five years the differential between Catholic and all male unemployment has remained stubbornly and consistently at 2 to 1. The unemployment differential does not mean that

Catholics are financially twice as badly off as Protestants, since the effects of unemployment are cushioned by welfare benefits. However, figures from the Northern Ireland Family Expenditure Survey referring to the situation obtaining in 1993 showed that average gross weekly income for Protestants was 17 per cent higher than for Catholics. Social security benefit accounted for 29 per cent of Catholic income, as against 17 per cent for Protestants. The relatively high figure for Protestants—where nearly £1 per £5 is derived from public welfare benefit—demonstrates that current policies are failing them. Large numbers of them are very poor, but proportionately many more Catholics are.

The position of women in the Northern Ireland economy remains undervalued and under-resourced, particularly in areas of high disadvantage. For large numbers, caring for their families and elderly relatives means giving up educational and employment opportunities. For large numbers of young women, after-school experience consists of training schemes and a choice between unemployment and early marriage. Those in work are in the main in part-time, poorly paid, insecure employment, their jobs an extension of the cleaning and catering they undertake unpaid at home. Yet the earnings of the female work force are the difference between chronic financial insecurity and downright misery for their families. Current government policies and privatisation in the public services threaten even their current marginal position in the economic sphere.

A report by the North's Equal Opportunities Commission in 1995 found that both Catholic and Protestant women earn less than men and have a much more restricted range of job opportunities, and that more Catholic women are poorly paid or unemployed.

Women have borne the brunt of the suffering and the violence of the last quarter-century, not only keeping together communities shattered by violence, imprisonment and poverty but also demanding change. Any new structures must give them an equal voice in the process of reconstruction and determining its goals. They must also address the needs of women as workers and carers by providing adequate child care provisions and appropriate care for the elderly. Work should not be seen in purely economic terms. Work has a social value, locating the person in his or her community; it also has a political value. The terms 'alienation' and 'marginalisation' have often been invoked in relation to Northern Ireland; their reality is apparent in the sense of abandonment by the state in the poorest areas of Northern Ireland. The work of reconciliation requires that their future not be like their past.

The political and economic history of Northern Ireland over the past twenty-five years might present a picture of unrelieved gloom, but this is not the case. Within communities ravaged by violence and want there is a dynamism and energy. For many years the most innovative programmes for necessary change have emerged at community level. The government for many years ignored these ideas and was reluctant to respond to grass-roots pressure for change. At worst they practised a policy of political vetting, selectively financing community projects and withdrawing funds from groups they deemed politically unsuitable, both nationalist and unionist. This further exclusion from decision-making has made the community groups more insistent, and there is ample evidence that pressure from below, aided by international pressure, is slowly changing government priorities. It is crucial, however, that the government does not attempt to control and dictate the speed of necessary economic change: other voices, not least those of the disadvantaged themselves, must be a central part of the process of change.

The dynamic of the demand for an equal voice in social and economic decision-making has been most evident in the most deprived nationalist areas, as a result of their deeper and longer experience of deprivation as well as their history of exclusion from the political process. More recently, however, as a result of their own political history and an awareness of the impact of both the conflict and poverty on their communities, such ventures have become a feature of loyalist communities. This has led to a remarkable congruence between the two communities in relation both to the importance of economic restructuring and the form it takes. Sinn Féin, for example, has said that it regards the promotion of economic and social development in Ireland as a key and integral part of the peace process and has indicated that economic development is needed not only to develop the peace process but also to develop and consolidate agreement on political structures. For their part, representatives of the Progressive Unionist Party and the Ulster Democratic Party, in exploratory dialogue with senior officials of the Northern Ireland Office, have also emphasised the importance of economic regeneration, pointing to the erosion of traditional industries and the impact of twenty-five years of violent conflict on working-class areas in both communities. They considered economic regeneration as an essential component of conflict resolution and social construction, and proposed that key objectives in disadvantaged areas should be to increase employment opportunities, enhance the employablity of people in those areas, and develop community regeneration through a multiple-strategy approach to employment.

These voices come from the areas of highest disadvantage but they are part of a growing consensus, including the Confederation of British Industry, the Irish Congress of Trade Unions, and the Northern Ireland Economic Council, that prosperity and economic growth must be inclusive. The European initiative could only have come about with the co-operation of the North's three members of the European Parliament as another indication of that consensus; and already this has involved reaching out to and across communities to ensure that the funding reaches areas where it is most needed.

In many, but not all, of the areas of disadvantage there exists an informal network of community groups, existing outside political structures. What is essential is that these become full partners in the enterprise of regeneration and that their perceptions of local needs and sustainable employment be integrated with the policies of the government and civil servants. They need to be strengthened and resourced in order that their needs be put at the heart of economic renewal, rather than being seen as the problem itself. It is also essential that they be encouraged to develop long-term plans and goals. Through supporting their agendas for change, and hence their belief in themselves and their belief that they can make things happen for their own communities, self-esteem, confidence and identity will be fostered.

Cross-community development must not be narrowly constructed: it needs building-blocks, and its development must be based on the recognition of political and cultural diversity. There is existing cross-community activity by women's organisations, prisoners' groups, and voluntary organisations, and this needs to be supported and resourced. The success of the ventures undertaken by the British and Irish governments, and promised by the European Union and the United States, depends on expanding the role of this community sector. Their exclusion in the past has made addressing both the political and economic problems more difficult. Their own endeavours have had to be mediated by other agencies, and they are determined to maintain control of their vision and ensure that it is not diluted by others. The detachment of government agencies from their daily realities must be replaced with an active engagement; it is only then that the language of change will produce the reality of change.

The necessity of securing 'social inclusion' for these groups figures centrally in the plans of the EU initiative, and the Task Force has consulted them in formulating its strategy. They require technical assistance in developing their own plans for tackling their social and economic problems. The question of how money is to be channelled to them and used most productively in their interests has produced some new formulations, but also tensions with the traditional providers of resources: government agencies and local authorities. Monika Wulf-Mathies suggested that the concept of global grants could be used and made available to intermediaries designated by the EU. Such intermediaries would include women's groups and community groups, which would be responsible for selecting and assisting projects.

This central role for such groups also places a responsibility on them. Some of them have developed considerable expertise over the years—often in the most difficult circumstances—in planning and submitting projects and negotiating with agencies. Others have less experience in these areas. As partnerships develop, they need to articulate the components necessary to carry their plans forward and to genuinely represent those most vulnerable to disadvantage. They need to be balanced in respect of sex, disability, race and religion.

The idea of community or area partnerships is increasingly becoming a feature of plans for urban and rural renewal in Ireland and elsewhere in Europe as a result of the failure of traditional economic planning to reverse rising unemployment and to address growing social inequities. It is by no means a new idea in Northern Ireland and has its origins in a number of community developments in the 1980s. A notable and successful example of such a partnership was the Divis Joint Development Committee, centred in Divis Flats in nationalist west Belfast, a by-word for official neglect and indifference. The committee ultimately won agreement from the authorites for the demolition of most of the complex, and was involved in the rehousing scheme for the area.

An important element that remains missing is the absence of forums that would include business, public authorities, trade unions and communities meeting as partners and engaging in decision-making as a full partnership. The South's National Economic and Social Forum, as well as its Area Partnerships, points to the kind of broad co-operation that has little institutional expression in Northern Ireland. This gap needs to be filled to ensure that community groups feel confident that they are full and equal partners and that responsibility and accountability are shared. Such bodies are particularly critical for long-term planning and to ensure that job creation is aimed at sustainable and targeted growth. They could have a much broader role in both jurisdictions, as well as providing arenas for sharing experiences between the jurisdictions. By learning to share responsibility we could also learn how to handle more effectively problems of diversity that are by no means unique to the North.

In recent years those responsible for the administration in the North have slowly come to realise that regeneration depends on the consent and active participation of communities themselves. It also increasingly recognises that, for political as well as economic reasons, government resources must be directed towards the most disadvantaged. As a result, the British government announced in February 1991 that Targeting Social Need (TSN) was to be a third spending priority, alongside security and the economy. The announcement came as a result of consideration of the relative economic positions of the Catholic and Protestant communities, using a range of indicators, including unemployment, income, education and training, qualifications, health, and socio-economic group. These showed that there remained significant differentials between the two communities and that there had been little change in these over a number of years, in spite of fair employment initiatives.

The new approach encapsulated in TSN requires all government policies to be assessed in relation to their differential impact on the Protestant and Catholic communities. This requirement began to be implemented only at the beginning of 1994, when government departments were instructed to begin an appraisal of the impact of their policies in relation to religion, sex, disability, ethnicity, and sexual orientation.

As a third public expenditure—and one that can now be more adequately resourced as security spending is reduced—TSN can be aimed at eradicating differentials by ensuring that resources are focused equitably and proportionately, and at areas and groups of greatest disadvantage. These aims were explicitly spelt out in the Northern Ireland Structural Funds Plan in 1993: 'Targeting Social Need ... addresses socio-economic needs such as unemployment, housing conditions and educational attainment wherever those needs exist but with particular reference to reducing unfair differentials between various parts of the Northern Ireland community.'

In the present situation TSN is a potentially powerful policy, because it specifically addresses disadvantage. Since Catholics suffer disproportionate disadvantage, the policy should have a particular impact on them, although it must also improve the position of the poorest Protestants. It is aimed therefore at greater social inclusion for both communities. Implementation of the policy is, as always, crucial. TSN needs to be integrated with the policies of the EU and the Irish Government and also with the wishes emerging from the communities themselves. It must also be integrated with overall economic plans. In the next three years British government spending in Northern Ireland will run at some stg£8 billion a year; it thus dwarfs any extra money from EU or other sources. An integrated approach to the use of this money, targeting disadvantage at the heart of economic policy and in partnership with the communities themselves, could make a dramatic difference to the future, to provide sustainable and reasonably well-paid jobs for those who have been on the periphery.

An important element in such partnerships is the private sector. A key to Northern Ireland's future lies not merely in attracting inward investment and supporting indigenous industries and development but in harnessing that investment to existing social need. I strongly endorse Maureen Gaffney's view in her contribution to this book that business can both 'do well and do good.' In Northern Ireland, equality is good for business. Economic justice is a key to underpinning the peace, which in turn improves the business environment. It is part of the job of governments to ensure that investment fulfils environmental and other social criteria. To this end, co-operation is as important as competition to successful investment and growth.

The prospects for strengthening the peace in Northern Ireland depend crucially on social and economic restructuring, with resources and planning aimed at those who are most disadvantaged, and their full involvement in decision-making. The new circumstances require the inclusion in the economic process of those who in the past have been excluded. The prospects of success are better than they have ever been; the consequences of failure are unthinkable.

14 A View from the South

Maureen Gaffney

The achievement of peace in Northern Ireland signals more than an end to hostilities. A historic opportunity now presents itself to both parts of this divided island to articulate a vision of what kind of society we want to live in and what civic and moral values we subscribe to, and to mount an energetic and positive challenge to the economic and social problems that have historically bedevilled both societies.

Politicians concern themselves in war and peace with matters of territory, law, formal structures, and relationships. But real and sustained peace only happens at the level of people's daily lives and well-being in the communities they live in. Central to that well-being is the urgent and unavoidable need to tackle three fundamental social problems: unemployment, poverty, and social exclusion.

We live in an increasingly divided society. We now know that the rising tide does not lift all boats. This suggests something more than social inequality: it points rather to flaws in the social fabric, to the structural nature of a process that excludes part of the population from economic and social opportunities and from full citizenship in society. The problem is not simply a matter of the disparity between the top and bottom of the social scale but between those who have a place in society and those who are excluded. Unemployment, particularly long-term unemployment, plays a key role in that process of exclusion.

The high level of unemployment is one of our major economic and social problems. Everybody knows that. What is less well known is that our short-term unemployment rate is not greatly out of line with that of other countries. Concealed in the overall figures for unemployment is a much more disturbing problem: the rise and persistence of long-term unemployment, defined as continuous unemployment for twelve months or more. In that regard we have a uniquely serious problem. In 1991 we recorded the highest rate of long-term unemployment in the OECD, with nearly one in ten of the work force without a job for more than a year. Our long-term unemployment rate was greater than the *total* unemployment rate in many OECD countries (for example, it is more than three times that of Germany and more than ten times that of the United States).

Between 1980 and 1993, the number of long-term unemployed rose from 35,000, or 2.8 per cent of the work force, to 135,000, or almost 10 per cent of the work force. This happened despite high levels of emigration. Moreover, unless remedial measures are taken, the level of long-term unemployment is expected to be no lower at the end of the decade than it is now, even given favourable economic prospects in the medium-term ahead.

Tackling this problem is the declared priority of the Government, which in 1993 established the National Economic and Social Forum (NESF)—an official consultative and advisory body on economic and social policy issues—to develop new policy initiatives, particularly those aimed at combating unemployment. Recognising the now demonstrated value of a partnership approach to economic and social planning, the NESF is a widely representative and democratic body, including as it does representatives of all the political parties, the traditional social partners (trade unions, employers, and farmers), and those traditionally outside the consultative process, including women, the unemployed, the disadvantaged, people with a disability, youth, the elderly, and environmental interests.

In its Report, *Ending Long-term Unemployment,* published in 1994, the NESF set out to describe the grim reality behind the figures for long-term unemployment and to make detailed recommendations to the Government.

Long-Term Unemployment: the Facts

The National Economic and Social Forum's Report revealed that over half of our long-term unemployed are in the 25–44 age group and one-fifth are under 25. These figures do not include the very large numbers of women who are not registered as unemployed but who are dependent on welfare payments and therefore may share many of the characteristics and problems of the long-term unemployed in their exclusion from the labour market. For example, in 1992, while there were 92,000 women registered as unemployed, an additional 44,000 were receiving the lone parent's payment and almost 70,000 were classified as dependent adults.

How long have they been unemployed? Labour Force Survey data showed that in 1992 more than half the long-term unemployed had been unemployed for over three years and two-fifths for more than five years. Our analysis also showed that the longer people are unemployed, the greater the probability of their remaining unemployed. So those unemployed for under a year have a 30 per cent chance of being unemployed a year later; for those unemployed for more than one year but less than two years there is a 61 per cent chance of remaining unemployed a year later. Those who have been unemployed for over two years have a 74 per cent chance of being unemployed one year later, and this probability rises to over 80 per cent for men aged 25–44 and to 90 per cent for men aged 45–54.

In terms of educational qualifications, the long-term unemployed are seriously disadvantaged compared with those in work. For example, almost 50 per cent of the long-term unemployed had no formal educational qualifications, compared with 25 per cent of the short-term unemployed and 15 per cent of those in work. Only 13 per cent had the Leaving Certificate, compared with 26 per cent of the short-term unemployed and 35 per cent of those at work. Only 4 per cent of the long-term unemployed had a third-level qualification, compared with 12 per cent of the short-term unemployed and 25 per cent of those at work. Those with the greatest educational disadvantage are the older long-term unemployed. In 1991 almost two-thirds of the long-term unemployed aged 35 or more were without any qualification.

The relationship between educational qualifications and labour market success is particularly strong for young people: as educational qualifications increase, unemployment rates fall sharply. For example, in 1992 the unemployment rate among young workers aged 15–24 who had no educational qualifications was 52 per cent, compared with 32 per cent of those with the Intermediate or Group Certificate.

Each year approximately 20 per cent of school-leavers leave the education system with no qualifications whatsoever or with minimal qualifications. Given current labour market conditions, and in the absence of new policy initiatives, it is almost inevitable that many of these young people will eventually become long-term unemployed.

Almost half the long-term unemployed come from a manual occupational background, compared with only 29 per cent of those at work. Over 20 per cent of the long-term unemployed are in the 'other' category, reflecting their perception that they have no occupational background, because of how long they have been out of work or because they may never have had a job at all.

Almost two-thirds of the long-term unemployed are classified as 'household head', compared with 42 per cent of the short-term unemployed and 45 per cent of those at work. Over half are married; thus, they are more likely to have dependants. Moreover, 53 per cent of the partners of unemployed men were themselves unemployed, compared with only 30 per cent of those whose husbands were working. So, many households affected by unemployment may be characterised by almost total exclusion from the labour market. Of the long-term unemployed, 38 per cent live in local authority housing, compared with only 22 per cent of the short-term employed and 10 per cent of those in employment.

Long-term unemployment therefore is concentrated in particular communities, among people who very often have families depending on them, who themselves suffer from significant educational disadvantage, and whose children are at risk of leaving school with no qualifications, thus perpetuating the cycle of disadvantage. The longer these people are out of work, the further they fall behind in the competition for jobs.

Long-Term Unemployment: the Costs

For those individuals, families and communities affected by long-term unemployment there will be no relief, unless radical measures are implemented that deal with their special problems. If we fail to tackle this challenge, the costs will be enormous. These costs include the significant effects of unemployment on the physical and psychological health of those directly affected. They include all the direct and indirect adversity caused by the resulting poverty: unemployment is the most important cause of poverty. They include the social costs: the depression, crime and alienation that arise in severely dispossessed and marginalised communities.

In a country that is traditionally characterised by a strong sense of community and solidarity, where there is justifiable pride in our quality of life, there is an increasing danger of allowing an underclass to develop, with whole clusters of families where neither parents nor their adult children have ever worked and who are profoundly alienated from society.

There are also significant economic costs, in the form of 7 per cent of GDP expended on unemployment benefits and forgone revenue from income tax and social security contributions, compared with an EU average of 4 per cent.

Long-Term Unemployment: the Causes

A broad range of factors is traditionally put forward to explain long-term unemployment. These include policy factors (such as the impact of employment legislation and unemployment benefit systems and the extent to which labour market policy is 'active' or 'passive'); the changing nature of work; the skill and education levels of the long-term unemployed; the barriers facing the long-term unemployed in finding and accepting work (such as recruitment practices, employers' reluctance, and unemployment traps); and, finally, persistence factors (such as loss of skills and the lack of influence of the long-term unemployed in the labour market).

The NESF in its Report examined these factors. In doing so it concentrated not on the causes of unemployment in general and issues such as the employment-intensity of growth but focused instead on the 'stock' (i.e. the absolute level) of long-term unemployment and on the reasons why it does not appear to respond to improvements in the overall employment and unemployment situation. In other words, we focused on the demand and supply-side factors that contribute to the persistence of long-term unemployment.

On the basis of our analysis of international thinking and policy responses, as well as our review of existing policy and programmes for the long-term unemployed in Ireland, we identified key deficiencies in policy objectives and interventions and put forward a comprehensive and integrated package of proposals to deal with the main dimensions and causes of our long-term unemployment problem.

The Employment Service: an Innovative Approach

The establishment of a comprehensive national and locally based Employment Service is the NESF Report's central recommendation. A variety of domestic and international evidence is cited to support the cost-effective and positive results of such a Service. This Service would be responsible for:

- implementing the proposed twin strategies of preventing long-term unemployment and reintegrating the long-term unemployed back into employment;

- providing an individually tailored guidance and placement service for unemployed people; and

- serving as the gateway to all employment and training programmes.

Registration by the unemployed would be voluntary, and the Service would be open to everybody: the unemployed and the unregistered unemployed (such as the spouses or adult dependants of unemployed people), as well as those in employment who were in need of its services.

The service would be responsible for establishing close links with local employers and mediating with them on behalf of its clients to secure appropriate placements and job opportunities. In fact the active co-operation, support and involvement of employers and trade unions is critical to the success of this initiative. In turn, the Service would have to be in a position to provide a quality service to employers to encourage them to use it to notify and subsequently fill vacancies.

Supply-Side Measures

The Employment Service's overarching aim would be to improve the *quality* of labour supply of the long-term unemployed and those at risk of becoming so, with the goal of creating a significant increase in the demand for their labour. Four important options should be available:

- First, pre-labour market assistance should be available to some clients to deal with those personal and social problems (for example literacy and interview skills) that need to be addressed before labour market interventions can be considered.

- Second, clients might need to be facilitated in acquiring specific educational or other qualifications that would help them compete in the labour market.

- Third, while training would be an important option for some clients, our review of existing policies revealed the limited effectiveness of general training; training would therefore only be used where it related to particular employment opportunities that had been identified and included employer involvement to ensure its relevance.

- Fourth, if training is to be effective it would need to be integrated with a period of related employment experience; again, employers would have a pivotal role here.

As a quid pro quo for their central involvement in the design and delivery of training there would have to be a commitment by employers to provide temporary employment experience that would build on the skills acquired on training programmes.

However, employment experience would not need in some cases to be linked to training. For example, for many people who are ready for employment in regard to education and skills but who are long-term unemployed or at risk of becoming so (i.e. those unemployed for between six and twelve months), their problem is simply a history of joblessness and lack of employment experience. A temporary employment experience in a real employment setting, with the status and working conditions of an employee and providing work that is appropriate to their skills and ambitions, might therefore be sufficient to help this group break into the labour market.

The Employment Service would have the resources to purchase directly such temporary job placements in the public and private sectors. These placements would be full-time and in general last for more than six months. The NESF estimated that no more than ten thousand placements would be required annually and that this should be publicly funded.

Demand-Side Measures

Even allowing for the positive effects of enhancing the quality of labour supply of the long-term unemployed and those at risk of becoming so, the NESF recognised that there would not be enough jobs available in the foreseeable future to deal with the very large number of people who are now long-term unemployed. Therefore it recommended that the Employment Service should take direct action to provide employment opportunities through a number of demand-side measures. These would include offering, as a 'last resort', to the long-term unemployed and/or their adult dependants a range of full and part-time longer-duration, contract-type employment opportunities in the public and voluntary sectors.

Contracts ranging from one to three years would be offered to those who have been continuously unemployed for a minimum of a year and, in limited circumstances, to those having difficulty in finding employment or experiencing recurring unemployment. As in the case of the employment experience option mentioned above, these contracts would be in a real employment setting, with the same status, wages and working conditions as an employee. The Employment Service would continue to liaise with the people availing of this option to assist them to find permanent jobs elsewhere in the economy.

The NESF also identified two other demand-side measures. First, there is the potential of the social economy to provide much-needed social services, thereby generating local job opportunities. Second, measures are needed to increase private sector demand for the skills of the long-term unemployed through continuing reform of the income tax and welfare systems (these issues will be dealt with in future Reports).

Critically, the NESF considered that its integrated package of proposals could be implemented within the Government's existing fiscal constraints. Thus, while the annual running costs of the Employment Service were estimated at an additional £30 million when fully operational with registration of 100,000 clients, all the other proposals could be implemented by a more creative and innovative use of existing resources.

Most important, this package of proposals was unanimously agreed on by all Forum members. Subsequently, a Government Task Force was established to examine the Forum's proposals; their first Interim Report was published in February of this year. This concentrated on developing a practical approach to the delivery of the Local Employment Service aspect of the Forum's Report. The Government has now decided to establish this Service initially in fourteen areas, with a specific budget allocation for this purpose. Thereafter the Service will be expanded throughout the country. At the end of this year the Task Force will report on the rest of the Forum's proposals.

Conclusion

The challenge facing the whole island of Ireland is to achieve the promise of the high ideals of equality and solidarity in an increasingly divided society. The challenge of creating that society cannot and should not be the burden of any one sector, even government. North and South have much to learn from sharing experiences on policy initiatives in this area. We are dependent too on business, at a national and international level, to revitalise a notion of corporate civic responsibility that can merge the twin goals of doing well and doing good. The relationship between business and society is interdependent, the well-being and prosperity of one affecting the well-being and prosperity of the other. There are many Irish and American businesses that have an honourable record in their civic responsibilities. But in the context of a new peace, that moment when, in the words of Séamus Heaney, hope and history rhyme, there is scope for an imaginative leap.

If we fail to respond creatively to this challenge of long-term unemployment, history will judge us harshly. According to Edmund Burke, each successive generation possesses their society's commonwealth only as temporary possessors and life-renters. Society, he said, is not a partnership in things of a temporary and expedient nature. Instead it is a partnership in every virtue and in all perfection, a partnership between those who are living, those who are dead, and those who are to be born. That kind of partnership now seems particularly relevant after twenty-five years of violence. What will be asked by future generations is how well all of us created that partnership, whether in shaping the new island of Ireland, in the words of W. B. Yeats, we could 'hold reality and justice in a single vision.'

Part 6

Improving the Island's Infrastructure

15 Transport: A Hard Road Ahead

Austin Smyth

According to an analysis undertaken by the author in 1989, the number of passengers travelling by rail between Belfast and Dublin, the two main population centres on the island of Ireland, was no more than 25 per cent of what would be expected between two cities of comparable size and level of prosperity within one state (see table 1). Even with the cessation of violence and the very significant rise in cross-border travel recently, it is evident that the political boundary between Northern Ireland and the Republic continues to dampen interaction between the North and the South.

Table 1: Travel propensity, 1987/88.

City pair	Index of propensity* for travel
Dublin–Cork	100
Dublin–Waterford	52
Dublin–Belfast	13

*Derives from the application of the gravity model for trip distribution
 estimation.
Source: Author's calculations.

With the growing integration of the European Union—and assuming peace holds—it can be expected that the demand for travel and the shipment of goods will continue to rise, although probably at a lower rate of growth than that experienced in the immediate aftermath of the ceasefires in Northern Ireland. This raises certain fundamental questions for the transport sector:

- Is the availability of cross-border links adequate for existing or projected demand?

- Is there an economic case for further improvements to cross-border transport?
- If so, what are the barriers, if any, to the realisation of such improvements?
- Are there examples of current or historical good practice in the planning and operation of cross-border transport?
- What new options are there in the provision of either infrastructure or services to meet any demands that might be made of the transport system?

Accordingly, the remainder of this chapter consists of:

(*a*) an overview of transport infrastructure and services, with particular reference to cross-border connections;

(*b*) an examination of the historical implications of the border for the quality of infrastructure and level of service currently offered on cross-border links;

(*c*) consideration of the role of the European Union in the development of transport in Ireland;

(*d*) a consideration of the case for improvements to cross-border transport;

(*e*) identification of potential measures that would lead to increased cost-effectiveness in the planning of cross-border transport;

(*f*) definition of potential options for reform of the regulations and control frameworks.

Overview of Transport Facilities

The geographical features of Ireland, both natural and human-made, create conditions not conducive to the provision of good levels of accessibility, either internally or externally. The island location off an island off the continent of Europe produces total dependence on sea and air transport for external links, with all the 'break of bulk', transhipment and related penalties associated with such a position. Internally the small total population and low population density throughout much of the island reduce the prospects for the cost-effective development of infrastructure and the provision of viable high-quality public transport services. Moreover, major historical events, including the Famine of the mid-nineteenth century and partition, have helped to create additional problems for transport which continue down to the present day.

Nevertheless, while in general such characteristics are common to both Northern Ireland and the Republic, differences of geography, historical conditions and political and economic forces have resulted in significant divergence in the current state of transport North and South.

I plan to review separately current levels of infrastructure and service endowment for external links and internal connections to the island. Inevitably, given the focus of this book, particular attention will be given to the latter, even though the development of external transport, both historically and in the future, has been and will continue to be greatly influenced by the degree of co-operation and harmonisation in the field of transport policy between the Republic and Northern Ireland.

By far the dominant mode of transport in both Northern Ireland and the Republic is road transport. The South is serviced by a network of more than 92,000 kilometres of road, while the North contains some 24,000 kilometres. This is equivalent to 1.33 and 1.70 kilometres per square kilometre, respectively, or more than 26 and 15 kilometres per thousand head of population, respectively. Placed in the context of the European Union, these figures would not suggest that either part of the island is poorly endowed with road infrastructure (table 2). Indeed, in the case of the Republic the figure per 1,000 population is twice the EU average, although it is some 25 per cent below the average based on an areal measure.

The European Commission has proposed a composite index incorporating a weighted average for both population and area. On this basis the Republic is still 44 per cent better endowed than the EU average. On all indicators, it also enjoys a supply of road space at least three times greater than Greece and Spain, double that of Portugal in terms of the areal indicator, and up to five times their supply in terms of population served. Likewise Northern Ireland performs favourably compared with all other 'objective 1' (economically disadvantaged) areas of Europe—except the Republic—and to the EU average.

These are somewhat crude measures, and by common consent (at least until recently) the road infrastructure in the Republic was seen as inferior to Northern Ireland and a major handicap to wealth creation. Such views reflect not so much the overall supply of road space but rather the quality of the network, including standards of maintenance. These variations between the North and South can be traced to the very large difference in investment in the road network in favour of Northern Ireland right up to the late 1970s or early 1980s. This encompassed not only new construction but also maintenance levels. However, in relation to cross-border connections the disparity in quality was not so great in design capacity, even if the maintenance differential was readily apparent to even the casual observer.

There are some 180 cross-border roads, of which until recently just over one in ten were officially designated 'approved crossing-points', monitored by the customs authorities on both sides of the border. However, no road link even today exceeds the relevant single-carriageway two-lane design standards prevailing in Northern Ireland and the Republic.

Table 2: Transport infrastructure endowment, European Union, 1990

	Road surface per km²	Road surface per 1,000 inhabitants	Composite indicator	Rail lines per km²	Rail lines per 1,000 inhabitants	Composite indicator
EC average	100	100	100	100	100	100
Northern Ireland	95	122	109	45	56	51
Republic	76	211	144	51	145	98
Greece	23	45	34	34	65	49
Portugal	42	58	50	63	87	78
Spain	23	43	33	51	97	74

Source: CEC (1995); Department of Environment (NI) transport statistics—various.

The railway system in the Republic consists of some 1,870 kilometres, while the network in Northern Ireland totals just under 340 kilometres. On a population basis these translate to approximately 0.54 and 0.21 kilometres per 1,000 population, respectively, or 0.027 and 0.024 kilometres per square kilometre. On a population basis the figure for the Republic represents the most generous provision in the EU (45 per cent greater than the EU average), while Northern Ireland's performance is close to the bottom of the EU league table. On an areal basis, however, the Republic's rail network is some 50 per cent below the EU average, a figure only a little higher than that of the North.

Once again combining the two indicators reveals a performance by the Republic well in advance of all other objective 1 areas and in line with the EU average. The figures for the UK as a whole are within a few per cent of those for the Republic. On the other hand, the performance of Northern Ireland puts it at the bottom of the EU league table with Greece. This apparent rather good performance by the Republic must be tempered when quality of service levels, including speeds and frequency, are taken into account compared with many of the wealthier countries of the EU.

Notwithstanding the favourable performance of the Republic in relation to rail transport, today there is only one cross-border connection, a feature that can be traced to policy on railways in Northern Ireland during the 1950s and 1960s.

Historically relatively little use was made of internal waterways for the transport of goods or people in Ireland. Today no commercial freight or public passenger services are operated on what remains of the canal network, although one cross-border canal was recently reopened for leisure traffic.

While air transport has exhibited remarkable growth in recent years, this has been almost entirely for external travel. Within the Republic the 1980s witnessed the development of an embryonic network of regional air services, which included two cross-border links to Londonderry and Belfast (City) airports. In neither case did the routes survive, a feature common to many domestic services within the Republic. However, a new service linking Londonderry with Dublin via Belfast was scheduled to start in the spring of 1995.

The geography of Ireland dictates total dependence on air and sea modes for external transport. However, important trends and changes can be noted. For air and sea, including both freight and passenger traffic, there has been a continuing upward trend in demand. While the dominance of sea continues to be eroded, particularly since the late 1970s and early 1980s, sea remains by far the most important form of transport for freight, both in volume and value. In the 1970s air transport overtook sea as the principal mode for passenger travel, a trend that gathered pace with the liberalisation of air transport and the collapse of 'classic' passenger traffic by ferry and train.

The dominant ports in Ireland—Belfast, Dublin, Larne, Dún Laoghaire,

Rosslare, Waterford, Cork, and Warrenpoint—are all on the east or south coasts. There is evidence of keen competition between Belfast and Larne on the one hand and Dublin and Dún Laoghaire on the other. Their performance is in part attributed to the quality of access offered by internal access routes in Northern Ireland and the Republic as well as to and from British west-coast ports and in part to the relative efficiency of the ports and road haulage industry north and south of the border. Port costs are markedly less for the Northern ports than for their Southern counterparts, a reason, say some commentators, why 'natural' traffic has leaked through ports in the Republic to their competition north of the border.

In the case of air transport, Northern Ireland is served by two substantial airports, Belfast International and Belfast City, as well as the very much smaller City of Derry Airport. The Republic's airports are dominated by Dublin, whose total of six million passengers a year exceeds that of all other airports in the state put together and which caters for almost double the combined throughput of Belfast International and Belfast City airports. This is reflected in an extensive network of air services to European destinations as well as to the eastern seaboard of the United States.

The Impact of the Border on the Development of Transport

The variations between Northern Ireland and the Republic in infrastructure endowment or service provision are not merely the product of economic, demographic or geographical differences. Significant differences in government policy north and south of the border, including differing emphasis between modes and levels of investment, have helped to reinforce divergence over the last three-quarters of a century. The creation of the two states in 1921 brought in its wake significant effects on cross-border transport, directly in the form of divergence in policy on transport at state-level infrastructure and service and indirectly through changes in trade and commerce and the organisation of administrative functions.

The direct effects attributable to the creation of the border manifest themselves today in the orientation and connectivity of the internal transport system. Historically the road network of Ireland in the nineteenth century focused on Dublin, radiating out in a southern, western and northern direction (see fig. 1). Overlaying this was a second major focus based on Belfast, which crisscrossed the routes emanating from Dublin in Counties Armagh, Monaghan, Tyrone, and Fermanagh. The effect of partition was to bring about a reorientation in the importance of corridors in favour of west-east movements over north-south flows. This was further enforced by the investment programmes north and south of the border but particularly in Northern Ireland during the 1960s with the development of the M1 and M2

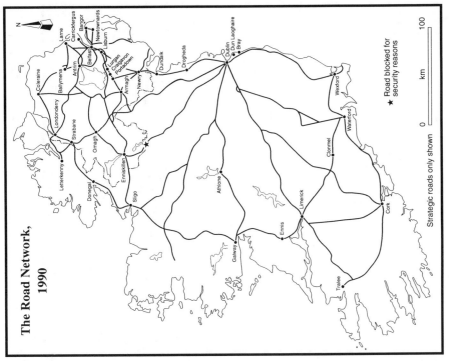

Fig. 2

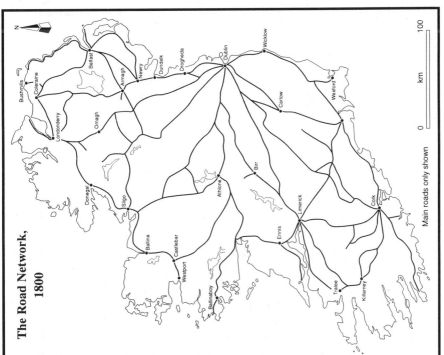

Fig. 1

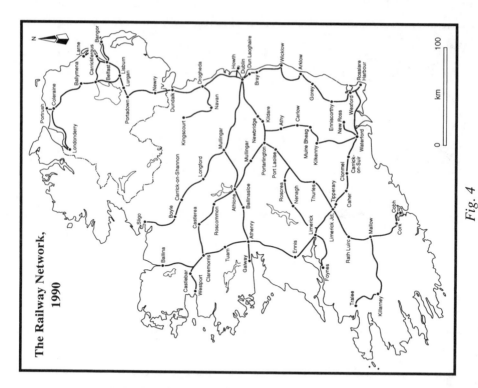

The Railway Network, 1990

Fig. 4

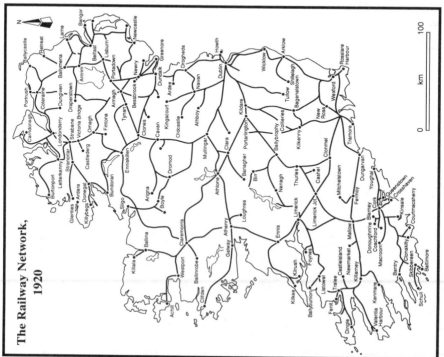

The Railway Network, 1920

Fig. 3

corridors and improvements to their linking A class roads (see fig. 2). The effect is manifest today, with indirect routings avoiding Northern Ireland proposed under the two most recent National Development Plans in the Republic to link Donegal with the midlands and Dublin area.

Today there are some 177 'viable' cross-border roads, in addition to some 50 lanes and tracks. Until the recent withdrawal of customs controls with the culmination of the '1992 process' throughout the European Community, only some 20 roads were 'approved' crossing-points. Because of the security situation in Northern Ireland since 1969, a significant number of these roads and tracks were physically closed to traffic. However, with the initiation of the ceasefires in Northern Ireland a large programme of reinstatement of these roads (and tracks) is now under way (table 3). This will involve the rebuilding or reinstatement of 104 crossings. By April 1995 a total of 80 schemes had been completed, 12 were under way, and a further 12 were at the planning stage.

In the case of rail transport, the current significant differences in infrastructure provision in Northern Ireland and the Republic represent a complete reversal of the position before 1921 (see figs 3 and 4). While this reflects a more benign attitude to railways and their financial liabilities in the Republic, the divergent policies manifested themselves in their most extreme form in relation to cross-border links. From a peak of some twenty connections across the border in 1922, today only one remains. The effect of a more financially oriented policy on railways in Northern Ireland, resulting in the withdrawal of almost all railways in Counties Down, Armagh, Tyrone, Fermanagh, and Londonderry, coupled with the massive road building programme there and the dampening effect of the border on traffic, forced a complete withdrawal of rail facilities from Counties Monaghan, Cavan, Leitrim, and Donegal, the only counties in the Republic now completely bereft of rail transport.

Moreover, the public road transport that replaced the railways throughout much of rural Ireland exhibits significant gaps in the network and reduced connectivity adjacent to the border, even though—in contrast to the road network—many of the through express coach services between Donegal and Dublin transit Northern Ireland rather than being diverted around Counties Tyrone and Fermanagh.

The effect of the border on infrastructure is one thing; equally marked has been the impact on demand for cross-border movement and consequently the supply of public transport services, particularly for longer-distance movement. Demand for inter-city travel is between 15 and 25 per cent of what would be expected for journeys entirely within either state. This is reflected in a relatively low frequency of service offered on cross-border services, after allowance is made for the population of the urban areas served.

Table 3: Cross-border connections, closures, and reinstatement programme

Classification (NI)	Number	Number closed for security reasons (1993)	Reinstatement (April 1995) Completed—In progress—Planned
Roads:			
A class	22	1	
B class	14	5	
Unclassified	141[3]	55	
Subtotal	177	61	
Tracks/lanes	48[4]	27	
Non-road features	4[5]	4	
Total	229	92[1] (104[2])	80—12—12

[1] Actual closures.
[2] Subject to closure order.
[3] Excludes 3 deemed 'non-viable' crossings.
[4] Excludes 32 deemed 'non-viable' crossings.
[5] Excludes 27 deemed 'non-viable' crossings.
Source: Northern Ireland Office.

As noted below, at a *strategic* level the low levels of cross-border travel can be attributed to the quality of road and rail links *only to a limited extent.* Hartshorne in his seminal analysis of boundary disputes in inter-war Europe attributes only low levels of cultural and historical associations between Northern Ireland and the Republic and only a very modest socio-economic connection. Heslinga (1979) broadly concurs with this view.

More recently Fitzgerald et al. (1988) identified a very steep 'distance decay' effect associated with cross-border shopping (a 1 per cent change in distance led to a 0.72 per cent fall in shopping trips across the border). For example, the probability of a shopping trip being made by a resident of the Republic living more than thirty miles from the border is 16 per cent of that of someone living within five miles of the border. Moreover, some two-thirds of shopping trips originating in the South were to Northern Ireland destinations within a few miles of the border. The most important deterrent to cross-border shopping was the security situation in Northern Ireland.

Confirmation of the limited effect of transport links on propensity for travel is reaffirmed by consideration of the imbalance in cross-border shopping movements. For instance, while 12 per cent of the population of the Republic reported making shopping trips to the North during the last six months of 1986, the equivalent figure for Northern Ireland residents going south was 5 per cent. If transport was the major consideration in influencing the propensity for movement, such differences would not be expected.

In the case of freight, once again the propensity for movement appears to be significantly reduced. Indeed the Confederation of British Industry (NI) and the Irish Business and Employers' Confederation suggest that enhanced trade between North and South could quadruple, yielding £3 billion in value and leading to the creation of up to 75,000 jobs. However, a number of commentators have expressed scepticism about the potential for increased trade: Scott and O'Reilly (1992) suggest that the level of cross-border trade is in line with that experienced between other small European countries and their nearest neighbours.

Reference has already been made to the effect of historical policy differences north and south on the particular fortunes of cross-border rail services and, to a lesser extent, roads. Such differences and their implications for cross-border interaction extend to air and sea travel. Historically, sovereign states have tended to facilitate or promote the development of indigenous shipping and air transport services. These 'flag carriers' have until recently enjoyed considerable protection from competition through various bilateral agreements with other countries with which they provided direct connections. In the case of the island of Ireland, therefore, it is not unexpected to find that while Northern Ireland has depended historically almost entirely

Table 4: Transport operational programmes: projected and actual expenditure, 1989–93, and projected expenditure, 1994–99

	Northern Ireland		Republic	
	Projected (1989 prices)	Outturn (1993 prices)	Projected (1989 prices)	Outturn (1993 prices)
All transport: Expenditure, 1989–93 (million ECUs)	211	254	1,064	1,325
	%	%	%	%
Rail	17.5	15.4	4.4[1]	n.a.
Roads	10.5	7.4	75.2	n.a.
Ports	45.0	57.4	8.2	n.a.
Airports	26.0	19.0	11.5	n.a.
Buses	0	0.8	n.a.	n.a.
All transport: Expenditure, 1994–99	(1994 prices) 208		(1994 prices) 3229	
%EU	67		58[2]	

[1] Relates to all public transport

[2] Based on National Development Plan estimates, Republic

Sources: Department of Environment (NI), 1989, 1993; Irish Government, 1993, 1994; Irish Government and Commission of European Communities, 1990; NI Structural Funds Plan, 1994.

on UK-registered carriers and operators, strategic and economic interests led to the formation of state-owned airlines and shipping companies in the Republic.

In both sectors, however, the increasing liberalisation of transport through the European Commission '1992 process' has placed the Republic's carriers under particular pressure, reflecting the small size of their indigenous markets. The effect typically has been to produce lower tariff levels for both shipping and air transport to and from Northern Ireland, even though for both air and sea services the Republic enjoys a more extensive network of services, something that cannot entirely be attributed to the greater size of the population south of the border.

The Role of the EU in the Financing of Developments in Transport

Notwithstanding the increasing harmonisation in regional development and transport policies at a European level, differences in policy priorities in Northern Ireland and the Republic remain. Together with significant divergence in funding availability since the mid to late 1980s in favour of the Republic, this continues to have important consequences for cross-border transport.

While up to the 1970s Northern Ireland spent significantly more on its internal road infrastructure than the Republic, the doubling of EC Structural Funds under the 1987 Single European Act and the pursuit of the 1992 process brought about a transformation in the scale of finance available for transport in the Republic in the late 1980s. For instance, between 1989 and 1993 the Republic planned to spend 1,064 million ECUs on transport, while the Northern authorities allocated 211 million ECUs, both under their respective EC Operational Programmes (table 4).

Despite this imbalance in the availability of funding, both the emphasis and the allocation of funds to cross-border projects were substantially greater in the Northern Ireland Transport Operational Programme (1989–93) than in its Southern counterpart, a particularly noteworthy example being the explicit commitment from the Northern Ireland authorities to the Belfast–Dublin rail upgrading project as part of the Trans-European Network Development Programme and the absence of any reciprocating commitment in the Republic's original Operational Programme on Peripherality (1989–93).

As far as transport is concerned, under the 1994–99 programmes the disparity has been increased as the overall funding received by the Republic from EU Structural Funds and the Cohesion Fund has risen to some 1,500 million ECUs, while in Northern Ireland the allocation to transport has been reduced to 139 million ECUs. In the 1994–99 programme the difference in

EU funding for transport between North and South, a ratio of more than 10 to 1 in favour of the Republic, makes it difficult to judge the relative priority given to cross-border projects in each state. No breakdown by transport sector or mode or even between external and internal links is provided in the Northern Ireland Transport Operational Programme (1994–99), perhaps reflecting the UK government's successfully pressed case for subsidiarity in the implementation of policy. Nevertheless, taking into account necessary carry-overs of financial commitments from the last programme, together with the presentation emphasis of the document, it would appear that a greater proportion of funding will go to projects with an explicitly cross-border basis than will be the case for the Republic.

The balance in investment allocated to external versus internal transport and between modes of transport should to a large extent be determined by systematic investment appraisal and project assessment. While, however, there are similarities in approach between sectors of the industry eligible for funding support and between transport north and south of the border, variations in the techniques, investment criteria and rigour of their application have produced and continue to produce anomalies, inconsistencies and misallocation of public sector resources in both Northern Ireland and the Republic. These factors tend to inhibit the implementation of cross-border projects in particular. Moreover, in Northern Ireland the long-standing question marks placed against the true 'additionality' of Structural Funds secured from the European Commission would appear to have skewed the selection of projects towards those schemes for which it would be less likely that public expenditure from the Northern Ireland block grant could be effectively clawed back by the Treasury in London. In particular, it would appear that such considerations may have adversely affected expenditure on entirely domestic road schemes within Northern Ireland.

Cross-Border Transport: the Case for Improved Infrastructure and Services?

It can be argued that overall the quality of cross-border transport is a product of recent historical levels of cross-border commercial, tourist, and VFR (visiting friends and relations) traffic. However, differences in internal policy priorities for transport North and South pursued over many years have combined to produce remarkable differences in the quality of infrastructure on each side of the border. Moreover, such differences in approach have tended to slow down the pace of improvement and harmonisation of standards. This state of affairs is seen in its most extreme in the railway system, where a policy in favour of road development in Northern Ireland during the 1960s—with the abandonment of much of the network in the south and west—brought about the inevitable abandonment of all lines in the border counties that crossed into Northern Ireland, with the single exception of the Belfast–Dublin route.

It is reasonable to conclude, therefore, that the supply of transport has tended to respond to demand, although in certain cases reductions in supply have tended to further dampen potential levels of demand. In addition, cross-border road closures for security reasons have undoubtedly had localised effects on cross-border activity.

With the growing integration of the EU generally, including linkages between Northern Ireland and the Republic—reinforced by the ceasefires—significant increases in demand for cross-border transport facilities can be expected. Already the rapid recovery of rail traffic—down 50 per cent between 1968/69 and the mid-1970s and now back to pre-'Troubles' levels—is posing capacity problems for the two state-owned railway companies. It is noteworthy that as recently as 1988 it was declared policy to reduce to a single track sections of the Belfast–Dublin cross-border line, with traffic little more than two-thirds of that today.

If repeated for cross-border transport overall, such significant changes in demand could pose serious questions for the current adequacy of key cross-border roads.

The important question, therefore, is what is the potential demand for cross-border trade and passenger travel. Even among economists and those involved in business there is wide disagreement on the scale of this potential. For transport economists and planners, no adequate analytical models at present exist. However, it would be true to say that were they to exist, cross-border transport models would point to the existence of very large increases in demand *if transport and accessibility parameters were the only determinants of traffic levels.* Such levels of demand if realised would overwhelm existing road infrastructure, particularly in the Belfast–Dublin 'corridor', while the current rail upgrading project would require further increases in capacity and could well justify further enhancement in terms of reduced travel times. In such circumstances, transport would constrain levels of economic development attributable to cross-border activity.

However, the other side to this argument is that any demonstrable or even perceived deficiencies in the existing or near programmed infrastructure are of limited significance in explaining current levels of cross-border economic activity. To answer the more fundamental question of why cross-border activity is so relatively low goes beyond the remit of this chapter. It would be too easy to attribute this to any marked extent to the current state of transport. Improvements to transport generally can therefore be regarded as facilitating increased cross-border activity but will not guarantee or produce it. At local level the reinstatement of the closed cross-border roads will enable previous patterns of activity to be restored, with potentially additional local benefits in the tourism and agricultural sectors.

If the barriers to such exchange of goods and movements of people do begin to come down, then in the medium to longer term it is possible to envisage implications for road development in strategic corridors, pressure for future enhancement of the rail link over that planned, and enhanced viability for regional and commuter air services between Dublin and the north-west or even a spinal cord of routes linking City of Derry and Belfast International or City Airports with those at Dublin, Cork, and Shannon. Regular direct services from Northern Ireland beyond Dublin would be unlikely. However, schedules could be developed that would make use of existing feeder services from the Republic's regional and other main airports to Dublin. With the growing liberalisation of air transport in the EU, it is also possible to envisage substantial increases in international air traffic from Northern Ireland using Dublin or Shannon as a hub as an alternative to airports such as Manchester and Birmingham.

An analogous situation could arise in sea transport, where there is already evidence of considerable amounts of Republic-to-Britain traffic favouring Northern Ireland ports rather than facilities in the Republic. In sea transport and indeed road haulage an all-island market for services is already evident, something that does not yet apply in air transport.

Cross-Border Transport: the Case for Technical Harmonisation and Integrated Planning?

Reference has already been made to the effect of differences in policy priorities on infrastructure quality north and south of the border and in particular on the rate of development or rationalisation of cross-border infrastructure and public transport services. This is reinforced by the effect that all political boundaries have on the propensity for movement across them.

The fact that the investment appraisal techniques at present in use make no allowance for the blocking effect of borders reduces the likelihood of cross-border schemes achieving a demonstrable rate of return that meets the criteria set by either state. Moreover, the pursuit of cross-border projects as two separate entities reduces the viability of improvement schemes by failing to exploit the synergy that may obtain. Such an approach may also promote duplication of investment and a failure to exploit potential economies of scale. This also applies to domestic infrastructure improvements either side of the border, where, given a more co-ordinated approach to planning, greater cost-effectiveness in the use of EU funding might be achieved.

Within the context of cross-border planning in the European Union the issue of differences in design standards, analytical and investment appraisal procedures and domestic policy priorities can be shown to have inhibited the development of cross-border infrastructure, not only in Ireland but elsewhere in Europe. A review of such issues in the context of Ireland might yield an insight into harmonisation measures that could be introduced to expedite projects.

Accordingly, the planning and implementation of cross-border transport infrastructure and service improvements in all sectors of industry on a cross-border basis is likely to enhance the viability of the schemes, reduce the costs of implementation, and increase the pace of progress towards completion. This is well illustrated by a comparison of the progress made in upgrading the Belfast–Dublin road and rail links. The latter was faced with possible closure in 1986, a policy of reducing to a single track much of the route between Portadown and Dundalk thereafter up to 1989, and now completion of a multi-million pound scheme by late 1996. Certainly without planning on a complete route basis, a policy of retrenchment would possibly have continued.

In the case of the road link, domestic considerations have prevailed. While these have afforded some benefit to cross-border travellers, the Newry–Dundalk section remains a bone of contention, not only because of differences in appraisal techniques, design standards and funding but also because of the absence of any agreement on the apportioning of the costs to the two governments. In this case, unlike that of the rail project, no joint team of planners or engineers to advance the scheme has been set up. An announcement was made in Summer 1995 that a new study of this section would be undertaken.

The setting up of project-specific dedicated task forces or supranational agencies needs to be reviewed from the point of view of their potential beneficial impact on progress on cross-border infrastructure and the co-ordination of investment in transport generally. Experience in other parts of the economy on the island of Ireland as well as the transport sector in other parts of the EU could provide practical lessons relating to the cost-effectiveness of such bodies.

Notwithstanding the importance attached by the United Kingdom government to the issues of sovereignty and subsidiarity, the role of the EU in fostering co-operation between North and South in the areas of transport cannot easily be overstated. The significance of EU funding for peripheral areas and particularly for the Republic means that there is increasing pressure for transport strategies in such areas to be compatible with and founded on an overall EU perspective. They must also be compatible with EU policies on the environment and social policy as well as regional development. However, the promotion of compatibility across the EU's internal borders also demands consistency in the allocation of funding, as the level of finance available has an important bearing on design and investment appraisal procedures and criteria.

In recent years there has been a considerable level of investment in transport infrastructure in the Republic, which has not been matched in Northern Ireland. While to some extent this could be regarded as redressing past imbalances in favour of investment in the North, the negotiation process at the European Commission or state level, together with the perceived needs from a Brussels perspective of Northern Ireland and the Republic, should be reviewed to establish whether the allocation of funds, including both the Structural Funds and the Cohesion Fund, has been equitable and whether they have led to distortions in the rate of development of transport systems in the two parts of the island. The implications of the Cohesion Fund, which does not extend to Northern Ireland, seems particularly relevant, given that the Republic's level of prosperity, in terms of Gross Domestic Product per head, is now on a par with Northern Ireland and is projected to overtake the North in this respect.

Cross-Border Transport: Some Options for Reform of the Regulatory and Control Frameworks and Planning

Thus far we have been primarily concerned with infrastructure. However, potential measures that could improve the quality of cross-border transport encompass not only technology and infrastructure but also the regulation and control of the industry. Issues of privatisation, market liberalisation and regulation and state subventions to transport operators are relevant. EU legislation for instance, provides access by competing organisations to operate international rail services. Clearly this could be of particular relevance to the island of Ireland. An initial step could be the creation of a single state-owned company to operate the upgraded Belfast–Dublin service after 1996. The cost savings achieved in the implementation of this scheme by the formation of a joint team from both North and South are well recognised by both governments A franchise arrangement to operate the service could also be offered to the private sector.

There are a number of local precedents for such a joint company. In 1953 the governments of the Republic and Northern Ireland set up a joint company, the Great Northern Railway (GNR), to run all the services of the former Great

Northern Railway (Ireland). Born out of financial difficulties faced by the private-sector GNR, this operated until 1958, by which time policy divergence on railways North and South had produced unsustainable tensions between the two governments, and the GNR Board was dissolved that year.

The increasing harmonisation of policy on transport between Northern Ireland and the Republic, and on rail in particular, in part brought about by the influence of the EU, would make such tensions much less likely than during the 1950s. Again based on EU practice, the development of a competitive cross-border bus market through the joint licensing of such routes by the authorities North and South could be examined to determine the cost-effectiveness of such a policy.

While road hauliers based in Northern Ireland have a significant share of the international road freight traffic originating in the Republic, hauliers from the Republic achieve a limited share of the market. An all-Ireland market in road haulage, the complete implementation of which will emerge with cabotage in the EU in 1998, should produce opportunities for economies of scale; in turn this could produce changes in market shares of haulage firms, North and South, and should produce reductions in costs to customers. The effect of such an all-island market will also depend upon harmonisation of taxation applied to the haulage industry and the competitive response of firms on either side of the border.

Conclusions

Overall the quality of cross-border transport is a product of recent historical levels of cross-border commercial, tourist and VFR traffic. For longer-distance travel these levels are typically less than 25 per cent of what would be expected from a completely integrated society and economy. However, transport has played little part in the dampening of demand for cross-border transport, with perhaps the single exception of the cross-border railway system, which was almost entirely closed down because of the policy of internal closures within Northern Ireland in the 1950s and early 1960s.

The creation of the border also brought about a reorientation of the road networks, emphasising east-west movements at the expense of north-south corridors, partly in a response to changes in the spatial pattern of demand and partly because of the very large investment in such roads in Northern Ireland from the early 1960s. However, the coverage provided by the road systems in Ireland is not poor by EU standards and is very much superior to that of the other peripheral countries enjoying objective 1 status.

The EU has helped to bring about a degree of harmonisation in transport policy on both sides of the border, but the very large imbalance in funding in favour of the South raises certain fundamental questions about fairness in the allocation of resources as well as more long-term questions about the cost-effectiveness of current plans. For the future, the growing integration of the EU, including Northern Ireland and the Republic, and the assumption that peace will prevail are likely to create particular pressures on key cross-border transport links in the medium to longer term.

In the short to medium term it would appear that there may be potential cost savings and other benefits to be achieved from planning strategic transport links on an integrated all-island basis, either through project-specific dedicated task forces or supranational agencies. At an operational level, potential benefits might be realised by bringing forward the promotion of all-island markets in freight and road passenger transport as well as by the creation of a single company to run the upgraded cross-border rail service. For these various examples, precedents dating from the 1950s already exist, including agreement between the Stormont government and Dáil Éireann on the setting up of the GNR Board and more recently between the two state-owned railway companies in their development of the current cross-border rail investment programme.

Further Reading

Baker, M., *Irish Railways since 1916,* Shepperton: Allan 1972.

Colby, C. (ed.), *Aspects of International Relations,* Chicago: Geographic University of Chicago 1938.

Department of the Environment (NI), *Transportation Programme, Northern Ireland, 1989–1993,* Belfast: HMSO 1989.

Department of the Environment (NI), *Transportation Programme, Northern Ireland, 1994–1999,* Belfast: HMSO 1993.

Dudley Edwards, Ruth, *An Atlas of Irish History* (2nd edition), London: Routledge 1991.

European Commission, *Competitiveness and Cohesion in the Regions: Fifth Periodic Report on the Social and Economic Situation and Development of the Regions in the Community,* Brussels: European Commission.

Fitzgerald, J., T. Quinn, and B. Whelan, *An Analysis of Cross-Border Shopping* (Paper 137), Dublin: Economic and Social Research Institute 1989.

Government of Ireland, *National Development Plan, 1994–1999,* Dublin: Stationery Office 1993.

Government of Ireland, *Operational Programme for Transport, 1994–1999,* Dublin: Stationery Office 1994.

Government of Ireland and Commission of the European Communities,

Operational Programme on Peripherality, Roads, and Other Transport Infrastructure, 1989–1993, Dublin: Stationery Office 1990.

Heslinga, M., *The Irish Border as a Cultural Divide,* Assen 1979.

Killen, J., and A. Smyth, 'Transportation' in R. Carter and A. Parker (eds.), *Ireland: Contemporary Perspectives on a Land and its People,* London: Routledge 1990.

Northern Ireland Structural Funds Plan, 1994–99, Belfast: HMSO.

Patterson, E., *The Great Northern Railway of Ireland,* Lingfield: Oakwood 1962.

Smyth, A., 'Development of Transport Strategies for Peripheral Areas of Europe' in Proceedings of Twenty-Second PTRC European Transport Forum, University of Warwick, September 1994.

Smyth, A., *Development of an Investment Strategy for Promotion of High-Speed Rail in Ireland: an Exercise in Joint Planning by two National Railways* (in press).

Smyth, A. and H. McGeehan, 'Missing Links: Inconsistencies in Investment Appraisal Criteria and their Implications for the Development of Trans-Frontier Infrastructure in the European Community' in Proceedings of the European Transport Planning Colloquium, Brussels, March 1992.

16 Telecommunications: Routes for the Information Superhighway

Gerry McAleavy and Gerard Parr

Telecommunications services, considered as infrastructure, differ radically from other basic services that support industrial productivity, such as transport, in that communication systems are as much a medium for public debate and exchange of ideas as they are a commercial utility. Indeed in the rapidly changing information-dependent society we inhabit today there is a close relationship between the ability of societies to facilitate the expression of new ideas and the generation of economic growth.

It is no small irony that telephone exchanges and cabling have been prime targets for destruction during periods of conflict. In his book *The Electronic Age: Telecommunication in Ireland,* Eamonn Hall has noted that 'the Anglo-Irish and civil wars had wrought havoc to the process of communication,' while the events of the past twenty-five years have resulted in a number of attacks on telephone exchanges in Northern Ireland. Dr Hall also records the view that the cutting of the trans-Atlantic cables at Valencia in 1922 was a factor that influenced the routing of TAT-1 (the first trans-Atlantic telephone cable) to Oban in Scotland rather than Ireland, suggesting that conflicts may have lasting effects in terms of economic development.

In the contemporary state the shaping of the telecommunications infrastructure and the accompanying regulatory structures is influenced by a complex web of governmental concerns. Of these the need for industrial and commercial development is but one issue to be weighed alongside the desire to maintain management control over the distribution of information resources and their content. Recent technological innovations mean that communications systems are no longer mere carriers of messages but are now central to the transformation of public discourse through the opening of new arenas for debate on a national and international basis (e.g. cable television, satellites, and desktop video conferencing). The synergy between personal and educational usage on the one hand and commercial usage of new communication systems, moreover, is illustrated by the 1993 Internet survey, which reported that there were 406,464 commercial 'host' computer systems, compared with 467,897 educational hosts and 93,456 governmental hosts. 'Competitive edge' is a key argument for soliciting funds in the US Congress for the National Research and Education Network—the foundation of the Internet. The fact that the Vice-President of the United States, Al Gore, is a leading advocate of the deployment of NREN demonstrates the need to have a major political figure driving and informing national policy in a technically literate manner.

In Ireland, North and South, the interrelationship between the industrial and interpersonal use of telecommunication services may be critical to the development of a culture and climate for economic development, particularly in rural areas.

The European Dimension

Telecommunication policies, North and South, are increasingly constructed within the framework of European Commission policies. The green paper *Towards a Dynamic European Economy* (1987) sets out the role of telecommunications as 'the basis of the future service economy,' noting the need to integrate national systems. It suggests that current statistics may underestimate 'by a considerable margin' the degree to which information-based services have grown, noting that up to 80 per cent of the cost of computers is made up of software and other services. It is estimated that by 2000 more than 60 per cent of EU employment will be 'information-related—and will therefore depend on telecommunications.'

Since it was claimed that the potential for exchanging services through telecommunications could offer a decisive increase in productivity for the whole economy, including manufacturing and agriculture, and that 'the telecommunications network is now developing into Europe's nervous system,' the implications for the entire Irish economic system, North and South, are considerable.

The green paper, meanwhile, goes further. It recognises that 'adequate telecommunications infrastructures and services are a sine qua non for the free expression and free flow of information in the Community in the future. The provision of telecommunications network infrastructure and tele-communications services will provide the conduit within which information can flow. The provision of information services and a free market for information content are indispensable requirements for putting tele-communications network infrastructures and telecommunications services to best uses.'

To gain maximum advantage from an effective infrastructure it is necessary to have widely accessible telecommunications services and a range of relevant industrial and commercial applications. The presence of these resources on their own, however, is not enough to ensure development: if coupled with an insensitive band of tariffs, the result may be to inhibit the uptake of the technology. Therefore it is imperative that the deployment of advanced infrastructure and services be complemented by the addition of attractive tariffs that will make it cost-effective to change traditional work practices within a particular organisation and enhance competitiveness in an ever-increasing global market.

Telecommunications Structures North and South

To promote the ideal of an integrated European telecommunications network, the EU has implemented a number of programmes designed to promote the development of advanced communications services to the peripheral regions, including Ireland, North and South. These programmes have included the Special Telecommunications Action for Regional Development (STAR) initiative and Télématique, intended for Europe's most economically disadvantaged regions. The implementation of these initiatives, allied to central government policies, has resulted in the development of a telecommunications infrastructure in the two regions that is extremely advanced, at least in terms of physical conduiting structures. Take, for example, the Northern Ireland STAR initiative (£7.5 million), which was integrated into British Telecom's £100 million modernisation programme and was completed in 1994. The development has given Northern Ireland one of the most advanced telecommunications infrastructures in the world (especially given its geographical coverage) by adopting optical fibre as the medium within the region and providing optical fibre links to Great Britain and the Republic. These links were potentially to open a host of new opportunities for computer-based industries offering Northern Ireland business a vital technological and marketing advantage for the single European market in 1992.

In the South, according to Eamonn Hall, Telecom Éireann has since 1984 adopted a policy of replacing co-axial cable with optical fibre on the main trunk routes and has co-operated with British Telecom in laying an optical cable between Portmarnock and Holyhead in 1988. An optical cable was laid between Wexford and Land's End and completed at the end of 1994, while the PTAT1-1 trans-Atlantic optical fibre cable was connected in 1989.

The significance of these developments can hardly be overstated. One result has been the development and provision of the integrated-services digital network (ISDN2), which can provide two channels each with a bandwidth of 64,000 bits per second, making possible the transmission of compressed video, voice, data and text to destinations in Ireland and abroad. At present ISDN2 is available from forty-four exchanges in Northern Ireland, and in recent months it has become widely available within the Telecom Éireann network. In addition, the two universities in Northern Ireland have upgraded the Joint Academic Network (JANET) communications system to SuperJANET, a high-bandwidth system currently capable of supporting 34 million bit/s data transfer (to be extended to 2.4 billion bit/s in the future), which will support the development of multimedia transfer and electronic data interchange (EDI) among the universities and associated learning communities. Moreover, the British government view is that SuperJANET, as a national superhighway, should not be monopolised by the academic community but rather should act as an enabler to encourage greater levels of technology transfer, innovation and diffusion of new concepts that could enhance job creation. Joint ventures between Telecom Éireann and AT&T or BT may well lead to similar developments in the Republic, which could result in parity of high-speed infrastructure between North and South.

There is, therefore, considerable potential for compatibility between the two telecommunications systems. There exists a formidable technological resource for encouraging best practice in industry to grasp the telematics challenge and for assisting rural areas in economic regeneration, expanding education and training capacities through distance learning, and creating new opportunities for public debate and communication between communities. For example, the European Open Learning for Cross-Cultural Education Network (ELNET) has 'involved the creation of a virtual European college allowing students and lecturers to communicate with each other electronically' and has demonstrated the potential both for cross-community understanding and the use of languages in business. The ACTOR project at the University of Ulster (sponsored by British Telecom and being implemented by the authors) is concerned with the use of ISDN2 communication systems to link vocational education colleges, North and South, to higher education in order to enhance training opportunities for communities in rural areas and to assist in the development of small and medium-sized enterprises.

The mere fact of the existence of a comprehensive telecommunications backbone, however, does not indicate either widespread awareness of the possibilities or any inevitability that economic development will take place, or that peripheral communities will experience benefits. What is needed now is a range of model applications that capture the attention and imagination of potential client groups and promote awareness of the technology available.

Market Opportunities and Obstacles

It is clear that the provision of information services is a major growth industry but that Irish companies will be required to operate in an increasingly competitive market. While consumers can note, through their daily purchasing experiences, the extent to which international companies have penetrated local markets, the consumption of information services is not easily visible, being carried out on behalf of the consumer by public libraries, government agencies, universities, and large corporations. It is unlikely, therefore, that there will be consumer resistance to international suppliers on the grounds of loyalty to a local product. Local companies may not be able to follow the traditional route of first developing a local market as a stepping stone to export markets, since we are rapidly moving towards a global information society.

Since small and medium-sized enterprises have traditionally tended to grow from a local market base, and development policies, both North and South, have often been underpinned by this assumption, it may well be time to rethink the governmental approach to enterprise in preparing SMEs in this sector for early participation in global markets. Equally, since 'enterprise skills' are becoming embedded in the education system, it will be important to reconsider whether present programmes are adequately preparing future entrepreneurs for a market where products may only be tradable through the use of advanced communications systems.

There is, furthermore, evidence that the returns from the recent investments in infrastructure have so far been poor in relation to the development of existing industries.

Investments in IT infrastructure in the remoter parts of Ireland, which have been heavily funded by EU programmes such as STAR, Télématique, and ORA, have so far produced few concrete signs of development. Research in Northern Ireland concluded that while STAR demonstration sites did successfully introduce information technologies to a large range of local companies, the percentage uptake of the new telecommunications services was quite low, especially for sectors such as textiles, clothing, and engineering. These findings are not encouraging for the prospects of promoting regional development of industry, particularly in rural and peripheral areas. It is reasonable to expect that the substantial investments should in any case have encouraged the growth of teleworking projects, providing 'back office' services to large companies through remote processing of administration.

The most recent findings from the Teleworker association, however, indicate that there are only four projects in Northern Ireland and thirteen in the Republic. Since the figures also show that there are four projects in the island of Stornoway in Scotland alone and thirty projects in Wales, it is clear that Ireland is lagging in this area. One reason for the lack of projects may be the failure to provide appropriate training. In Northern Ireland there are only two teleworking courses available, and neither is provided through any of the seventeen colleges of further education (one is provided at the Kinawley teleworking project in Enniskillen, and the other is at Springvale Training Ltd in the Belfast area).

Strategic Development

The evidence so far demonstrates the futility of hopes that the provision of broad-band communications infrastructure alone is sufficient to revitalise industry, restore competitiveness, and regenerate peripheral areas. While the poor results so far may be due to a wide range of factors, including lack of awareness of the potential of the technology, lack of capital, technophobia, absence of expertise and training, and the feeling that advanced communications systems are only for large corporations, there may also be a structural problem relating to the mismatch of system design and the needs of SMEs. It is of key importance, therefore, that policies are devised, in collaboration with a wide range of communities, industrialists, and stakeholders, to address the kinds of strategic infrastructure architecture that can provide cybernetic networks designed to serve problems and needs rather than require users to devise reasons for adopting technological systems. A significant barrier to this process is the absence of debate in the political or economic arena concerning the new communication systems, which tend to be viewed as technical rather than economic or social issues. In the United States, by contrast, organisations representing disadvantaged groups, such as the National Association for the Advancement of Colored People, have as a principal aim the provision of optical fibre technology to ghetto areas.

In Ireland the tradition of political dissent has tended historically to have an anti-technology stance, and this is reflected in modes of discourse where terms such as 'mechanistic' and 'robotic' have derogatory connotations. Equally the backgrounds of most established political figures are unlikely to have included any substantial technological education. While Ireland, North and South, continues to produce substantial numbers of graduates, technology is not one of the popular options. The Northern Ireland Economic Council has pointed out that Northern Ireland has the lowest proportion of students of any UK region studying science and technology subjects.

The crucial task for the future is to consider what processes might be appropriate to enable businesses and communities to articulate the purposes and aims that might be achieved through the new communication infrastructures. Consideration of the outcome of this process can provide the basis for the design of the kinds of communications architecture that can begin to address community and industrial needs.

A critical perspective, which is increasingly held, is that designers of communications systems use design methods that highlight technical aspects but ignore work implications, and that traditional methods of designing computing systems are not adequate when applied to the new communications technologies. Since organisations in Ireland will be importing many communication systems, there will be limitations with respect to the design parameters, but it is important to note that the software of many telecommunications products can be re-engineered, through the application programming interface. It will be important, both in responding to the needs of users and in valuing local identities and sense of ownership, to ensure that user interfaces are customised to fit a wide variety of needs. At a time when the Framework document is addressing the notion of embracing cultural and political difference, it would be ironic if the adoption of common policies in relation to communications systems were to lead to the insidious imposition of normative values through the mistaken notion that systems design is a value-free process.

The concerns of the Government in the Republic on the issue of cultural identity and the media are raised in the draft green paper by Michael D. Higgins, Minister for the Arts, Culture, and the Gaeltacht, which addresses the challenges posed by the interaction of local and global cultures. There is, however, the danger that any future engagement with these concerns would tend to focus on the highly visible media, such as television, video, and radio, while neglecting the potential of the particular forms of telecommunication to shape national and community identities. To take one example, the traditions, North and South, of the production of cultural artefacts (novels, dramas, poetry, and musical composition) can be enhanced and can contribute to economic development through the new technologies of electronic publishing and the provision of on-line data-bases, provided the opportunities are recognised and the technology is configured to appeal to this community of users.

When an appropriate architecture is in place it will be important to consider a model of change that is sensitive to the cultures and values that inform organisations and communities, while taking account of the need to ask users to confront current working practices in the light of the new possibilities offered by advanced communications systems. There are considerable risks for the less-protected members of the work force in adopting new forms of technology, particularly in the case of teleworking. Workers may find that changing the location of work from office to home may also entail a change in employment status, from being an employee to becoming self-employed, or social deregulation by technical means.

As a response to this process, two German academics cite the policies of the German Social Democratic Party, which they claim are based on 'concerted action' by an alliance of stakeholders, including the telecommunications industry, trade unions, consumer groups, and data protection officials, to develop a consensus about technical and regulatory changes. In the light of government policies on privatisation in recent years in the UK this may seem a rather utopian position. It should be noted, however, that an informal alliance has recently been formed consisting of British Telecom, the Communication Workers' Union, and the British Labour Party, to demand that BT be permitted to build a national network of high-capacity optical fibres.

Conclusion

The experience of telecommunications thus far in supporting economic development on both sides of the border indicates that the issues are considerably more complex than might be imagined by those whose vision is restricted to technical solutions. Put another way, there are no pure technical decisions to be made in this area: rather there is an urgent need for the development of policies on what particular configurations of communications facilities can best provide solutions to the problems faced by communities and businesses. There exists a real risk that the need for policy formulation in this area will not be perceived as a priority, especially given the existence of a high-level infrastructure in the form of advanced transmission and switching systems. It is crucial, however, that the notion of infrastructure be widened to include a consideration of the interaction of the social and economic issues if the potential of new communication technologies to regenerate rural areas and generally contribute to economic growth is to be realised.

In this respect the notion of difference between North and South may have creative possibilities for policy generation, given the opportunity for engagement between the recently privatised sector in the North and the state-controlled service in the South. Telecommunications, as an enabling technology, has a role to play as a provider of parity of access to financial, educational and scientific information on the global scale, making all borders transparent.

Part 7

Selling the Island

17 Tourism: A Product with Big Potential

Paul Tansey

The Nature of the Tourism Product

Tourism is a unique business. It is immobile and immovable. Unlike most other traded goods and services, it cannot be delivered to consumers in their local shopping centres or on their doorsteps: rather than the product travelling to the consumer, the consumer must travel to the product. The enjoyment or consumption of tourism can only take place at the location where it is made available. The delights of Donegal or the Glens of Antrim can be sampled only by being there.

This defining characteristic is the source of both the strengths and the weaknesses of tourism. On the credit side, it is the influx of tourists and the cash they carry that generates incomes and jobs, foreign exchange earnings and economic growth in the host economy. On the debit side, however, the location-specific nature of tourism ensures that if the destination is deemed dangerous, then tourists will stay away in droves.

Twenty-five years of violence flashed on television screens to homes across the world constituted the greatest negative advertising campaign ever mounted against Irish tourism. Moreover, it was not only the development of tourism in Northern Ireland that was stunted as a result: what economists term negative 'neighbourhood' or 'spill-over' effects ensured that tourist expansion in the Republic suffered also, at least until the mid-1980s.

If violence was the most significant, albeit unspoken, barrier to tourism growth for a quarter of a century, then peace is the antidote. Even in its most passive form, where peace is interpreted as no more than the absence of violence, its achievement removes the most significant obstacle to long-term tourism growth on the island of Ireland. A more positive interpretation of peace, with the emphasis placed on co-operation rather than on mere co-existence, could see tourism evolve into a major industry throughout the island of Ireland.

197

A New Framework for Agreement, the joint document prepared by the British and Irish governments, represents a step in the positive co-operation direction. For it points out: 'Both Governments consider that new institutions should be created to cater adequately for present and future political, social and economic inter-connections on the island of Ireland, enabling representatives of the main traditions, North and South, to enter agreed dynamic, new, co-operative and constructive relationships.'

Moreover, tourism neatly fits the criteria that the Framework document suggests would be within the executive competence of a North-South body: 'By way of illustration, it is intended that these proposals would include at the executive level a range of functions, clearly defined in scope, from within the following broad categories:

—sectors involving a natural or physical all-Ireland framework;

—EC programmes and initiatives;

—marketing and promotion activities abroad; and

—culture and heritage.'

The Tourism Industry's Potential

Assuming the continuance of peace and allowing for greater co-operation in marketing the island of Ireland abroad as a tourist destination, what of the market itself?

At the outset, it must be made clear that potential tourism expansion offers no panacea for the economic ills besetting Ireland, North and South. For a start, international tourism, and particularly European tourism, is now a mature business, with little scope for exponential growth rates. Growth in world tourism is decelerating, and Europe's share of the world market is declining. The pace of expansion in international tourism is forecast to average 3.8 per cent annually through the 1990s, while in Europe, tourist arrivals are expected to grow by 2.7 per cent each year.

In addition, Ireland will never command a position as a major tourism destination, and for one simple reason: the sun cannot be induced to shine for sufficiently long periods. In essence, Ireland's best hope is to carve out a successful niche in the total international tourism market.

Lest this sounds excessively pessimistic, the prospects for developing a successful niche for the Irish tourism product are good, and for the following reasons:

First, the international market for foreign holidays is becoming less monolithic, more fragmented. The days when sun, sand and sea alone could sell holidays are over.

Second, to some extent market fragmentation mirrors growing fears that excessive exposure to sunshine causes health problems, and particularly skin cancer.

Third, more diverse patterns of tourism reflect a degree of demand saturation on the part of consumers with established products. Ten successive years on the Costa del Sol and consumers are ready for something different.

Fourth, social costs, particularly time losses and congestion, are detracting from the original value of many established tourism products in traditional sunspot destinations.

Fifth and finally, institutional and economic changes are working to the advantage of the Irish tourism product. In Europe, working weeks are becoming shorter and holidays are growing longer. With the economy of the European Union now in the early stages of an upswing, advances in real disposable incomes are in prospect. These factors, together with the proximity of Ireland to the population centres of Europe, make the island an ideal and feasible location for short-break second holidays.

In summary, while Ireland can never hope to usurp the supremacy of sunspot destinations, real opportunities exist to capitalise on changes in consumer tastes, incomes, and leisure time. The development of a strong niche position in the international tourism market, while it would not solve endemic unemployment problems North or South, can make a concrete contribution both to raising incomes and to expanding employment.

But strong market niches are not automatic entitlements for small players in the big game of international tourism: they must first be created, then defended. Market niches are successful and defensible where they offer highly differentiated products, consistent and superior quality, and value for money.

Strengths of the Irish Tourism Product

In a diverse and increasingly differentiated international tourism market, Ireland possesses sufficient strengths to build and defend a profitable market niche. Paradoxically, the comparative advantages enjoyed by Irish tourism in the present are the legacy of economic failures in the past. The elements of Ireland's comparative advantage in tourism, which serves as the foundation for building competitive advantage, can be enumerated thus:

1. Ireland is empty. Sustained mass emigration over a century and a half, particularly from rural areas, has left the country denuded of people. Population densities North and South approximate more closely to the Scandinavian countries than to those of the European heartlands. In a literal sense, Ireland can offer foreign visitors a genuine opportunity to get away from it all. Moreover, the descendants of those who left in previous generations form a potential target market for tomorrow's tourists.

2. *Ireland is old.* Civilisation in Ireland stretches back to the third millennium BC. Each succeeding historical epoch has left its mark on the Irish mind as on the contours of the countryside. This provides a sound basis for developing both cultural and historic tourism products. For the past, too, is a foreign country.

3. *Ireland is green.* Ireland's largely agrarian economy was barely touched by the Industrial Revolution. Apart from the rise of Belfast in the nineteenth century, heavy industry bypassed the rest of the island. Ireland, then, is green in two senses: for in addition to great scenic beauty, the country—largely by default, it must be conceded—is environmentally friendly.

4. *Ireland is accessible.* Physical proximity to the high-income population centres of western Europe provides Ireland with the opportunity to mine a rich seam in international tourism.

These comparative advantages, and the differentiated tourism products they allow, are not automatic guarantors of competitive success, for only effective management and imaginative innovation can transform potential into performance.

Tourism in the Republic: a Case Study

Tourism performance in the Republic has been transformed over the past decade. After languishing for years in the long shadows cast by the Northern Ireland Troubles, tourism in the Republic struggled back to its feet in the second half of the 1980s. It was assisted by the buoyant economic conditions prevailing in the principal source markets for overseas tourism during this period. For expansion in real personal disposable incomes is the principal force driving the growth in international tourism.

Moreover, the economic boom in Britain, the United States and continental Europe coincided with a determined effort to deregulate international air fares. The high cost of gaining access to the Republic had for long constituted a major impediment to expanding the overseas tourism sector. Taken together with the deceleration in the rate of domestic inflation—consumer prices have not risen by more than 5 per cent annually since 1985—the Republic was edging its way towards price-competitiveness.

Thus, at one and the same time, foreign consumers' incomes were rising and the price of holidaying in the Republic was falling. The Irish tourism industry took off as a result.

Recent analysis by the *Economist* has charted the rapidity of the expansion in the Republic's tourism base. Of fifteen European countries surveyed, including the principal sunspot destinations, earnings from international tourism grew fastest in the Republic. Between 1980 and 1992, earnings from overseas tourism increased at an annual average rate in excess of 10 per cent, leaving the Republic first, ahead of Portugal and Sweden. Britain was placed thirteenth in this European tourism league.

The pace of overseas tourism growth in the Republic slowed in 1991 and checked in 1992, reflecting the reverberations of the Gulf War on the demand for international tourism and the onset of recession in both Britain and the United States. However, growth resumed smartly in 1993 and continued into 1994.

Tourism Expansion: its Impact on the Republic's Economy

The spending power of tourists, foreign and domestic, is the channel through which tourism makes its impact on national income and national employment levels. Foreign tourism is inherently more valuable to the economy than domestic tourism, since it represents injections of fresh cash into the community. Domestic tourism, on the other hand, principally represents a reallocation of domestic spending.

The economic impact of tourism can be assessed under five separate headings.

1. Impact on gross national product. The spending of tourists, foreign and domestic, creates successive waves of direct, indirect and induced expenditure in the host economy. When the re-spending of part of the additional tourism tax revenues accruing to the exchequer are included, Deane and Henry found that in 1992, tourism's contribution represented 6.9 per cent of the Republic's GNP.

Despite the exceptional growth in recorded GNP in recent years, Tansey, Webster and Associates recently estimated that tourism's share of GNP increased by 1.5 percentage points between 1986 and 1993.

2. Impact on employment. Tourism expenditure supports employment. However, the disparate nature of the tourism product makes it difficult to quantify the jobs sustained by the sector. Using input/output techniques, Deane and Henry estimated that tourism supported 86,000 full-time job equivalents in the Republic's economy in 1992, equivalent to 7.6 per cent of the national work force.

Utilising a comparable approach, Tansey, Webster and Associates estimated that by 1994, tourism-supported employment had risen to 95,600 in 1994, an advance of one-fifth on the full-time equivalent numbers working in the sector in 1990. Jobs supported by tourism now account for one-eighth of total services employed in the Republic.

3. Tourism's contribution to the balance of payments. Overseas tourism and associated carrier receipts generate extensive foreign exchange earnings. Moreover, since the domestic value-added component in tourism products is large, the import content is low. Deane and Henry estimated tourism's direct contribution to the Republic's export drive at 6 per cent in 1992.

For the years 1990–93, Tansey, Webster and Associates show that tourism has generated a current payments surplus ranging between £400 and £500 million annually, even where residents' expenditure on foreign holidays are included. In 1993, tourism accounted for 56 per cent of all export earnings from services.

4. Tourism as an extra tax collector for the exchequer. Since foreign tourism injects new money into the economy, and since expenditure by foreign tourists tends to be concentrated on highly taxed goods and services, overseas tourism generates extra cash for the exchequer. Deane and Henry calculated that when direct, indirect and induced taxation effects are taken into account, 45p out of every initial pound spent by foreign tourists ultimately ended up in the exchequer's coffers.

Using the same methodology, Tansey, Webster and Associates estimated that tax revenues derived from all tourism, foreign and domestic, provided the Government with almost £900 million in gross tax receipts in 1993, approximating to 7.8 per cent of all tax revenues raised that year.

5. Tourism's impact as a regional stabiliser. Many of the areas of greatest scenic beauty and many of the established tourism centres in the Republic lie in the country's less-developed regions. Bord Fáilte found that in 1993 almost half (47.5 per cent) of all overseas holidaymakers spend some time in Cork and south Kerry. In terms of total tourism revenue in 1993, the west and north-west together earned one in five of all tourist pounds spent, as did Dublin. The south-west captured one in every four pounds expended by the tourists.

Earlier, Tansey, Webster and Associates identified the four poorest regions in the Republic as the north-west and Donegal (85 per cent of national per capita incomes), the midlands (86 per cent), the west (87 per cent), and the north-east (87 per cent). Tourism revenues were found to be particularly important in sustaining personal incomes in two of these regions, the north-west plus Donegal and the west. In both regions, tourism revenues were assessed as accounting for around 10 per cent of personal incomes, rapidly approaching the income conferred by agriculture. Similarly, tourist-supported employment was estimated as accounting for roughly one in every ten jobs in the north-west and Donegal, the south-west, and the west.

By creating and sustaining employment and income streams in the Republic's less-developed regions, tourism expansion acts as an unseen instrument of regional policy, effecting regional stabilisation by stealth. The expansion of tourism in the Republic over the past decade has paid handsome dividends in jobs and incomes, balance of payments, and regional stabilisation.

Tourism's Economic Impact in Northern Ireland

The Northern Ireland tourism industry was among the first casualties of the 'Troubles'. Scott and Guy have found that visitor numbers rose steadily during the 1960s 'but then more than halved between 1969 and 1972 as a result of the impact of the beginning of the current period of violence and instability.' Thereafter visitor numbers remained relatively flat for four years. Since 1976 there has been a steady upswing in numbers, allowing the previous peak of the late 1960s to be surpassed in the late 1980s.

Over the twenty years to 1992 the growth in Northern Ireland's real tourism revenues and in visitor numbers has matched performance in the Republic. However, this has been insufficient to reverse the loss of market share suffered as a result of the initial shock of violence.

In the late 1960s one in every three visitors coming to Ireland was bound for Northern Ireland, with the remaining two destined for the Republic. Within two years Northern Ireland's share of all visitors to the island had dropped from 33 to 20 per cent. As Scott and Guy put it, 'little of this share has been regained since the early 1970s, since the similarly of growth rates since the 1970s means that Northern Ireland has simply not fallen further behind. If, in the absence of the "Troubles", one can assume that the market share of the 1960s had been maintained, there has been a substantial "loss" in income in Northern Ireland, representing also a hindrance to the process of economic development in Northern Ireland since 1969.'

As a result, tourism looms less large in the economy of Northern Ireland than in all other economies of the European Union.

Moreover, tourism is of far greater importance to the Republic's economy than to the economy of Northern Ireland. Scott and Guy used three alternative methods to estimate the impact of tourism on the Northern Ireland economy in 1990. They then compared the Northern Ireland economic impact of tourism relative to Professor Eamon Henry's findings for the Republic in 1989. The results are shown in table 1, augmented by Deane and Henry's results for the Republic in 1992.

Table 1: Economic impact of tourism

Category	Northern Ireland 1990	Republic 1989	Republic 1992
Tourism as percentage of GDP/GNP*	1.2–1.3%	3.4–6.0%	6.9%
Tourism jobs (1,000)	4.9–10.5	37.4–64.5	86.0
Tourism jobs as percentage of total employment	0.8–1.8%	3.4–5.9%	7.6%

*Gross National Product in the Republic.

As can be seen from table 1, tourism's relative contribution to national income is three to five times higher in the Republic than in Northern Ireland over the period surveyed. Employment supported by tourism is also far more significant in the Republic, whether measured in absolute or relative terms.

More recently, tourism growth in Northern Ireland appears to have gathered momentum. The Northern Ireland Tourist Board now estimates that tourism comprises 2 per cent of the North's gross domestic product.

The Weaknesses of Irish Tourism

Despite the advances of recent years, tourism in the Republic still suffers from serious weaknesses, impediments that must be overcome if the industry is to become a long-term source of economic growth.

In 1992, Tansey, Webster and Associates identified two major and related sources of weakness in the Republic's tourism industry: excessive seasonality, and low profitability. Excessive seasonality—a short tourism season crowded into the midsummer months—resulted in low rates of annual capacity utilisation of tourism assets. In turn, insufficient utilisation of capacity stunted profitability. This is a vicious circle from which it is difficult to break out. For without higher rates of return on tourism assets, the industry can neither attract new investment funds into the sector nor generate sufficient funds internally to finance investment programmes from own resources. And extra investment in marketing, in product quality and in new product development offers the best hope of counteracting excessive seasonality.

Almost all the other barriers to tourism growth identified by Bord Fáilte—capacity constraints, inadequate marketing budgets, the small scale of most tourism enterprises, and the small number of high-profile visitor attractions—can be traced ultimately to the excessive seasonality/low profitability nexus.

Some progress has been made in the intervening years. Tourism expansion in the past two years has increased room occupancy rates. The new Operational Programme for Tourism under the Community Support Framework, 1994–99, has acted as a spur to new investments, both in marketing and in product development. Yet, despite these improvements and initiatives, much remains to be accomplished to secure the industry's future.

These essentially commercial difficulties are likely to be mirrored in Northern Ireland, where the industry is less developed. Moreover, the physical difficulties confronting the tourism industries North and South of the border are precisely the same. As a small, peripheral island, it can be difficult and costly to gain access to Ireland. Direct access points are few. Indirect entry to the island can prove costly both in time and money.

In an international context, the small size of the tourism industries North and South imposes significant scale diseconomies on marketing, advertising and promotional expenditures.

Tourism's Contribution to the Peace Dividend

The explosion of violence in Northern Ireland in the late 1960s sent the tourism industry into a slump. Moreover, the economic costs were not contained within Northern Ireland: violence in Northern Ireland deterred many prospective tourists from visiting any part of Ireland. As a result, tourism languished in the Republic for fifteen years after 1969, recovering only in the later stages of the 1980s.

However, if tourism was one of the first economic casualties of violence in Northern Ireland, it can also be one of the first beneficiaries of the peace. For the simple absence of violence will, if maintained, act to dismantle the biggest barrier to tourism growth throughout the island of Ireland.

Clearly, as the major sufferer from the conflict, the tourism industry in Northern Ireland stands to be the biggest winner from peace. Nor are overseas markets the only source of tourism growth for Northern Ireland. Initially, the major impetus to tourism growth in the North may stem from a much-accelerated flow of visitors and holidaymakers from the Republic.

But peace is a positive-sum game. The Republic can also capitalise on the ending of violence in Northern Ireland and on the high-profile and positive publicity generated by the peace process in the major source markets for the Republic's tourism. For the broad coincidence of tourism growth rates north and south of the border from the early 1970s to the late 1980s clearly indicates that the Republic's tourism drive was also retarded by the 'spill-over' effects of Northern violence. The international publicity accorded to the peace process will serve to quell the fears of potential overseas visitors, while highlighting Ireland as an international tourism destination. In technical terms, this can be seen as an exercise in making the market for Irish tourism function more effectively by the filling of information gaps, both for consumers and investors.

Thus, even in the absence of any policy initiatives for concrete co-operation, tourism on an all-Ireland basis stands to gain substantially from a continuance of peace.

However, policy-makers North and South would be remiss if they did not seek to capitalise on the unique opportunity now presented to them. Three areas suggest themselves as potential areas for co-operation.

1. Improving the quality of the tourism product. Initiatives in this area would focus on widening the range of consumer choice and hence providing overseas visitors with better value for money. In particular, such initiatives could centre on offering visitors 'Holidays in two countries for the price of one.' Such a venture would require that tourist information be provided to potential visitors on an all-island basis.

2. Joint marketing, information and publicity drives. Already under way, marketing co-operation would not only serve to promote tourism on an all-island basis but would work to overcome the diseconomies of small scale now afflicting tourism promotion North and South.

3. Promoting private sector co-operation at the level of tourism segments. Cross-border enterprise co-operation in the marketing and packaging of activity holidays (golf, waterways, equestrian holidays), of cultural and historic tourism and of sheer relaxation (country house holidays) could help to overcome some of the identified barriers to tourism development. In effect, such co-operation, by increasing the range of products available to visitors, would mitigate the absence of high-profile tourism attractions. It would also help individual tourism businesses to escape the constraints imposed by the small scale of their operations and the consequent difficulties in financing adequate marketing budgets. Individual enterprises are the keys that unlock the economic benefits of tourism. But there is strength in numbers.

Peace has come dropping slow. It is important that its continuance not be jeopardised by the imposition of grandiose structures. Much better that border crossings be built on the firm foundations of mutual economic benefits. Tourism meets this test, for the expansion of tourism will lead to an improvement in the general welfare of all on the island of Ireland.

References

Bord Fáilte Éireann, *Perspectives on Irish Tourism, 1989–1993: Regions*, Dublin: Bord Fáilte 1989, 11.

Bord Fáilte Éireann, *The Economic Effects of Irish Tourism, 1989–1993: Regions,* Dublin: Bord Fáilte 1989, 11.

Bord Fáilte Éireann, *Developing Sustainable Tourism: Tourism Development Plan, 1994–1999,* Dublin: Bord Fáilte 1994, 12.

Deane, Brian, and Eamon Henry, 'The Economic Impact of Tourism' in *Irish Banking Review,* winter 1993.

Frameworks for the Future, part II: A New Framework for Agreement: a Shared Understanding between the British and Irish Governments to Assist Discussion and Negotiation Involving the Northern Ireland Parties, 1995, 28.

Northern Ireland Tourist Board, *1994: a Year of Opportunities and Challenges,* Belfast: NITB 1995.

Scott, Ronnie, and Nigel Guy, *The Economic Impact of Tourism in Northern Ireland* (Working Paper no. 2), Belfast: Northern Ireland Economic Research Centre 1992, 10–14.

Tansey, Webster and Associates, *Tourism and the Irish Economy,* Dublin: Irish Tourist Industry Confederation, 1991.

Tansey, Webster and Associates, *A Strategic Framework for Tourism Enterprises,* Dublin: Irish Tourist Industry Confederation 1992.

18 Inward Investment: Getting the Best from Foreign Capital

Douglas Hamilton

There is arguably no aspect of industrial policy in Ireland, North and South, that receives more attention than inward investment. When new inward investment projects are first announced, they receive high-profile publicity, and expectations around their potential can be substantial, especially in terms of job creation. On the other hand, of course, the spectacular failure of projects such as the car manufacturer De Lorean in Belfast and, more recently, the computer company Digital Electronics in Galway has also given inward investment publicity, but of a far less favourable kind.

Inward investment has been viewed by both governments as a crucial, if not the key, component of industrial policy. The successful attraction of inward investment by the Industrial Development Board (IDB) in Belfast and the Industrial Development Authority (IDA) in Dublin is seen as a fundamental aspect of the respective governments' attempts to generate much-needed employment and to develop industrial capacity. In this context, inward investment is a major sector of the economy, North and South; it acts as a key component of policy, and, of course, it accounts for substantial public resources.

To get a full understanding of the role of inward investment, this chapter has a number of aims. The first is to look at the extent of foreign ownership, North and South, and more specifically to examine its characteristics in terms of nationality and breakdown by industrial sector. The second aim is to examine the record of the IDB and IDA in attracting inward investment in terms of the number of jobs created, the methods employed to attract the investment, and the associated costs involved. Third, and perhaps most fundamentally, it is important to consider the contribution inward investment has made to the development of a dynamic and self-sustaining industrial base. Finally, in the context of the possibility of peace, stability, and an agreed political settlement arising from the 'peace process', it is worth considering what the future might hold, especially in terms of the development of an island economy and greater economic integration. In particular, some issues are raised concerning the prospects for inward investment and the type of policies and institutional structures that could be developed.

The Extent of Inward Investment

The main source of information on the role and contribution of inward investment in Ireland relates to manufacturing employment. Inevitably, this restricts the scope of the analysis: other important aspects of foreign ownership are output, trade, investment, profitability, and capital flows. Nevertheless employment is a key variable in terms of policy and general industrial structure. Moreover, an employment analysis of externally owned companies allows comparisons to be made between Northern Ireland and the Republic, for which similar data is available.

Northern Ireland

The most recent information shows that in 1990 there were just over two hundred externally owned manufacturing plants in Northern Ireland, employing over 41,000 people. The level of employment in externally owned business represented a small decline since 1986 but a huge fall, of over 46,000 or 53 per cent, on the position in 1973. This substantial haemorrhage of external manufacturing employment means that such plants now account for around 40 per cent of the overall manufacturing base in Northern Ireland, down from 53 per cent in 1973 (fig. 1). In other words, employment in externally owned plants fell much more rapidly than the overall level of manufacturing employment. Indeed, of the overall decline of almost 60,000 manufacturing jobs during this period, almost 80 per cent took place in externally owned plants. Interestingly, however, if British companies are excluded from the analysis, the proportion accounted for by foreign firms actually increased, from 14 per cent in 1973 to 17 per cent in 1990.

The decline in manufacturing employment during the 1980s was due almost entirely to either the closure of plants or the contraction of employment in British companies (fig. 2). In 1973 there were almost 300 British-owned manufacturing plants in Northern Ireland, employing just under 65,000 people. By 1990 only 23,300 were employed in 120 plants, a fall of 41,000 or 64 per cent. British companies are still important to the Northern industrial base (around one in five jobs), but in the context of manufacturing investment and employment there has been a sustained economic withdrawal of British capital over the past twenty years.

Fig. 1: Externally owned manufacturing employment as percentage of total manufacturing employment

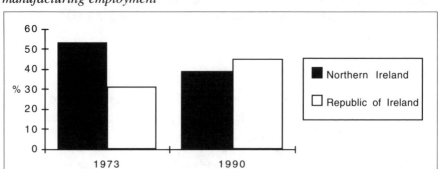

Perhaps surprisingly, there were only 30 American-owned plants in 1990, employing just over 9,000 people—less than 10 per cent of overall manufacturing employment. There were 20 plants from the rest of the EU, employing just over 3,000. Unlike other parts of the UK, Northern Ireland has not been able to attract a substantial number of plants from the Far East: around 1,500 were employed in only a handful of plants in 1990. It would appear that Far East companies have quite different approaches from American companies when it comes to locating in Europe and that financial incentives are far less important to their production strategies. More important seems to be the presence of other Far East companies and the availability of factors such as high-quality sub-suppliers.

Fig. 2: Employment in externally owned manufacturing plants in Northern Ireland, by nationality

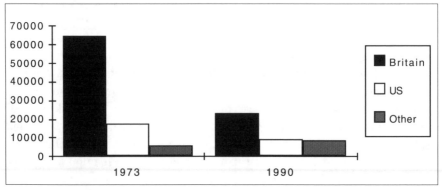

A final aspect of the nationality of externally owned plants is that, largely as a result of take-overs, firms from the Republic are a growing feature of the Northern Ireland industrial base. In 1990 there were almost thirty such manufacturing plants, employing almost 3,000 people, with much of this in the food industry, though not exclusively.

In terms of the industrial sector, most externally owned employment in Northern Ireland—around one-third—is in textiles and clothing (table 1). This proportion has been maintained despite the long-term trend of employment decline in this traditional industry. Only twelve externally owned plants, employing just over 7,000 people, were in the more modern electrical and instrument engineering industry.

Table 1: Percentage shares of employment in externally owned manufacturing plants or companies in Northern Ireland and Republic by industrial sector, 1990

Industry	Northern Ireland	Republic of Ireland
Mineral products	2	4
Chemicals & synthetic fibres	7	12
Metals & engineering	27	46
Food, drink, & tobacco	17	14
Textiles & clothing	34	13
Paper, printing, & publishing	4	2
Other manufacturing	8	8
Total manufacturing	100	100

In the Republic there were 980 externally owned companies in 1990, employing over 90,000 people. Almost half of this employment was in US-owned companies, with one in five employed in British companies (table 2). Almost 14,000 were employed in companies owned in the rest of the EU and, as in Northern Ireland, only a relatively small number (2,000) in companies from the Far East. As a proportion of total manufacturing employment, 45 per cent were employed in externally owned companies, a substantial increase from 31 per cent in 1973 (fig. 1).

Table 2: Employment in externally owned manufacturing plants or companies in Northern Ireland and Republic by country of ownership, 1990

	Northern Ireland		Republic of Ireland	
Nationality	Employ-ment	Percentage of total	Employ-ment	Percentage of total
Great Britain	23,259	57	16,900	19
United States	9,282	23	43,800	48
Canada	951	2	2,800	3
Republic of Ireland	2,718	7	—	—
Rest of EU	3,155	8	13,900	15
Far East	1,496	4	1,900	2
Other	224	1	11,400	13
Total	41,085	100	90,700	100

With regard to the industrial sector, just under half of all externally owned employment was in metals and engineering, with between 12 and 14 per cent in each of three industrial groupings: chemicals and synthetic fibres; food, drink, and tobacco; and textiles and clothing (table 1).

In summary, the experience of inward investment in Northern Ireland stands in stark contrast to that in the Republic. Since the early 1970s, externally owned employment in Northern Ireland has halved, compared with an increase of almost 30 per cent in the Republic. The result of this period of fundamental restructuring in industrial ownership is that the Republic now has a much higher proportion of foreign-owned employment (45 per cent) than Northern Ireland (39 per cent)—the reverse of the situation in the early 1970s. Moreover, in contrast to Northern Ireland, inward investment in the Republic is associated with more modern industrial sectors. This suggests that given similarly generous incentive packages, whether it be in the form of capital grant subsidies in the North or tax concessions in the South, much of this difference can be attributed to the continuing political conflict in Northern Ireland over the last twenty-five years.

Government Policy Towards the Attraction of Inward Investment and its Effectiveness

The attraction of inward investment has been a major component of industrial policy North and South for many decades. In the North a wide range of incentives has been available, the main policy instrument being high rates of capital grants, at anything up to 50 per cent of overall investment costs. Other incentives include the provision of advance factories, industrial derating, and various types of grants with specific aims, such as the promotion of R&D activity.

In the Republic the main policy instrument for the attraction of inward investment has been tax incentives, in particular a 10 per cent rate of corporation tax. Relatively high rates of grant assistance, particularly for capital investment, have also been available over a long period, though there has been some reduction in the use and level of grants since the late 1980s. These assistance packages add up to two of the most generous in what is a highly competitive European market. With so many countries and regions actively attempting to attract inward investment to their own areas through the use of assorted incentives, the cost of pursuing this type of policy in Ireland has necessarily been high. This has particularly been the case in Northern Ireland, which, not surprisingly, has found overseas marketing difficult as a result of the political conflict.

In Northern Ireland over the period 1980 to 1993, just over 13,000 jobs were 'promoted' by the IDB in new inward investment projects, an average of 930 jobs a year. These are jobs that foreign companies planned to create over an agreed period (normally about five to six years) with financial assistance from the IDB. This compares with an equivalent figure for the Republic of almost 116,000 jobs approved by the IDA over the same period. In other words, the Republic managed to attract almost nine times as many jobs through new inward investment as Northern Ireland.

An important issue in this regard is that actual job targets set by the IDB and the IDA for assisted new inward investment projects have rarely been fully met. While there have been wide variations between companies, the overall record of inward investment in Northern Ireland for the period 1982–88 was that only one in five jobs planned for ever materialised. Of particular concern is that American companies performed particularly badly in this regard. The record in the Republic is not much better, with only one-third of IDA job targets in new foreign-owned plants being met by the end of the period 1981–90.

Almost £220 million was offered to new inward investment projects in Northern Ireland over the eight-year period 1986/87–1993/94. This accounted for around 30 per cent of overall investment costs in the projects and gives a cost per job 'promoted' of almost £24,000. This compares with average male earnings in Northern Ireland of just over £16,000.

In the Republic it is more difficult to estimate the cost of inward investment policy, because of the use of tax concessions. However, grants totalling almost £430 million were paid to new inward investment projects over the period 1981–90. In addition, it is estimated that in 1991 alone tax relief for all industry located in the Republic amounted to £600 million, almost all of which would be accounted for by new inward investment projects. In the North, therefore, not only has inward investment policy led to a relatively small level of job creation but these jobs have been attracted at a high cost. In the Republic the IDA has had more far more success in attracting inward investment, but this has been achieved with a substantial outlay (in the case of tax relief, a loss) of public resources.

The Wider Role and Contribution of Inward Investment to Industrial Development

Despite the less than buoyant picture of inward investment in Northern Ireland presented above, both in performance and policy effectiveness, it is surprising that inward investment policy has never been put under close public scrutiny by the government or the IDB. This is especially so given the considerable amount of public funds that has been expended on this area of industrial policy over many years. Indeed the recent reviews of industrial policy by the Department of Economic Development and the IDB in the first half of the 1990s devoted little attention to inward investment policy. The general attitude of the government seems to have been that the attraction of inward investment is a necessary and justifiable policy and one that will be of clear benefit to the development of the industrial base and the creation of sustainable employment. Yet the little that is known about the operation of foreign investment in Northern Ireland suggests that a more detailed assessment would be worth while.

In the Republic there has been a much more extensive debate and analysis around the role and contribution of inward investment in overall industrial development. However, many of the policy implications arising from this discussion have not filtered through to affect official policy. In 1982 the 'Telesis' report, commissioned by the National Economic and Social Council, argued that the balance between the support for foreign and indigenous industry was weighted too much towards the former. This, it was argued, had the result that industrial policy had been insufficiently concerned with the development of indigenously owned industry.

With only refinements to policy taking place during the 1980s, rather than fundamental changes to strategic approaches, the Culliton review group, which reported in 1992, repeated the earlier recommendation of Telesis that the grant budget for internationally mobile industry should be further squeezed. Again the reason for this was not so much an objection to foreign investment per se, more the need to develop more fully indigenously owned Irish industry, especially in higher-value-added sectors. Nevertheless it was acknowledged that foreign-owned industry had not performed well in making a contribution to the economy beyond job creation. Moreover, the Culliton report specifically stated that the attraction of foreign investment was not a sufficient basis for developing a national advantage in advanced industries that would create increased employment opportunities and raise living standards.

Much more needs to be known about the effectiveness of inward investment policy and the role such investment plays in its wider contribution to economic, industrial and social development in Ireland. A number of important questions can be raised. For example, what are the pros and cons of offering capital grant subsidies as opposed to tax concessions? Different policy incentives will inevitably have an effect on the types of projects attracted and their subsequent contribution to overall industrial development. Do capital grants tend to encourage capital-intensive projects with low employment content? Similarly, do tax concessions, as currently offered in the Republic, necessarily lead to the attraction of unsophisticated assembly-type plants with low levels of skills, little if any R&D input or technology transfer, few linkages with the rest of the economy, and, perhaps most important, the repatriation of excessive levels of profits through transfer pricing? Are particular policy incentives more effective at attracting certain nationalities of firms? Why is it that plants from some countries perform differently from those from others?

Finally, does the way in which foreign ownership is introduced into the economy make a difference? For example, rather than the traditional route of brand-new green-field branch plants, recent experience suggests that mergers and take-overs are becoming increasingly important. In terms of overall industrial development it is important to know how these newer processes compare with the more traditional green-field location of foreign-owned branch plants.

The most fundamental question is over the contribution that inward investment can be expected to make to sustainable economic, industrial and social development. It is essential that agreed priorities and expectations are stated in any overall economic development strategy, both on the role of inward investment and on policy directed at its attraction. The experience of elsewhere, and the Republic in particular, is that while inward investment has an important role to play in promoting industrial development, it will not be sufficient by itself. Without the development of indigenous industry that can link into and benefit from foreign-owned plants, sustainable industrial development is unlikely to take place. The task, therefore, is not simply the attraction and development of inward investment, a policy that is hard enough by itself, but the integration of foreign industry into the wider industrial development needs of the economy.

Peace, Political Stability, and an Agreed Political Settlement

The potential that now exists for peace, political stability and an agreed political settlement offers the opportunity of much-increased inward investment, both in quantity and quality. If it is assumed that the North under more 'normal' conditions could attract as many jobs as the Republic, then, after allowance is made for its smaller size, it is estimated that the overall level of jobs arising from new inward investment in Northern Ireland would be over four times greater than has been the case since the early 1980s. This means that, rather than 'promoting' just over 900 jobs each year (the number of jobs firms plan to create with assistance), the IDB would have promoted almost 4,000 a year. If it is further assumed that only about half of these jobs ever materialised (an optimistic assumption on recent experience), almost 20,000 extra jobs might have been created in new inward investment projects since the beginning of the 1980s. More stable political conditions could, therefore, be expected to have a substantial employment impact in Northern Ireland in the future.

A further important issue is that not only is the *quantity* of investment from abroad likely to increase significantly but also the *quality* of that investment. It has been noted already that inward investment in Northern Ireland has been heavily concentrated in the more 'traditional' industries of textiles and clothing. In contrast, the Republic has attracted investment in the more modern industries of computers, electronics, and pharmaceuticals. While there have been problems associated with this investment in the form of low linkages with the rest of the economy and very high rates of profit repatriation, these industries would seem to have greater long-term viability. Furthermore, in a period of political stability it would seem likely that the types of projects attracted would be less risky in their longer-term viability. An important consequence of inward investment being attracted on the basis of very high rates of grant assistance (up to 50 per cent of overall investment costs) is that the company incurs relatively low sunk costs. This can have the consequence of easy entry being accompanied by easy exit. If inward investment can be attracted in more 'normal' conditions and with lower rates of grants, then it seems likely that less risky projects would be obtained.

A final potential consequence for inward investment policy concerns the opportunity and benefits that would arise from increased policy co-operation between the IDB and the IDA, if not their replacement by a single body. Indeed the Joint Framework Document, produced by the Irish and British governments, seems to suggest that industrial promotion could be an activity appropriate for North-South institutions, at least in the context of harmonisation, and possibly even as an executive function.

With regard to the co-ordination of policy incentives, there would be substantial benefits from standardising tax incentives and grant rates and promoting the island as one location. This might mean the IDB being able to offer tax concessions in line with the IDA in the South or, probably more sensibly, the two agencies standardising and reducing their current generous aid packages. As already stated, a number of reports and studies have suggested that the incentives package in the Republic is over-generous. One reason for this is that the IDA has competed with the availability from the IDB of high grant assistance in the North. Moreover, this competition for prospective inward investment projects has led to a bidding-up of offers, the only beneficiaries of which have been the inward investing companies themselves. If policy were co-ordinated, not only could a more effective policy be introduced but budgetary savings would also be realised.

An important benefit of co-operation between the two agencies, especially if a single all-Ireland body were established, would be that a more coherent location policy could be implemented throughout the whole of Ireland. In particular, a single body would be far better placed to address more fully the wider developmental needs of the economy. Rather than inward investment projects being stand-alone branch plants with few linkages to the rest of the economy, there would be increased opportunity and scope for foreign-owned plants to become more deeply embedded into the existing industrial base on an all-Ireland basis. This could lead to substantial and wider benefits for the island economy additional to those arising simply from the activities of the plants themselves.

In conclusion, it is important to state that inward investment will continue to play an important part in the Irish economy, North and South. This is especially likely to be the case if peace, stability and an agreed political settlement can be realised and sustained. Nonetheless, there remains considerable scope for greater understanding of the role and contribution that inward investment can make to the economy and consequently lessons for policy. Only if analysis and discussion continue and are extended will the full benefits of foreign investment be gained and built upon. With an economic environment more conducive to industrial development, the drawbacks, difficulties and risks often associated with inward investment and that have been all too common in Ireland, North and South, could be avoided and reduced.

The views expressed are those of the author and not necessarily of the Northern Ireland Economic Council.

Part 8

Selling into the Island

19 Lever Brothers: The Reality of a Single Market

Shane Molloy

In this chapter I will set out why Lever Brothers decided to combine its businesses on the island of Ireland where before Northern Ireland had been served from Lever (UK) in Kingston, Surrey, while the business in the Republic had been managed from Dublin.

Essentially, cross-border similarities in the structure of the grocery trade made it more effective for Lever in Ireland to become one organisation. More importantly, it enabled Lever to give much greater attention to two growing markets and for Northern Ireland particularly to receive the focus it deserved as a significant part of the new company.

Lever Ireland: Some Background

Lever Ireland is responsible for the marketing and selling of such market leaders as Persil, Domestos, Jif, Comfort, Surf, Radion, Lux, and Dove. It began operating on an island-of-Ireland basis in January 1993 and continues to grow at a constant rate of over 5 per cent a year. In a detergent market (fabric cleaning and care, dishwashing, household and personal wash) worth, at retail level, about £140 million, it has a share of 37 per cent.

While one of its dishwashing brands is manufactured in Ireland, most of the Lever lines are supplied by its factories throughout Europe, particularly those in Britain. Lever has a tight management structure, with two-thirds of its team in marketing and sales; in total, sixty-two people are employed on the island, as well as a number indirectly involved through the use of third-party support in warehousing and distribution, primarily in Northern Ireland.

Over half the homes in Ireland will have at least one Lever brand in use at any time. Lever brands are marketed to consumers through supermarkets and other retail outlets. On the island of Ireland, wholesalers are a critical intermediary part of the distribution channel. Lever is a consumer-driven business in an industry where success is achieved only through an effective working relationship with its trade partners.

At the time of writing (spring 1995) there is a backdrop of two major changes in the commercial and social life of the island of Ireland. Chronologically, the first is the collapsing of economic borders between the member-states of the European Union, the nearest of which to me in Dublin was that at Newry. More dramatically there are the ceasefires, which have held since the early autumn of 1994; the effect of these is to etch away at the suspicions that had developed between the two parts of Ireland and to encourage more people from the Republic to visit Northern Ireland, and vice versa.

Interconnected Markets

The grocery industry has always had a cross-border dimension. Southern consumers have flocked to Newry and other shopping centres at different times in recent years, attracted in equal measure, it seems, by the perception and the reality of bargains. A minority of trade customers have regularly taken advantage of 'grey' trade opportunities—price differentials between the two markets. Both the numbers involved and the scale of the trading increase when currency movements are especially sharp. Additionally, many businesses market the same or similar brands North and South. Many of these are multinationals or British businesses that include Northern Ireland in their UK organisation while having a separate entity managing the Republic. Others are companies that have an Irish character and a presence in both parts of Ireland.

Lever Brothers, which originated in the second half of the nineteenth century in Britain, has a long history in Ireland. It incorporates one of the older companies founded in these islands, John Barrington and Sons of Dublin, which moved into the manufacture and sale of soap in 1775. While never a major supplier, Barrington's enjoyed success for many years throughout Ireland and even built an export business to Scotland before becoming part of Lever early in the twentieth century. So, Lever in Ireland was originally just one organisation. During the 1920s, however, the business adapted to the new political structures. A separate company was set up in the Republic; Northern Ireland continued to be part of the UK business.

Although links remained close, market and brand differences evolved over the years between Ireland and the UK. As a general rule, with its higher income per household, the British market tended to be more advanced. For example, the market penetration of front-loading automatic washing machines, which led to the development of low-suds washing powder brands such as Persil Automatic, went ahead at a much faster rate in the UK than in the Republic. On the other hand, although at a lower level than washing machines, dishwashers were found in more homes south of the border than in either the North or Great Britain. (The demand for more dishwashers seemed to come from the greater number of large families in the South and the pressure on Dad to relieve everyone from the drudgery of washing up!)

Increasingly we have seen indications of market convergence through the last decade. Partly this is because consumer trends are on a much more similar time structure these days. The influences for this are many: we are all more European, both as a result of greater experience and knowledge of other countries through travel, emigration, immigration, and especially the media, in particular television; the income gap is slowly closing; and, of course, companies like Lever are highly committed to European harmonisation of their products and brands.

European Influence

The European backdrop is of fundamental importance. Traditionally, Lever's interests in Europe were managed on a country-by-country basis, each company having full profit and strategic responsibility for its own market. During the 1980s it became clear, however, that this approach was a hindrance in the drive for a sharper competitive edge. Effort was being diluted by fragmentation of focus in innovation, branding, advertising development, and achievement of the lowest-cost producer position.

Lever's response to the emerging situation took a very concrete form. In 1990 it fused the national companies of sixteen countries into one organisation—Lever Europe—which is managed from Brussels by a team of general managers. Since then the European structure has gone through a series of further developments that have brought into existence both business units and product category management teams. Crucially, a new organisational culture is being forged. Lever Europe is responsible for the strategic direction of Lever's detergent business in Europe, its profitability, and manufacturing. The national companies are now marketing, sales and operations businesses (MSOs) responsible for delivering sales, share and profit targets through the implementation of European plans, events, and activities.

For the MSOs this means that their prime areas of involvement are customer service, pricing, media planning, consumer promotions, and trade activity.

Two Markets or One Market?

These changes had a fundamental impact on Lever culture. In essence, the local companies became operational units, focusing on using their local knowledge and understanding to ensure the best possible transfer of European plans into their markets. Strategy became the prerogative of the European organisation. These developments prompted examination of the most appropriate geographical arrangements for several of the countries and regions in Europe.

As outlined earlier, there were signs for some time of a convergence in markets on the island of Ireland. A good example is the similar trend in the fabric cleaners market, where Radion had a very successful launch in both parts of Ireland. It achieved a significant market share more quickly than in any other European country, including Great Britain. Again, the fabrics cleaners market, which in many countries has seen concentrated products take over from conventional powders, sees a different pattern in Ireland. Both North and South, consumer demand for the conventional product holds at the expense of concentrated products, both liquids and powders.

The Consumer

In a wider sense, some of the key structural and cultural aspects of the Republic and Northern Ireland are closer to each other than either is to Britain.

- Ireland—North and South—has a significantly younger population than Great Britain; family sizes are larger.

- Far more women work full-time at home.

- The urban-rural split is quite different: 14 per cent in the Republic and 8 per cent in Northern Ireland are involved in agriculture, compared with 2 per cent in Great Britain.

- Population is much more thinly spread in Ireland.

- The number out of work, particularly young people, is much higher on the island of Ireland.

While these structural differences will very probably continue, the latest trends are for them to become less acute. Family sizes are getting smaller in both parts of Ireland; the numbers in farming are declining all the time; and so on. Nevertheless these structural factors and their consequences (a greater number of dependants, less income per household) continue to have sufficient impact to alter the shape of a market in terms of product forms and brands preferred. Value brands, such as Surf, have a much greater appeal to Irish consumers on both sides of the border than is the case in Great Britain or indeed in many other European markets.

For all that, there are signs of a merging media market encompassing both islands, not just both parts of Ireland. Social and cultural attitudes would support the qualitative research studies that find that consumers on this side of the Irish Sea are much more sensitive to music, rhythm and colour than their Anglo-Saxon counterparts. There are some very good examples, where budgets have permitted it, of advertising campaigns developed specifically for the Irish markets that have built on these elements; the most successful instance of this is the very different approach adopted for the Guinness brand in Ireland compared with Great Britain.

Media

The other side of advertising is the media channel. While press is not particularly important as an advertising medium on an island-of-Ireland basis—aside from the British tabloids—television has been a driving force in the development of the one-market concept. There can be little doubt that the existence of a common television market has helped the convergence of consumer behaviour and attitudes. The penetration of the Republic (over 60 per cent of all homes) by UTV has been the critical element. While RTE has made some small progress in gaining viewers in the North, it has had nothing like the same success.

For several years, some leading advertisers had pursued an Irish 'single market' media strategy. Lever experimented with this before setting up a formal system in 1990. This was done on the initiative of the Irish company, to optimise both the level, phasing and balance of advertising expenditure with Lever UK. The approach had mixed success, as it required disproportionate input from the British company, when UTV was only a minor participant in the UK media market—and most of the benefits were going to Lever in the Republic.

Effective management of the media overlap opportunities generates a saving of more than 10 per cent in advertising expenditure. The key to achieving savings is to eliminate duplication of coverage.

Essentially there are three distinct television markets on the island of Ireland: those households receiving (*a*) UTV or Channel 4 only, (*b*) RTE only, and (*c*) both UTV or Channel 4 and RTE. There are also homes receiving HTV and S4C from Wales instead of UTV and Channel 4, but they are a minority. More recently the satellite channels and indeed the breakfast stations add another dimension. From an advertiser's viewpoint, the increase in the number of channels is a mixed blessing: on the one hand it widens coverage to viewers quite hard to reach normally—as in the case of Channel 4 programmes—but on the other it fragments audiences. Also, costs are higher, because it requires more spots to reach the same audience size.

For Lever brands, where, most often, we want to communicate with mass-market consumers—for example all toilet soap buyers—the optimisation of media buying has now become a science as we strive to construct the most cost-effective advertising schedule. This is the case even in a small media market, by European standards, like the island of Ireland. However, the ability to manage one media strategy is a significant step forward, as distinct from trying to co-ordinate two separate approaches.

Consumers: the Conclusion

Of course there are fundamental differences between the North and South, but from a commercial point of view they are overshadowed by the common characteristics. All that said, neither the media opportunity nor the similarities between consumers North and South were the defining reasons why we chose to operate on an all-island basis. The critical factor was the way the trade functioned and its largely common customer base. To understand why Lever decided that one organisation could be more effective on the island of Ireland, we need to look at the similarities between the grocery trade on both sides of the border.

The Trade

Most of the major retailers were either part of retailing interests operating only on the island of Ireland or were unique to one or other part of Ireland. Broadly, and this applied even to symbol group franchise holders, strategies were being pursued that crossed the border or to which the border was irrelevant. Meanwhile, British multiples were either not in Northern Ireland or were withdrawing.

The shape of the distributive grocery trade for detergents is very similar North and South: the multiple-to-wholesale split in Northern Ireland is of the same order as that in the Republic, which is broadly 55-45. In Great Britain the split is about 85-15. At the same time the practice of branch delivery was dominant in Ireland; and while subsequently there has been a movement towards central warehousing in Northern Ireland, as far as the consumer is concerned similar marketing and promotion strategies continue to apply.

In effect the differences in the trade structures between Northern Ireland

and the rest of the UK required a different service structure, even while Northern Ireland was still within the ambit of Lever UK. One significant statistic highlighted the situation: Northern Ireland contributed 2.5 per cent of total UK sales but accounted for nearly 15 per cent of both sales calls and delivery points.

In this context it is appropriate now to examine, in general terms, the financial aspects of a combined island-of-Ireland organisation.

Financial Aspects

The strength of the financial proposition for a single organisation was borne out because in the event, in the Lever experience, it generated higher sales, more competitive prices to our customers and consumers, and a cost-effective structure. It simplified the operations of the UK Lever organisation and added critical mass to the Irish business. It ensured that Northern Ireland, because of its greater importance in the new island structure, received much greater focus, which in turn generated higher turnover. This allowed marketing investment to be increased, with further benefits being derived from economies of scale to the advantage of the whole island.

Competitively, it was a window of opportunity that added value to the Lever business at a time when competitive pressure both from our industry rivals and trade customers was pushing profitability in the wrong direction.

Practical Factors

Forgoing sales revenue is not easily agreed in any organisation, especially one undergoing structural development on a significant scale. Lever UK rightly regarded itself as the custodian of the Lever reputation in Northern Ireland. It undertook, with us, a very detailed programme of hand-over, ensuring that customers and other appropriate organisations were kept fully informed at all times in the process. Understandably, despite the strong case put forward, they were a little reluctant to give up any business, and it was perhaps fortuitous that the person in charge of Lever detergent business on a worldwide basis was an Irishman, Niall Fitzgerald. Once he was convinced of the merits of the business case for the transfer of management and profit responsibility, he was ideally placed to provide reassurance and encouragement as appropriate.

The grocery industry operates in a demanding climate, with an underlying tension between retailers, wholesalers, and suppliers. This is usually healthy, and, in the case of the formation of the new Lever structure, support was positive and a key element in its success. The battles have not changed, and issues of pricing and margins may never be resolved to the satisfaction of participants in the industry, but it is clear that keeping close to the market is an essential factor in maintaining an effective working relationship with customers.

A substantial expansion in the size of a company—in the case of Lever Ireland, 30 per cent—puts enormous strain on all the people involved, especially when the increase in numbers employed was far smaller. Yet when a team is totally committed to growing the business on the clearly measurable targets of sales revenue, profit, and market share, then some complicated and tough plans can be achieved in a very positive manner. This was the Lever experience in what was known as 'Project Cheltenham' (the original proposals were written during the racing festival of the same name). We were hungry for the opportunity, and having been given the chance were determined to make it a success. This was a critical motivational factor.

One Market: One Company

The North and the Republic share with Great Britain a largely common television culture. The story for the rest of our lives in the two parts of Ireland is quite different. In those parts of our lives where we interact with our neighbours we are closer to each other than either of us is to Great Britain. As I have pointed out, Northern Ireland shares many demographic, occupational and social characteristics with the Republic. Our patterns of trade are similar.

It is the policy of Lever Europe to benefit from economies of scale throughout the continent while making the best use of the ability of operating companies to focus on the unique characteristics of individual countries or regions. The move to operate on an all-island basis for the island of Ireland was a practical expression of this policy. Its success has led to other regional organisations being formed, for example a Nordic one, comprising Denmark, Finland, and Sweden. This began operating as a combined business unit at the beginning of 1995; and further developments along the road to an even more integrated European organisation can be expected as the single market evolves.

Appendix 1 A Questionnaire Survey of Selected Firms already Operating on an All-Island Basis

D'Arcy Smyth & Associates, Dublin

To help create a broader picture for readers of the benefits and pitfalls of evolving new all-island operational and management structures for their business, D'Arcy Smyth & Associates undertook a small-scale survey aimed at indigenous companies whose public profile suggested that they were operating on an 'all-island' basis. For the purposes of this survey we defined this as 'the desire (or determination) of management to co-ordinate and integrate their production, sales, marketing, distribution and administrative operations North and South to the greatest extent possible, with the principal point of "local" control for the whole operation also being on the island.'

The survey's objective was simple: to elicit as much advice and guidance of such all-island operations as the respondents were willing to share.

Thirteen questionnaires were distributed to chief executive officers and managing directors. The firms selected were a mixture of those with head offices in the North and South.

Five companies did not reply for logistical reasons (managing director away, etc.). Two companies felt that, although they were operating both North and South and indeed had done so successfully for a long time, they did not fall within the survey's terms of reference for operating on an all-island basis.

Six companies did reply—a 46 per cent response, which is high for this kind of survey. The following is a general profile of the respondents:

Sectors: Food, manufacturing, construction, publishing, clothing, and consultancy.

Size: Large (over 200 employees), medium (50–200 employees), and small (under 50 employees).

Location: Headquarters throughout the island, in both urban and rural locations.

Orientation: By virtue of operating on an all-island basis all are exporters, as that term has been traditionally defined and understood. However, from their answers it is clear that most of the respondents also market their goods or services beyond the island.

Therefore, as this brief outline illustrates, while small in number the respondents do represent a reasonably broad range of commercial activities and perspectives.

Question 1

simply asked each company to confirm its formal title and to describe its all-island activity.

Question 2

requested respondents to *'list the principal reasons for carrying out these activities on an all-island basis.'*

A wide and informative range of motivations was listed. One company was totally pragmatic: 'efficiency, cost-effectiveness, market development, and profitability.' Another had a most impressive company-specific rationale developed: '(*a*) Manufacturing to customer specification is so much easier to service; (*b*) no customer is more than 300 miles away, and personal contact is vital; (*c*) inward investment in manufacturing is stronger in the Republic; (*d*) it is easier to keep the competition at bay from outside the island and therefore create a niche market.'

A third company saw the all-island dimension as representing a desire to make use of the expertise and knowledge of its industry, gained in one part of the island, in the acquisition of compatible businesses in the other.

Two further interesting reasons from a Northern perspective were, firstly, the high level of imports into the Republic from the UK (in this company's sector), which made it *de facto* an important market, and, secondly, the fact that the company's founder, originally from the North and now living in the South, wished to utilise in a commercial context the many personal contacts developed while being reared and educated there.

Finally, one company saw itself as 'serving the whole of Ireland.'

Question 3

'To the extent that you can, please describe the principal barriers and/or operational difficulties which you have had to overcome or come to terms with to operate on an all-island basis.'

The completion of the single market by removing customs and border controls was specifically mentioned by three of the six respondents as a barrier now removed. One company cited price differentials in its product as the major obstacle. The 'poor road structure between points on an "all-island" [basis], also poor rail' are cited by another company, and because of necessity 'before the peace initiatives … often used England for warehousing.'

However, most interesting was the reference to non-economic barriers by three of the respondents. One company stated frankly: 'Initially, the main barriers were sectarian and national—Irish or British! These have considerably weakened since mid-1970. Now if you provide the service, you are accepted.'

Another, having stated that 'there are no real barriers to trading on an all-island basis; we can deliver direct to our customers with no transhipment within twenty-four hours. If your service, quality and price are competitive, the business grows by referrals,' qualified this somewhat by pointing out that 'on two occasions in the past we have lost substantial business due to new personalities in our customer organisation with strong republican/nationalist tendencies, but this is very isolated, and not a real issue.'

A third company, having stated that 'barriers is too strong a word,' acknowledged the importance of being aware of cultural differences, both perceived and real, between North and South. However, they believe that, having been sufficiently conscious of these, they 'have always found the Northern/Southern Ireland situation to be compatible once it came to economic issues.'

Question 4

'If there have been benefits from this process (i.e. carrying out activities on an all-island basis) to your company (which you can share with others), please list them here in order of merit.'

A wide variety of benefits was listed by respondents:

(a) 'Better understanding and communication.'
(b) 'Speed of delivery to customers, particularly in this world of quick responses.'
(c) 'The various bodies in Northern Ireland, especially those interested in job creation, are over-anxious to assist, both with advice and cash grants, all bona-fide job creating projects.'
(d) 'Customer confidence based upon performance (in overcoming difficulties) in guaranteeing in-house generating capacity to keep production uninterrupted.'
(e) 'Responding immediately [to customer demands] by personal visits.'
(f) 'The UK diplomatic service appears to be much more commercially oriented than the Irish equivalent.'

This last point is particularly interesting. It suggests that an all-island company has the possibility of tapping into the commercial support services, both internal and export-related, of the respective governments. For many reasons, including tradition, political culture, and available resources, the type and extent of this support varies significantly between the two jurisdictions. Therefore, in a practical sense, all-island companies could 'enjoy the best of both worlds.'

Question 5 (*a*)

'*Overall, are these benefits outweighing the costs right now?*'

Four companies indicated that the benefits were outweighing the costs. One felt simply that 'any cost we have is the basic cost of doing practical good business, and whether it is in Northern Ireland or Southern Ireland or England we would be doing the very same thing.' Therefore they felt there was 'no extra cost other than normal costs, because we are on an all-Ireland basis.'

One company gave no specific answer.

Question 5 (*b*)

'*If no, would you like to specify what both governments could do to either reduce the costs or improve the benefits?*'

Respondents offered some straightforward and practical advice to both governments:
(i) 'A level playing field with regard to tax benefits on exports (of manufactured goods) as in the Republic would [remove] some of the anomalies in pricing and purchasing policies.'
(ii) 'Having a similar corporation tax structure would be beneficial.'
(iii) 'There should be an all-island look at the various attractions in bringing industry to the island.'

Question 6

'*Please list, in order of priority, the three main conclusions you would draw from your experience to date of operating on an all-island basis.*'
(*a*) *First priority.* Interestingly, three of the respondents ventured a cultural dimension to their first conclusion:
(i) 'If free from political interference, individuals of all persuasions can work together even in the same office harmoniously and peacefully.'
(ii) 'Always make sure to understand the culture where you are operating.'
(iii) The political situation 'makes the situation different.'
That said, three others did not:

(iv) 'Increased market providing higher profits.'
(v) 'The Republic is an exciting market, but because of its international basis one has to be internationally competitive and give a service which any company outside the island cannot match.'
(vi) 'Customer satisfaction.'

It is worth noting that there was no clear division along 'traditional' lines (i.e. North v. South, manufacturing v. services) in whether a respondent mentioned a cultural dimension or not. Neither did the prioritisation of this aspect follow any discernible pattern. Indeed most respondents had quite different thoughts and priorities. Perhaps this variation reflects both the relatively small number of respondents and the fact that each is pioneering a new business approach rather than travelling a well- worn path.

(b) Second priority. In listing the second most important factor, every respondent got right down to business basics:
(i) 'Stick to the economic factors that concern you and your business.'
(ii) 'Efficient and cost-effective manufacturing and delivery operation.'
(iii) 'Expansion of sales.'
(iv) 'Deliver what [you] promise better than others' and you will be accepted by all, 'thereby overcoming any initial suspicion.'
(v) Once more though the cultural dimension also arose: 'The myth of payment difficulties in the Republic only indicates an inherent lack of good credit control in the supply company. Our payment experience in the Republic, selling in sterling only, has been excellent.'

(c) Third priority. For their third priority some respondents once more gave answers that extended beyond the purely business:
(i) 'It is an optimistic strategy for the future.'
(ii) 'Keep the politicians quiet and the enmity between the differing factions in the North will disappear in due course.'
(iii) Try at all times to promote 'a level playing pitch from the point of view of the state agency development initiatives' and to ensure that companies already operating on an all-island basis have an input to this process.

Others, however, kept their focus firmly on the business dimension:
(iv) 'A larger staff and skills market.'
(v) 'Call on a regular basis with potential customers (with one order it took seven years of calling).'
(vi) 'Make deliveries personally' (analyse the market and existing

suppliers) and 'if a customer wants you to call, do this within twenty-four hours.'

In summary, a range of interesting and universally positive views, including some useful and pertinent reminders of the difficulties to be circumvented.

Appendix 2 Facts and Figures April 1995

Nuala O'Donnell and Niamh Sheridan

PHYSICAL STATISTICS

	Northern Ireland	**Republic of Ireland**
Total land area	14,139 sq. km	70,282 sq. km
Percentage of land cultivated for agriculture	80.5%	63.2%
Population density	112/sq. km	51/sq. km
Highest mountain	Slieve Donard (823 m)	Carrantuohill (1,040 m)
Largest lake	Lough Neagh (396 sq. km)	Lough Corrib (168 sq. km)
Longest river	Bann (129 km)	Shannon (370 km)
Average annual rainfall	800–1,600 ml/year	800–2,800 ml/year
Average annual sunshine	3.2–3.8 h/day	3.56–4.65 h/day
Average annual temperature: Summer	14.5–15.5°C	15.5–18°C
Winter	4–5°C	4.5–5.5°C

DEMOGRAPHIC STATISTICS (1991)

	Northern Ireland	Republic of Ireland
Population	1,577,836	3,525,719
Percentage—		
Aged 19 and under	32.5%	36%
Aged 20–39	29%	28%
Aged 40–64	26%	24%
Aged over 65	13%	11%
Birth rate		
(per 1,000 of population)	16.5	15
Death rate		
(per 1,000 of population)	9.5	8.9
Marriage rate		
(per 1,000 of population)	5.8	4.8
Marital status		
(percentage of population):		
Single	49	56
Married	42	39
Remarried	1	*n.a.*
Widowed	6	5
Divorced	2	*n.a.*
Distribution of population:		
Belfast (travel-to-work area)/		
Dublin (city and county)	52%	29%
Average number of children		
per family	2.14	2.08
Numbers in full-time education (1993):		
Full-time students	388,633	976,000
of whom—		
Pupils in primary school	50%	54%
Pupils in post-primary school	38%	37%
Students at third level	11%	9%

MACRO-ECONOMIC STATISTICS

	Northern Ireland (£Stg)	Republic of Ireland (£IR)
GNP (1993)	*n.a.*	£28,563 M
GDP (1993)	£12,360 M	£32,290 M

Gross national product figures do not exist for Northern Ireland, as a region of the United Kingdom. The GDP figure given is provisional.

Inflation rate (1994)	2.3%	2.4%

Unemployment rate:

Live register (Jan. 1995)	12.3%	14.3%

Percentage employed (1993):

Manufacturing	24%	27%
Services	38%	37%
Agriculture	6%	12%
Public sector	32%	24%

International trade (1993)

			Percentage change 1992–93
Imports	*n.a.*	£14,796 M	12%
Exports	*n.a.*	£19,671 M	18%
Imports from NI		£419.2 M	–10.5%
Exports to NI		£707.9 M	–14%

Trade data is not available for Northern Ireland. A recent survey showed that total exports from the region in 1990 were £4,126 M. In that year exports from the Republic were £14,336.7 M.

Industrial disputes (1993)

Number	7	47
Days lost	15,723	61,300

Exchange rate (19 Apr. 1995): IR£1 = Stg£1.0262.

PAY RATES

	Northern Ireland (£Stg)	Republic of Ireland (£IR)
Industrial workers (average gross earnings):		
Male	£249.30	£297.33
Female	£161.70	£183.81
Public service (selected pay scales):		
Lowest grade	£6,928–9,826	£7,833–11,636
Highest grade	£87,435	£62,773
Primary teacher	£11,883–20,145	£13,315–24,995

For primary teachers in Northern Ireland, additional increments are available, up to a maximum of £32,160. In the Republic, increments depend on qualifications.

Political representatives:		
Local councils	*Allowance for expenses*	*Allowance for expenses*
Parliamentary representatives:		
Prime Minister/Taoiseach	£76,234	£89,573
Government minister	£63,047	£71,343
Junior minister/Minister of state	£44,611	£51,532

TAX RATES

	Northern Ireland (£Stg)	Republic of Ireland (£IR)
Income tax:		
Bands of taxable: income	Lower rate (20%): £0–3,200	Standard rate (27%): £8,900
	Basic rate (25%): £3,201–24,300	Higher rate (48%): on balance
	Higher rate (40%): over £24,300	

In the Republic, married couples are taxed as a unit, so the tax bands for married couples are simply those of a single person doubled.

Tax Rates

	Northern Ireland	**Republic of Ireland**
	(£Stg)	(£IR)
Allowances:		
	Personal: £3,525	Single person: £2,500
	Married couple: £1,720	Married couple: £5,000

SOCIAL INSURANCE CONTRIBUTIONS:

Northern Ireland (national insurance)

Weekly earnings	Employer	Employee
Below £59	0%	0
£59–104.99	3%	2% of £59+
£105–149.99	5%	10% of earnings
£150–204.99	7%	Between £59 and £440
£205–440	10.2%	
Above £440	10.2%	

Republic of Ireland (pay-related social insurance)

Weekly earnings	Employer
£0–231	9%
Over £231 but under 25,800 p.a.	12.2%
Over £25,800 p.a.	0%

Weekly earnings	Employee
£30–60	Nil
£60.01–178	First £50: nil; balance: 5.5%
£178.01–231	First £50: 2.25%; balance: 7.75%
Over £231 p.w. but under £21,500 p.a.	First £50: 2.25%; balance: 7.75%
Over £231 p.w. & over £21,500 p.a.	First £50: 2.25%; balance: 2.25%

Self-employed

The self-employed both North and South pay the prevailing rates of income tax and are responsible for the assessment of their tax burden. The social insurance contributions paid by the self-employed differ from the employed; in the Republic the maximum charge is 7.25%, compared with 6.3% in the North.

Corporation tax

Two rates of corporation tax apply, North and South; a standard rate along with a small companies rate in Northern Ireland, and a manufacturing rate in the Republic.

	Northern Ireland	**Republic of Ireland**
Standard rate	33%	38%
Small companies	25%	
Manufacturing rate		10%

In Northern Ireland the small companies rate applies to all firms with taxable profits of less than £300,000. For profits between £300,000 and £1,500,000 the rate varies from 25 to 33%; above £1,500,000 a rate of 33% applies. In the Republic the 10% rate applies to all manufacturing and certain other activities, e.g. financial services in the International Financial Services Centre in Dublin and certain computer services.

Value-added tax

Standard rate	17.5%	21%
Special rates	0	0/2.5%/12.5%

The VAT registration threshold for goods in the Republic is £40,000 and for srvices £20,000. One threshold of £46,000 applies in Northern Ireland.

Excise duties

Beer, per 1% alcohol per pint	5.41p	7.825p
Still wine, per litre	£1.40	£2.15
Petrol, per litre	36.14p	29.934p

BUSINESS EXPENSES

Premises	Northern Ireland	Republic of Ireland
2,500 sq. ft centrally located	Belfast	Dublin
Purchase price per sq. ft	£40–100	£55–125
10,000 sq. ft warehouse	Derry	Limerick
Purchase price per sq. ft	£25–35	£15–30

Costs may vary widely depending on the age, condition and location of the building, the availability of car parking, and other amenities.

BUSINESS EXPENSES

	Northern Ireland	Republic of Ireland
Telecommunications		
Per 3-minute call:		
Local calls	£0.15	£0.115
UK	£0.30	£1.08
United States	£1.19	£2.49
Germany	£1.06	£1.29

Customers in border areas of Northern Ireland and the Republic can make cross-border calls for the price of a local call.

Electricity

The rate charged per unit of electricity depends on the status of the user. There are four different rates for Northern Ireland and three for the South.

Per unit of electricity:		
Domestic	9.70p	7.65p
Small commercial	9.66p	*n.a.*
Industrial	5.68p	8.04p
Large industrial user	4.72p	4.71p

Post:		
First-class inland	25p	32p
Air mail within EU	25p	32p

Courier delivery:		
10 kg package to London	£25	£35
10 kg package to Paris	£63	£63

VAT is charged on courier services in Northern Ireland at 17.5% and in the Republic at 21%.

Transport costs

Flights (business fare):	from Belfast	from Dublin
to London	£216	£236
to Brussels	£310	£622
Cheapest rate (subject to restrictions):		
to London	£100	£65
to Brussels	£99	£179

BUSINESS EXPENSES

	Northern Ireland	Republic of Ireland
Freight charges (40 ft container)	from Belfast	from Dublin
to Rotterdam	£430	£710
to New York	£1,690	£1,700

Rates may vary widely depending on the commodity. These rates are an approximation of the average cost of shipment of non-hazardous materials. Shipment costs to New York are subject to tariffs and therefore depend on the commodity.

It did not prove possible to obtain information on other business expenses, such as audit, insurance and legal fees, as no standard fee exists. Fees are negotiated between the client and company and vary widely depending on the nature of the work and the client-customer relationship.

Accommodation and Social Expenses

	Northern Ireland	Republic of Ireland
Accommodation		
One-night stay per person, sharing:		
Four/five-star hotel	£65–70	£70–110
Two-star hotel	£30–40	£25–40
Eating out (dinner, *Michelin Guide* restaurant)	£21.50	£25–30
	excl. service	+ 15% service
Theatre	£7.50–9.50	£10–13

Based on weekend rates; cheaper tickets are available on weekdays.

House Prices

	Northern Ireland	Republic of Ireland
New house	£50,250	£54,935
Existing house	£34,914	£53,868

The gap between existing and new house prices in Northern Ireland is due to the larger average size of new houses.

CROSS-BORDER ORGANISATIONS
The following is a selected list of organisations that operate on a 32-county basis.

Cultural
Association for the Visual Arts in Ireland
AWARE
Comhaltas Ceoltóirí Éireann
Comhar na Múinteoirí Gaeilge
Conradh na Gaeilge
Creative Activity for Everyone (CAFE)
Joint Committee for Church Music in Ireland

Charitable
Barnardo's
Co-operation North
Concern
Order of Malta
Oxfam
Protestant Aid and the Brabazon Trust
Royal National Lifeboat Institution
Salvation Army
Samaritans
Simon Community
Society of St Vincent de Paul
Trócaire

Environmental
Botanical Society of the British Isles (BSBI), Irish Section
Conservation Volunteers Ireland
Foyle Fisheries Commission

Political
Irish Association for Cultural, Economic and Social Relations
New Consensus International
Political Studies Association of Ireland

Governing bodies of sport
Association of Adventure Sports
Badminton Union of Ireland
Ból-Chumann na hÉireann

Croquet Association of Ireland
Cumann Cluiche Corr na hÉireann
Equestrian Federation of Ireland
Federation of Irish Cyclists
Gaelic Athletic Association
Gaelic Camogie Association
Golfing Union of Ireland
Handball Council of Ireland
Irish Amateur Boxing Association
Irish Amateur Rowing Association
Irish Amateur Swimming Association
Irish Basketball Association
Irish Blindsports
Irish Canoe Union
Irish Clay Pigeon Shooting Association
Irish Cricket Union
Irish Federation of Sea Anglers
Irish Hockey Union
Irish Ladies' Golf Union
Irish Ladies' Hockey Union
Irish Rugby Football Union
Irish Sailing Association
Irish Schools Athletic Association
Irish Schools Swimming Association
Irish Squash Racquets Association
Irish Surfing Association
Irish Table Tennis Association
Irish Triathlon Association
Irish Underwater Council
Irish Water-Polo Association
Irish Water-Ski Federation
Irish Windsurfing Association
Irish Women's Cricket Union
Irish Women's Squash Racquets Association
Ladies' Gaelic Football Association
Motorcycle Union of Ireland
Mountaineering Council of Ireland
National Athletic and Cycling Association
National Coarse Fishing Federation of Ireland
National Community Games
National Target Association of Ireland

Racquetball Association of Ireland
Schoolgirls' Basketball Association of Ireland
Special Olympics Ireland
Speleological Union of Ireland
Tennis Ireland

Support groups
Alcoholics Anonymous
Gingerbread

Trade unions
Irish Congress of Trade Unions

Amalgamated Engineering and Electrical Union
Amalgamated Transport and General Workers' Union
General and Municipal Boilermakers
Graphical, Paper and Media Union
Irish National Teachers' Organisation
Manufacturing, Science and Finance Union
National Union of Journalists
Services, Industrial, Professional and Technical Union
Transport Salaried Staffs' Association

Youth organisations
Boys' Brigade
Catholic Boy Scouts of Ireland
Catholic Guides of Ireland
Church of Ireland Youth Council
Girls' Brigade
Girls' Friendly Society in Ireland
ICTU Youth Committee
YWCA of Ireland

Other trade and professional organisations
Booksellers' Association of Great Britain and Ireland
Chartered Association of Certified Accountants, Irish Region
Chartered Institute of Irish Journalists
Electrical Contractors' Association
Institute of Chartered Accountants
Institute of Chartered Secretaries and Administrators
Institute of Directors, Ireland

Institute of Information Scientists, Irish Branch
Institute of Internal Auditors UK, Irish District Society
Institute of Personnel and Development
Institute of Personnel Management
Institute of Petroleum
Institute of Professional Auctioneers and Valuers
Institution of Chemical Engineers
Institution of Engineers of Ireland
International Fund for Ireland
Irish Auctioneers' and Valuers' Institute
Irish Book Publishers' Association
Royal Town Planning Institute
Society of Irish Foresters

Other
Catholic Marriage Advisory Council
Irish Federation of University Women
Peace Train Organisation
Union of Students in Ireland

Nuala O'Donnell is currently a Research Assistant at the Economic and Social Research Institute. She holds a Bachelor of Commerce (Economics) and a Master of Economic Science degree from University College Dublin.

Niamh Sheridan holds a Bachelor of Commerce (Economics) and a Master of Economic Science degree from University College Dublin. She is currently employed as a Research Assistant at the Economic and Social Research Institute.

Index